AF315606

The Scots Philosophical Monograph Series

While this monograph series is published on behalf of the Scots Philosophical Club, refereed by a panel of distinguished philosophers in the Club, and has as one of its aims the provision of a publishing outlet for philosophical work being done in Scotland, it is nevertheless international. The Club is committed to bringing out original works, written in a lively and readable style, and devoted to central areas of current philosophical concern, from philosophers working anywhere in the world.

As a deliberate policy we have specified no areas of the subject on which the series is to concentrate. The emphasis is on originality rather than, say, on surveys of literature, commentaries on the work of others, or exegesis. Historical works are included only in so far as they also contribute significantly to topical debates.

As well as our debt to the referees and consulting editors, we have to acknowledge a very real debt to the universities of Glasgow, Edinburgh, Aberdeen, Stirling and St Andrews who—despite the current stringencies— have given financial support to the series.

Series Editors: Andrew Brennan, Alan Millar

Consulting Editors:
J R Cameron *Aberdeen*
Neil Cooper *Dundee*
Robin Downie *Glasgow*
R W Hepburn *Edinburgh*
Bernard Mayo *St Andrews*
Neil Tennant *Stirling*
Crispin Wright *St Andrews*

Scots Philosophical Monographs Number Ten

TOWARD AN ONTOLOGY OF NUMBER, MIND AND SIGN

Scots Philosophical Monographs Number Ten

TOWARD AN ONTOLOGY OF NUMBER, MIND AND SIGN

CHARLES B DANIELS
JAMES B FREEMAN
GERALD W CHARLWOOD

Series Editors
Andrew Brennan & Alan Millar

ABERDEEN UNIVERSITY PRESS
HUMANITIES PRESS: NEW JERSEY

First published 1986
Aberdeen University Press
A member of the Pergamon Group

British Library Cataloguing in Publication Data

Daniels, Charles B
Toward an ontology of number, mind and sign.—
(Scots philosophical monographs, ISSN 0144-3062; 10)
1. Ontology
I. Title   II. Freeman, James B   III. Charlwood, Gerald W
IV. Series 111   BD311

ISBN 0-08-032462-2
ISBN 0-08-032461-4 (flexi)

Humanities Press Inc, USA
ISBN 0-391-03397-2
ISBN 0-391-03398-0 (Pbk)

PRINTED IN GREAT BRITAIN AT
ABERDEEN UNIVERSITY PRESS

Contents

Preface

Ontology is the study of the basic categories of being, of what are the basic kinds of things and how they do and do not relate to one another. In this monograph we adopt an ideal language ontological approach. The general idea is the traditional one of constructing a language that will perspicuously mirror the world—being in all its categorical splendour. A detailed description of our ontological approach and the criteria we appeal to for ideal languages are provided in the beginning in Chapter 1. Indeed, in Chapter 2 a language is presented that by the criteria we adopt does qualify as 'ideal'.

Why have we chosen the topics of number, mind and sign, rather than, say, time, for ontological investigation? In the case of the ontology of number, at least, it will become clear how an interest in this subject is almost automatic, given the ontological criteria we advocate. Number aside, however, why choose mind and language rather than, say, time? The honest answer is that that's what we're interested in. Gut appeal also 'explains' why an inside-out view of the relationship between mind and language is taken, rather than an outside-in view, one in which there is no mind prior to language immersion and acquisition.

There is much in this monograph of a highly technical nature, incomprehensible to those without fluency in Symbolic. In all cases we've done our best to remove the technical to the Appendices.

The co-authors of Chapters 1 and 5 are Charles B Daniels, James B Freeman and Gerald W Charlwood, of Chapter 2 and Appendix 1 Daniels and Freeman and of Chapters 3 and 4 and Appendices 2 and 3 Daniels and Charlwood.

We wish to thank Professors Bas van Fraassen, Kit Fine, Alasdair Urquhart, Robert K Meyer, Hector-Neri Castañeda, J Michael Dunn, David Kaplan, John Perry, John Pollock and Jonathan Bennett for help they have given us along the way. We gratefully acknowledge the Canada Council for grants S74-0551-S1 and S76-0824 and the Social Sciences and Humanities Research Council of Canada for grants 410-78-0453-R1 and R2. Finally we wish to thank the Series Editor of Scots Philosophical Monographs, Andrew Brennan, for very helpful suggestions.

1

Ontology

Section 1
Ideal languages

The study of ontology is the study of the basic categories of what there is.

Our approach to this study will lie within the 'ideal language' tradition. We find especially interesting and fruitful the method used in the work of Nino B Cocchiarella, in which ontologies are displayed within the logico-syntactic structure of formal languages.[1]

How, then, does a language display an ontology? What makes language relevant to ontology? What makes a language ontologically 'ideal'?

An ontologically ideal language represents what has ontological status by its bound variables. As Quine says in Chapter 1 of his *From a Logical Point of View* [2], to be is to be the value of a (bound) variable. And how natural, since ontology is the study of the categories of what—*there is*!

We follow Cocchiarella, however, in noting first that this is not tantamount to saying that *to exist* is to be a value of a (bound) variable and second that this criterion of ontological status (being) does not carry with it a commitment to the view that all the items that do have ontological status fall into *one* ontological category.

Section 2
Being and existence

Some philosophers distinguish between being and existence. For them there are things that don't exist—to name but a few: Pegasus, Othello and (for some of them) Plato (because he's dead). These philosophers would note that the last sentence makes use of two different quantifiers, 'there are' and 'there exist'. This is important for them, for it allows them to say 'There are things that don't exist', i.e., 'There are things x such that there exists no y identical to x'.

Other philosophers resist this view. For them there is no distinction between being and existence. And when push comes to shove, what they've got in mind is existence. To them it seems to be a conceptual truth that there are no things that don't exist, i.e., that all things exist. They treat 'There are some things that don't exist' as if it said 'There exist some things that don't exist'.

Quine is such a philosopher and worth quoting, Wyman is his mythical opponent in the debate:

> Wyman, by the way, is one of those philosophers who have united in ruining the good old word 'exist'. Despite his espousal of unactualized possibles, he limits the word 'existence' to actuality—thus preserving an illusion of ontological agreement between himself and us who repudiate the rest of his bloated universe. We have all been prone to say, in our common-sense usage of 'exist', that Pegasus does not exist, meaning simply that there is no such entity at all. If Pegasus existed he would indeed be in space and time, but only because the word 'Pegasus' has spatio-temporal connotations. If spatio-temporal reference is lacking when we affirm the existence of the cube root of 27, this is simply because a cube root is not a spatio-temporal kind of thing, and not because we are being ambiguous in our use of 'exist'.[2]

Wyman, for Quine, represents those philosophers who wish to preserve a distinction between being and existence. What Wyman might say in answer to Quine is not hard guess:

> I agree with one point Quine seems to be making. The distinction between being and existence does not make sense for every ontological category. The questions of whether there is or exists a cube root of 27, or whether there is or exists a prime number between 7 and 11, do not seem to be different ones. Indeed, the so-called 'existence' proofs in mathematics are to my mind really concerned with *being*, with whether or not *there are* certain entities. Again, although Quine would not like the example, to say that there is or that there exists a certain property, for example, the property of *Quinizing*, is to say the same kind of thing.
>
> In my view, where the distinction does make sense is within one of the basic ontological categories, a category of individuals that contains Quine, me, Pegasus, and Plato, but *not* the cube root of 27, the time the first rocket landed on the moon, and the property of *being Quine*. Indeed, I suspect one might do worse than to hold that it is a mark of this particular ontological category that the distinction between being and existence applies to its members. That existence comes with being in space at the present moment is an attractive view. But angels also seem to belong in this ontological category. And rumor has it they can have existence (in addition to being) without occupying space.[3]

Quine continues:

Wyman's overpopulated universe is in many ways unlovely. It offends the aesthetic sense of us who have a taste for desert landscapes, but this is not the worst of it. Wyman's slum of possibles is a breeding ground for disorderly elements. Take, for instance, the possible fat man in that doorway; and, again, the possible bald man in that doorway. Are they the same possible man, or two possible men? How do we decide? How many possible men are there in that doorway? Are there more possible thin ones than fat ones? How many of them are alike? Or would their being alike make them one? Are no *two* possible things alike? Is this the same as saying that it is impossible for two things to be alike? Or, finally, is the concept of identity simply inapplicable to unactualized possibles? But what sense can be found in talking of entities which cannot meaningfully be said to be identical with themselves and distinct from one another?[4]

Let us see what Wyman might say in response:

A series of questions, of course, is not an argument. To see that these questions have no force, let me just answer them as Quine poses them:

(1) If the doorway Quine is referring to is an existing one, say the one to his office, then he is in a better position to answer his questions than I am. The only fat men and bald men that can be in an existing doorway are existing fat men and bald men. Quine should take a look.

(2) The number of possible men in an existing doorway is the number of existing men in the doorway, no more, no less.

(3) Question for question: How are existing things alike? I guess they're alike in certain ways; they share certain properties and relations. It is the same with non-existing things. These, too, are alike in certain ways; they share certain properties and relations.

(4) Is the concept of identity simply inapplicable to unactualized possibles? Things in the category we've been discussing are identical when they share *all* properties and relations. Of course, how we can tell when they do this is a difficult and perplexing matter, having a long and controversy-laden philosophical history. But why not simply answer it in the manner of Descartes? We know the identity of a thing, not with our senses and not with our imaginations, but with our intellects.

Wyman *can* respond sensibly to the questions that Quine poses.

But Wyman aside, we find merit in Cocchiarella's analysis of existence,[5] which is concerned solely with the existence of just those kinds of basic individuals that Wyman seems to be talking about. For Cocchiarella certain attributes or properties entail the existence of the individuals that have them. An individual exists when there is some existence-entailing attribute it has.

On this analysis, existence and indiscernibility have a special, interesting status. An entity exists when there is some existence-entailing attribute it has; and given the standard second-order comprehension principle for attributes, *having some existence-entailing attribute* itself qualifies as an existence-entailing attribute. Similarly when b is indiscernible from a, i.e., has all the attributes a has, *having all the attributes a has* itself qualifies as one of the very attributes a has that b has as well.

For Wittgenstein there are two and only two kinds of ontological category, the category of what is and is not the case and the category or categories of what remains the same whatever's the case. In a Wittgensteinian ideal language ontological status is reflected in the latter kind of category by constants, names—one name for each category member; in the former, ontological status is reflected by complex signs, one for each possible fact.[6]

For us what reflect ontological status are not constants or complex signs, but (bound) variables.

There is another consideration that further supports the view we put forward, the view that 'There are some things that don't exist' not only makes sense, but is true. Sometimes we wish to quantify into fictional contexts, as in the true statement, 'There are at least two purely fictional characters that lived at 221b Baker Street in a city on the Thames in more than one of Sir Arthur Conan Doyle's stories'. Actually Holmes, Watson *and Mrs Hudson* lived at 221b Baker Street in more than one story. Unless we quantify over things that don't exist, we shall have to say something outrageous—like, for example, that Holmes and Watson existed and were in reality Conan Doyle's brain states, or that *we're* making up a story when we make this statement—to explain how there could be two such entities that lived at 221b Baker Street in more than one story.

One final point. It is really quite misleading to talk about quantifying over possibilia. It smacks too much of Meinong and *im*possibilia. It tempts us to confuse the issue of whether being and existence are the same with the quite separate matter of providing an adequate analysis of Meinongian definite descriptions like 'the first person to discover a method of trisecting the Euclidean angle with ruler and compasses alone'—descriptions we can easily have in our thoughts, but *cannot* fit to anything, existing or being— outside of stories.

What we are claiming is just that the assertion 'There are some things that don't exist' is not only possibly true, it is true. That's our central point.

Section 3
A universal genus

For Wittgenstein there is *no* universal genus, an ontological category to which *everything*, all ontological items, belongs.[6] Indeed, Wittgenstein insists that the two sorts of category in his ontology are radically disjoint—no (possible, or impossible) fact can be an object, no object a fact.

Frege has what at first blush does look like a universal genus.[7] The category of things that can be referred to seems to be a universal genus. Not only do nominative expressions refer to items in this category, sentences do as well. 'The True' and 'Snow is white' refer to the same object.

Yet while such expressions as 'whiteness' or 'the property of being white' also refer to items in this category, the predicate 'is white' does *not* find its semantic correlate here. Indeed, the nominative expressions 'whiteness' or 'the property of being white' do not have the same semantic correlate as the predicate 'is white'. Frege's discussion about the 'reference' of predicates can be read as a denial of a universal genus.

Naive set theory perhaps reflected the idea that there is one such all-encompassing ontological category.

Natural language, at least English, also may tempt us toward an ontology having a universal genus. The expressions 'What...refers to' or 'The semantic correlate of...' seem to capture everything.

Then, too, when we say 'everything', don't we mean *everything*? If to be is to be the value of a (bound) variable, 'everything' should capture all the things there are and corral them in one universal genus, or so it would seem.

Semantics, as it is normally done, also gives one a nudge in this direction. In semantics items of language are 'related' to other items. As such, the objects of these language–world relations, the relata, whether they happen to be individuals, properties, propositions or relations themselves, tend to be seen as being all of a sort—*objects of* (*semantic*) *relations*—and hence deserving of being lumped together in one big ontological category.

Wittgenstein was very alert to this tendency, and many of his more mystical pronouncements in the *Tractatus* can be taken as underscoring his view that this cannot be done—because there is no universal genus. One can refer to, name, objects; one asserts or denies facts. Not vice versa.

While ordinary language, with its nominative phrase 'the fact that...', tempts us to think we're referring to facts, it may also tempt us to think that at times we are saying, stating or asserting individuals—as in the statement 'Harry Truman' (uttered in response to the instruction 'State which President is famous for playing the piano'). Yet, for Wittgenstein, ordinary language is misleading ontologically. The philosopher's job is to show what, for ontological purposes, a more perspicuous, less misleading language might look like.

But, as Cocchiarella points out, having accepted Quine's dictum that to be is to be the value of a (bound) variable, we have *not* thereby committed ourselves on the issue of whether or not there is to be one, or more than one, kind of variable in an ontologically ideal language, or on the logico-syntactic structure of that language.

Cocchiarella, for example, explores a language in which there are two sorts of variables, one ranging over individuals and the other over properties, and in which the category of individuals includes the category of properties.

The point of this section is this: in holding that to be is to be a value of a (bound) variable, *we are not committed to a universal ontological genus.* In a completed ideal language project, every distinct category of being to which an ontologist is committed will be represented in the language by a distinct category of variable. Indeed, in the ontologies that will be suggested in the following, the various ontological categories will all be radically disjoint.

Section 4
Linguistic excess

The second demand we place upon ontologically ideal languages is that *they contain no syncategorematic constants.*

An ontologically ideal language should mirror the world, not represent it as having something over and above what it does have. There should be no more categories in the language than there are categories of being in the world. If a language contains constants that in their employment in it fail to represent things with ontological status, i.e., values of some variables in the language, then the language cannot be ideal. It 'talks about' something (!) that isn't there to be talked about.

The '$\in$' of set theory does not represent a value of the variables of set theory. But this feature of its language is not crucial, since what is normally written '$x \in y$' can, with no loss or ambiguity, be written 'xy', doing away with the constant '$\in$' completely.

This is indeed the test. If constants of a certain sort are not necessary, away with them! If we cannot do away with them, if it's simply a fact that they, or other constants like them are needed, then we should take this fact seriously and quantify over whatever it is that forces us to have them.

Thus if we are attracted to first-order languages and believe them to reflect the ontology of the world, we must either quantify over what their predicate constants represent, or get rid of the predicate constants. If '$\exists$', '$\forall$',

'∼' and '⊃' appear in an ontologically ideal language, we shall expect that language to contain variables that range over what '∃', '∀' '∼' and '⊃' represent. And the same, of course, goes for punctuation marks. But the case of '∃' is of special interest, since we started by saying that ontology is the study of the basic kinds of things *there are*. Well, what kind of thing is it that this ontologically important 'there are' represents? We shall see.

Section 5
Identity

A third requirement for an ontologically ideal language is that for each ontological category a notion of identity be definable.

The inability of philosophers to provide such a notion for certain categories has often tended to make the categories suspect. Rhetorical questions are asked, like 'What is the criterion of identity for these "propositions" you say you believe in?', 'What is the criterion of identity for properties?' or '...is the concept of identity simply inapplicable to unactualised possibles?'. These questions are rhetorical, but the rhetoric can be unsettling.

Yet aside from alleviating uneasiness and embarrassment brought on by rhetoric, it is important that a language which purports to mirror the world in some way shows us when, for each ontological category, we have two items and when one—when the possible fat man in the doorway is the possible bald man and when, so to speak, he's not.

That identity be definable in an ontologically ideal language will not, of course, entirely alleviate the uneasy feeling brought on by the question 'But what's your criterion of identity for...?', since the word 'criterion' is used and brings with it an inevitable epistemological smell. When we search our souls, we often cannot provide a fully satisfying answer to the question of how we *know* when we have identity. How *do* we know that, say, the largest object on my sofa shares *all* its properties and relations with the only thing now thinking with relish of fried mice?

Questions like this we do not even attempt to answer. We note, however, that at least part of what's required for one to be identical to the other is for the one to share all properties and relations with the other.

Another part is to have some indication of when there *is* the one and when the other. This forms the basis for a fourth demand we place on an ontologically ideal language.

Section 6
Ontological adequacy

The fourth requirement is that there be a full, adequate comprehension principle for each ontological category.

Ideal languages should not only tell us what entities there are but also the categories they display should be 'full'. If some wffs stand for propositions, every wff ought to do so. If some wff in which there are n free individual variables stands for an n-ary property, every such wff ought to.

In set theory some wffs in one free variable stand for sets, e.g., '$x \neq x$', but not all do, e.g., '$x \notin x$'. Set theory has the theorem '$(\exists y)(\forall x)(x \in y \leftrightarrow x \neq x)$'; but as Russell pointed out, '$(\exists y)(\forall x)(x \in y \leftrightarrow x \notin x)$' leads to contradiction. Thus the scheme

$$'(\exists y)(\forall x)(x \in y \leftrightarrow A)'$$

where y is not free in A, is not acceptable.

In many cases, the present requirement bears upon the last. Suppose, for instance, that we drop from second-order logic the normal comprehension principle for attributes, i.e.,

$$'(\exists f^n)(\forall x_1)\ldots(\forall x_n)(f^n x_1 \ldots x_n \leftrightarrow A)'$$

where 'f^n' is not free in A and 'x_1', ..., 'x_n' are distinct individual variables. Instead suppose we have:

$$'(\exists f^n)(\forall x_1)\ldots(\forall x_n)(f^n x_1 \ldots x_n \leftrightarrow g^n x_1 \ldots x_n)'$$

where 'g^n' is an n-place predicate constant or variable other than 'f^n'. Universal instantiation will be allowed only to predicate constants and variables.

Now where 'f' is a monadic predicate variable, 'a' and 'b' are individual constants, 'C' is a complex sentence containing one or more occurrences of 'a' and 'C*' is what results when 'b' is substituted for 'a' at one or more occurrences, the following three sentences might well be jointly satisfiable: '$(\forall f)(fa \leftrightarrow fb)$', 'C' and '$\sim C*$'. Here what the constants 'a' and 'b' denote are indiscernible in the sense that they share *all* attributes (since what counts as an attribute is severely restricted), but their denotata are discernible in the sense that there is a context in the language true of one that is not true of the other. This anomaly disappears with the addition of a full, adequate comprehension (and substitution) axiom.

Section 7
Summary

An ontologically ideal language, then, has the following four features:

(1) Ontological categories are represented by the various kinds of bound variables it displays.
(2) It contains no syncategorematic constants.
(3) A notion of identity is definable for each ontological category displayed.
(4) For each such category there is a full, adequate comprehension principle.

In Chapter 2 we shall present a language which not only qualifies as ontologically 'ideal', but displays an ontology of number—in the sense that Peano arithmetic an be developed in it.

Section 8
Truth

We conclude this introductory discussion with a few cautionary words concerning truth. From an ontologist's point of view, there are several different notions of truth.

(1) For Frege truth is an *individual* or *object*—an item referred to by both the nominative phrase 'the True' and by sentences like 'Snow is white'.
(2) For others truth has been seen to be a property or relation, the object that has this property or relation being referred to by a nominative phrase. This is the view of truth of modern semantics, in which we find 'M $\Vdash$ "A"' and 'O $\in$ V("A")', The object that is true is referred to by the quote 'A'.
(3) Finally there is a view of truth that might be called 'modal', in which truth is represented by a sentence operator, *not* a predicate. What is true is what a sentence asserts. The model in English is the phrase 'it is true that' or 'truly', as in 'Truly, A'. Here what is true is not referred to by a nominative phrase or a quote. 'Truly, "A"' does not make sense, since it lacks a predicate.

In Daniels and Freeman[8] we showed that notions (2) and (3) were distinct. We did so by arguing that under a certain ontological assumption—that there is some independent property[9]—the cardinality of truths and falsehoods under view (3) exceeds that of truths and falsehoods under view (2).

This distinction is important in the present discussion. Let us suppose we have a language that qualifies as ontologically ideal. There are two ways we can regard it. We can assess it semantically from the point of view of a metalanguage; and we can, so to speak, 'immerse ourselves' in it.

By doing the first we may radically distort the role the language is meant to play as ontologically ideal. Suppose in our ontology, (a) there is more than one ontological category, (b) all ontological categories are radically disjoint and (c) there is a category of propositions, represented by sentence variables in the ideal language. Certainly Wittgenstein would subscribe to (a) and (b).

For the purposes of evaluation as to truth in a metalanguage, the sentences of the ideal language will be treated as representing *objects*, values of the *individual* variables of the metalanguage. Yet if our object language is taken seriously in its role as ontologically ideal, its sentences, and in particular its sentence variables, *do not* range over the kinds of things that its individual variables do. Indeed, what its individual variables range over cannot be truths and falsehoods, since its categories are radically disjoint and the latter lie within the range of its *sentence* variables.

The ontologically appropriate notion of truth is the one that will be reflected in the object language itself by a sentence operator—view (3).

Of course, metalanguage analyses can be given and often in interesting ways. But in playing this game—and interestingly enough Cocchiarella speaks of it as '*toy* talk'—we cease to treat the object language as ontologically ideal.

In what follows we shall often play at 'toy talk', confident that these cautionary words will suffice to prevent misunderstandings. In their primary roles the languages we sketch out are meant to be taken as *mirroring* the world and not merely, by means of *individual* variables and constants, *talking about* it.

2

Number

Section 1
Quantifiers

In first-order logic, a quantified sentence is a sentence of the form $(\forall x)A$, where A is itself a sentence. The question of what in a quantified sentence is the *quantifier* can be answered two ways: first, that the quantifier is the complex expression '$\forall x$'; second, that it is the primitive symbol '$\forall$'. In our attempt to form an ontologically ideal language, we must be clear about which is which.

If we take the first notion, the requirements we have adopted do not demand that what '$\forall x$' refers to be a value of a quantified variable of the language, since '$\forall x$' is a complex expression, not a constant.

But '$\forall$' is a part of the complex expression '$\forall x$' and is itself a constant, so if we find that it or constants like it are needed (they are), we shall have to make '$\forall$' categorematic—a representative of a value of a variable of the language.

So with Borkowski[1] and Bostock[2] we shall call the primitive symbol '$\forall$' a 'quantifier' and treat it as categorematic in the ontologically ideal language we construct.

This has beneficial consequences. On the first notion of quantifier, when a language has more than one style of variable, like second-order logic with its individual and predicate variables, '$\forall x$' and '$\forall f$' are *different* quantifiers. There are, so to speak, two different notions of 'all' in the language. On the notion of quantifier we adopt, '$\forall$' represents the same thing—whatever variable it is associated with there's just one 'all'.

Let us generalise. A *quantifier* is an expression that takes m well-formed formulae (wffs) and n variables (of any sort) into a wff, $m \geqslant 1$, $n \geqslant 0$. Thus we speak of a m–n quantifier.

That $n \geqslant 0$ is handy, since when $n = 0$, '$\sim$' counts as a 1–0 quantifier, as does '$\square$' in a modal language. '$\rightarrow$' is a 2–0 quantifier. '$\forall$' is, of course, a 1–1 quantifier.

In our ideal language, then, for each m $\geqslant$ 1 and n $\geqslant$ 0 there will be a denumerable class of m–n quantifier variables.

Section 2
Identity

One of our requirements is that a notion of identity be definable in an ontologically ideal language for each ontological category. How, then, is this to be accomplished for the categories of m–n quantifiers? Given a constant 'Q' in the same category as '$\forall$', for instance, how are we to define '$\forall = $ Q'?

$\forall$ ought to be identical to Q when $\forall$ and Q are not discernible. When we have a context C in which '$\forall$' occurs, we should at least have C*, where 'Q' occurs in place of '$\forall$' in one or more places, and vice versa. Thus where v is any variable, we should have $(\forall v)$A if and only if we have (Qv)A. Eliminating parentheses by writing $(\forall v)$A as $\forall v$,[3] $\forall$ should be indiscernible from Q for *all* Av, 'Av' being what's left over when '$\forall$' is removed from '$\forall$Av'.

This can be accomplished in the manner of Borkowski[4,5] by introducing for each m $\geqslant$ 1 and n $\geqslant$ 0 a denumerable set of m–n variables that syntactically can take the place of a string of m wffs followed by n variables. We call these *saturated* variables. The special case where m $= 1$ and n $= 0$ is the class of propositional variables. The quantifier variables introduced in the last section we call *unsaturated* variables.

Thus where v is any variable, P is a 1–1 saturated variable, and when A is a wff, both '$\forall$Av' and '$\forall$P' are wffs. Indeed, since P is a variable itself, both '$\forall$AP' and '$\forall$P' will be wffs. Restoring parentheses for ease of reading, both '$(\forall$P$)$A' and '$\forall$P' will be wffs.

Returning to the question of how to define identity for the categories, both saturated and unsaturated, that have been introduced, we can now say

$$\text{'}(\forall = Q)\text{'} =_{df} \text{'}(\forall R)(\forall P)(R\forall P \leftrightarrow RQP)\text{'}$$

where 'R' is a 1–0 unsaturated variable and 'P' a 1–1 saturated variable.

In general, where 'Q_1' and 'Q_2' are m–n unsaturated expressions

$$\text{'}(Q_1 = Q_2)\text{'} =_{df} \text{'}(\forall R)(\forall P)(RQ_1 P \leftrightarrow RQ_2 P)\text{'}$$

where 'R' is a 1–0 unsaturated variable distinct from both 'Q_1' and 'Q_2' and 'P' is an m–n saturated variable.

It remains to provide a definition of identity for saturated variables, constants and expressions. It will help to have an informative way of writing what is left when the initial quantifier of a wff is removed. The wff can be of the form

$$QA_1 \ldots A_m v_1 \ldots v_n,$$

where Q is an m–n quantifier, $A_1, \ldots, A_m$ are wffs and $v_1, \ldots, v_n$ are variables. Removing Q, we write

$$\langle\langle A_1, \ldots, A_m\rangle, \langle v_1, \ldots, v_n\rangle\rangle$$

so as to preserve the information that Q is an m–n quantifier.

The class of m–n saturated expressions will contain all m–n saturated variables and constants and all formulae

$$\langle\langle A_1, \ldots, A_m\rangle, \langle v_1, \ldots, v_n\rangle\rangle$$

as just defined. We shall call this set $\Sigma[m, n]$. Notice that $\langle\langle p_1, \ldots, p_n\rangle, \varnothing\rangle \in \Sigma[n, 0]$, $\langle\langle p_1, \ldots, p_{n-1}\rangle \cdot \langle p_n\rangle\rangle \in \Sigma[n-1, 1], \ldots,$ $\langle\langle p_1\rangle, \langle p_2, \ldots, p_n\rangle\rangle \in \Sigma[1, n-1]$, where $p_1, \ldots, p_n$ are 1–0 saturated variables, i.e., propositional variables.

Given $P_1, P_2 \in \Sigma[m, n]$,

$$\text{'}(P_1 = P_2)\text{'} =_{df} \text{'}(\forall Q)(QP_1 \leftrightarrow QP_2)\text{'}$$

where Q is an m–n quantifier variable that is not free in either P_1 or P_2.

The presence in our language of 1–1 saturated variables, while it allows us to define identity for quantifiers, prevents us from appealing to the usual definition of '∃' as '∼∀∼'. While '$(\forall v)A$' and '$\sim(\forall v)\sim A$' ('∀Av' and '∼∀∼Av') both qualify as wffs, where 'P' is a 1–1 saturated variable, '∀P' also qualifies as a wff, as does '∼∀P'. But '∼∀∼P' is not well formed. '∼' cannot be attached to a 1–1 saturated variable or constant to get a 1–1 saturated expression. Thus in our ontologically ideal language '∀' and '∃' turn out not to be interdefinable. '∀' and '∃' must both be taken as a primitive 1–1 quantifier constants.

Section 3
Comprehension axioms

The language we have been describing has for each $m \geqslant 1$ and $n \geqslant 0$ a class of (unsaturated) quantifier variables and constants and a class of saturated variables and constants. For each such category a notion of identity is definable.

We must also ensure that there is an adequate comprehension principle for each category.

Let $S \in \Sigma[m, n]$ for $m \geq 1$ and $n \geq 0$, and let P be an m–n saturated variable that does not occur free in S. We should then have as a comprehension axiom:

AxComp1 : $(\exists P)(P = S)$.

As a special case where $m = 1$ and $n = 0$, we have the comprehension axiom for propositions, which are, of course, represented by 1–0 saturated expressions:

$(\exists p)(p = S)$.

Furthermore, where $S \in \Sigma[m, 0]$, $m \geq 1$, let $p_1, \ldots, p_m$ be distinct 1–0 saturated (propositional) variables that do not occur free in S. We should also have:

AxComp2 : $(\exists p_1) \ldots (\exists p_m)(\langle \langle p_1, \ldots, p_m \rangle, \varnothing \rangle = S)$.

Let A be a wff, let Q be a m–0 unsaturated variable that does not occur free in A and let $p_1, \ldots, p_m$ be distinct 1–0 saturated variables. Then we have:

AxComp3 : $(\exists Q)(\forall p_1) \ldots (\forall p_m)(Qp_1 \ldots p_m = A)$.

Finally, where A is a wff, Q is an m–n unsaturated (quantifier) variable that does not occur free in A and P is an m–n saturated variable, we have:

AxComp4 : $(\exists Q)(\forall P)(QP = A)$.

This language qualifies as ontologically ideal in the sense we have set out. A detailed technical exposition of its features can be found in Daniels and Freeman.[6,7]

While this language does qualify as ontologically ideal, the reader may still see it as flawed—since it contains neither individual nor predicate variables. We have not included these since our purpose at this point is to investigate quantifiers, including such numerical quantifiers as 'for exactly five' and 'for exactly three plus two'. Within an ideal language framework, this can be done without individual or predicate variables, a fact which in itself is of interest.

Section 4
Numbers

Any philosophy of mathematics should make clear what kinds of things numbers are. To what ontological category do they belong?

For us numbers are 'quanta'. They are to be found among the values of quantifier variables. Linguistically our claim means that numerical expressions 'one', 'two', 'three' should be symbolised by formal representations of the numerical quantifiers 'for exactly one', 'for exactly two', 'for exactly three'. In this we follow Borkowski and Bostock.[8,9]

Adopting this ontology seems to forestall certain problems other views have as to how natural numbers apply to the world. When we count the cows in a field and ascertain their number to be nine, there is no mystery in going on to say 'There are exactly nine cows in the field'. Numbers apply to the world in the way 'all' and 'some' do. We do not have to put cows and numbers into the same ontological bag and with the help of a one-to-one relation on some things in the bag, pair cows with numbers.

The language we have been describing has, thus far, just the two 1–1 unsaturated constants '$\forall$' and '$\exists$'. What kind of thing is it that, say, '$\exists$' 'represents'? What is it that adding '$\exists$' to 'Av' says?

These questions, and their answers, lead us into an area that to the unwary can prove treacherous, as we noted in section 8, Chapter 1. The idea that our word 'represents' itself must represent a single relation between bits of language and bits of the world, we have already given reason to suspect. It tempts us too much to the view that there is a universal genus—a category of 'what can be referred to'.

Of course it would be foolish to deny that the language we are discussing can be modelled. We *can* provide it with a semantics of the traditional kind. In doing so, however, we are not viewing it as an ontologically ideal language, one which in its quantificational categories 'mirrors' reality. Models, as Cocchiarella has been heard to say, are just toys.

Let us consider the notions of identity discussed earlier. The first thing to notice is that they are not one, but many. Identity of 1–0 saturated entities is one thing, of 3–2 saturated entities another, of 2–3 unsaturated entities yet another.

Indeed, in the case of 1–0 saturated entities, identity does fall into an ontological category, the same category as the entity 'represented' by '$\rightarrow$'. It is 'represented' by a 2–0 unsaturated expression; and one instance of the comprehension axiom is:

$$(\exists q)(\forall p_1)(\forall p_2)(qp_1p_2 = (p_1 = p_2))$$

where q is a 2–0 unsaturated variable. In most cases, however, the '=' we have introduced does not 'represent' anything. It is a sign that, like all defined signs, can be eliminated.

It may not be a bad idea to think about the word 'represents' in a similar way. First, there may be more than one notion involved. Secondly, the word in the metalanguage may not have any ontological correlate.

But enough. Notice having been posted that we may well be about to slip away into a Wittgensteinian realm of the unsayable, let us nonetheless try to answer the question, 'What is it that adding "$\exists$" to "Av" says?'. What it says depends upon what 'Av', $[\langle\langle A\rangle, \langle v\rangle\rangle]$, itself is taken to say.

Given that '$\forall$' and '$\exists$' are the *only* 1–1 unsaturated constants we need to deal with, 'Av' could be thought to 'represent' a bunch or set of propositions, the set $\{V'(A): V'$ differs from V at most at the variable $v\}$, V being the normal sort of valuation. Then '$\exists$' would 'represent' the union or the (perhaps infinite) 'disjunction' of its members. This is the approach we used in Freeman and Daniels.[10]

But when we assimilate 'for exactly one', 'for exactly two' etc., to 'for all' and 'for some', this approach will not work. The number of things having a certain feature need not correlate in any particularly nice way with the number of propositions that say of those things that they have the feature.

Take, for example, $\forall \vee p \sim pp$, i.e., $(\forall p)(p \vee \sim p)$. In classical logics,[11] there is just one proposition in the set that '$\vee p \sim pp$', $[\langle\langle p \vee \sim p\rangle, \langle p\rangle\rangle]$, 'represents'. Yet the number of propositions p such that $p \vee \sim p$ would certainly be at least two and very probably more.

Another alternative, one in line with type theory, would construe V('Av') as a function from the category of v into propositions. The problem with this view is that it gives us *too much* information. If V('Av') is a function from the entities v ranges over the propositions, to ascertain what V('Av') is, we must know what entities are mapped to what propositions, even when 'v' happens to be a 1–1 saturated variable, the kind of variable that has as its value the very sort of thing that 'Av' stands for.

But in saying 'There are exactly N v such that A', we do not have to know this. We just need to know *the number* of v's such that A, i.e., that N v's are such that A, not *which* v's are such that A.

Kit Fine has suggested to us a way of understanding what 'Av' says that constitutes a 'golden mean' between these two views. All we really need to do is to connect each proposition in our original bunch with a natural number, intuitively the number of v's that satisfy 'A' *at that particular proposition*—or, in the case where there is no such natural number N such that N v's satisfy 'A' at that particular proposition, with something else. Where X is a proposition, V('Av')X will equal card $\{V': V'$ differs from V at most at v and $V'(A) = X\}$.

Not all propositions have to be in the set $\{V'(A): V'$ differs from V at most at v}. Any such 'missing' proposition $V(\langle\langle A\rangle, \langle v\rangle\rangle)$ sends to the number 0. For example, $V(\langle\langle \sim\exists pp\rangle, \langle p\rangle\rangle)$ will send the proposition $V(\exists pp)$ to 0, since $V(\exists pp) \notin \{V'(\sim\exists pp): V'$ differs from V at most at p}.

Now 'There are exactly N v such that A' will be *true* when the sum of the numbers $V(\langle\langle A\rangle, \langle v\rangle\rangle)$ takes the true propositions into equals N, i.e., $\Sigma\{V(\langle\langle A\rangle, \langle v\rangle\rangle)(X): X$ is a true proposition} = N. It is easy to see that 'There is some v such that A' will be true when this sum does not equal 0.

Thus we can have as 1–1 unsaturated constants, the constants '∀' and '∃', and '0', '1', '2', . . ., representing 'for no', 'for exactly one', 'for exactly 2', ...

Axioms for these numerical quantifiers can now be given.

Let s be a 1–1 saturated variable, $u, v, v_1, \ldots, v_n$ be variables of the same sort and A be a wff. Where $e_1, \ldots, e_n$ are expressions all of the same category,

$$'\neq (e_1, \ldots, e_n)' =_{df} '((e_1 \neq e_2) \wedge \ldots \wedge (e_1 \neq e_n) \wedge (e_2 \neq e_3)$$
$$\wedge \ldots \wedge (e_2 \neq e_n) \wedge \ldots \wedge (e_{n-1} \neq e_n))'.$$

Then as axioms we have:

AxN1. $(\forall s)(0s \leftrightarrow \sim\exists s)$.
AxN2. $(1v)A \leftrightarrow (\exists v)(A \wedge (\forall u)[A[v/u] \rightarrow (v = u)])$, where u does not occur free in A and v is free for u in A.
AxN3. $(Nv)A \leftrightarrow (\exists v_1)\ldots(\exists v_n)(\neq(v_1, \ldots, v_n) \wedge A[v/v_1] \wedge \ldots \wedge A[v/v_n] \wedge (\forall u)$ $(A[v/u] \rightarrow [(u = v_1) \vee \ldots \vee (u = v_n)]))$, where none of $v_1, \ldots, v_n, u$ occurs free in A and v is free for $v_1, \ldots, v_n, u$ in A—N, of course, representing in the object language what n does in the metalanguage.
AxN4. $(\forall s)(Ns \rightarrow \sim Ms)$, where $N \neq M$.
AxN5. $(\exists s)Ns$, for all $N \in \omega$.

One problem remains. We have said that in modelling our language in the usual way, 1–1 saturated expressions 'represent' functions that take propositions into numbers. How do we reflect this feature *in* our language? How are we to reflect in our language that what the 1–1 saturated expression 's' 'represents' takes the proposition that the wff 'A' 'represents' into the number that the 1–1 quantifier 'Q' 'represents'?

We do so by introducing a new class F of *functorial* variables, variables that take an m–n saturated expression and an m–0 saturated expression into an m–n unsaturated expression. In the category of 1–1 functorial letters will be a constant 'α' such that 'αsA' will be a 1–1 quantifier, a complex unsaturated expression. In English we can read 'αsA' as 'the thing into which s takes the proposition A'. Let Γ be the class of unsaturated expressions, both primitive and complex.

It may turn out that for some numerical quantifier 'N' we have 'αsA = N'. This will say 'The thing into which s takes A is the number N'.

Where a_1 and a_2 are m–n functors in the class F, s_1 and s_2 are m–n saturated variables and p is a m–0 saturated variable, we can define identity for the new class as:

$$\text{'}(a_1 = a_2)\text{'} =_{df} \text{'}(\forall s_1)(\forall p)(\forall s_2)(a_1 s_1 p s_2 = a_2 s_1 p s_2)\text{'}.$$

Where A is a wff, a_1 is a m–n functor variable, s_1, p and s_2 are as above, and a_1 does not occur free in A, the comprehension axiom for functors is:

$$(\exists a_1)(\forall s_1)(\forall p)(\forall s_2)(a_1 s_1 p s_2 = A).$$

Where δ_1 and δ_2 are m–n unsaturated expressions and s is an m–n saturated variable that occurs free in neither, identity is defined as

$$\text{'}(\delta_1 = \delta_2)\text{'} =_{df} \text{'}(\forall s)(\delta_1 s = \delta_2 s)\text{'}.$$

A full comprehension axiom for m–n unsaturated expressions has already been given.

We are now in a position to give axioms for the constant 'α'. Let $u, v, v_1, \ldots, v_n$ be any variables of the same sort, $p, p_1, \ldots, pk$ be 1–0 saturated (propositional' variables and s, s_1 and s_2 be 1–1 saturated variables. Where $A_1, \ldots, A_n$ are wffs

$$\text{'}[\wedge \langle 1 \leqslant i \leqslant n \rangle A_i]\text{'} =_{df} \text{'}(A_1 \wedge \ldots \wedge A_n)\text{'}$$

and

$$\text{'}[\vee \langle 1 \leqslant i \leqslant n \rangle A_i]\text{'} =_{df} \text{'}(A_1 \vee \ldots \vee A_n)\text{'}.$$

The axioms are:

Axa1. $(\forall s)(\forall p_1)\ldots(\forall p_k)[(\neq (p_1,\ldots,p_k) \wedge [\wedge \langle 1 \leqslant i \leqslant k \rangle (\alpha(s,p_i) = M_i)] \wedge [\wedge \langle 1 \leqslant i \leqslant k \rangle p_i] \wedge (\forall p)(((\alpha(s,p) \neq 0) \wedge p) \to [\vee \langle 1 \leqslant i \leqslant k \rangle (p = p_i)])) \to Ns]$, where $M_i \neq 0$ and $N = \Sigma\{M_i : 1 \leqslant i \leqslant k\}$.

Axa2. $(\forall s)[Ks \to (\exists p_1)\ldots(\exists p_k)([\wedge \langle 1 \leqslant i \leqslant k \rangle (\alpha(s,p_i) \neq 0)] \wedge [\wedge \langle 1 \leqslant i \leqslant k \rangle p_i] \wedge (\forall p)([(\alpha(s,p) \neq 0) \wedge p] \to [\vee \langle 1 \leqslant i \leqslant k \rangle (p = p_i)]))]$.

Axa3. $(\forall s)(\forall s \leftrightarrow (\forall p)((\alpha(s,p) \neq 0) \to p))$.

Axa4. $(\forall s)(\exists s \leftrightarrow (\exists p)((\alpha(s,p) \neq 0) \wedge p))$.

Axa5. $(\forall s_1)(\forall s_s)[(\forall p)(\alpha(s_1,p) = \alpha(s_2,p)) \to (s_1 = s_2)]$.

Axa6. $(\forall s)(\forall p)([Ns \wedge (\alpha(s,p) \neq 0) \wedge p] \to [(\alpha(s,p) = 1) \vee \ldots \vee (\alpha(s,p) = N)])$.

Axa7. $\alpha(\langle\langle A \rangle, \langle v \rangle\rangle, A[v/u]) \neq 0$, where v is free for u in A.

Axa8. $(\forall p)[(\exists v_1)\ldots(\exists v_n)[\neq(v_1,\ldots,v_n) \wedge [\wedge \langle 1 \leqslant i \leqslant n \rangle (A[v/v_i] = p)] \wedge (\forall u)((A[v/u] = p) \to [\vee \langle 1 \leqslant i \leqslant n \rangle (u = v_i)])] \leftrightarrow (\alpha(\langle\langle A \rangle, \langle v \rangle\rangle, p)$

= N)], where v is the only variable occurring free in A and v is free for u,
$v_1, \ldots, v_n$ in A.

Axa9. $(\forall p)\,[(\alpha(\langle\langle A\rangle, \langle v\rangle\rangle, p) \neq 0) \to (\exists v)(p = A)]$, where v and p are distinct variables.

Section 5
More numbers

Granted that zero and the positive integers seem to find a natural home among quanta, as values of quantifier variables, it does not seem immediately obvious that a similarly comfortable place can be made for the negative integers and the rationals. What sense are we to make of the quantifiers 'for exactly minus four' and 'for exactly two-thirds'?

Actually it is a rather simple matter to make sense of these quantifiers by extending the ideas just presented, i.e., that $V(\text{'}Av\text{'}) = \text{card}\{V' : V'$ differs from V at most at v and $V'(A) = X\}$ and that 'There are exactly N v such that A' will be *true* when the sum of the numbers $V(\text{'}Av\text{'})$ takes the true propositions into equals N.

For the whole range of the integers we turn to those quantifiers that take two wffs and a variable into a wff, those in the 2–1 unsaturated category. Where A and B are wffs and v is a variable, $V(\text{'}ABv\text{'})$, $[V(\langle\langle A, B\rangle, \langle v\rangle\rangle)]$, might be thought of as a function that takes pairs of propositions into a pair (at least) of numbers, i.e., $V(\text{'}ABv\text{'})\langle X, Y\rangle$ might be $\langle V(\text{'}Av\text{'})(X), V(\text{'}Bv\text{'})(Y), ?\rangle$. The '?' might, for instance, be $\text{card}\{V' : V'$ differs from V at most at v and $\langle V'(A), V'(B)\rangle = \langle X, Y\rangle\}$. (There is no point in *losing* information we might retain.)

At any rate, where 'I' represents an integer, we shall have '(Iv)AB', ['IABv'], when the number of v's such that A less the number of v's such that B equals I.

Rationals can be treated in a similar way as values of 4–1 unsaturated variables. Where 'R' represents a rational number, we shall have '(Rv)ABCD', ['RABCDv'], when R equals the difference between two fractions: the number of v's such that A divided by the number of v's such that B, and the number of v's such that C divided by the number of v's such that D.

Section 6
Peano arithmetic

Our language allows us to say things like 'There are exactly n v such that A'. It does not yet, however, provide the wherewithal for such sentences as

'There are exactly $i+j$ v such that A' or 'There are exactly $i+j$ v such that A if and only if there are exactly n v such that A'.

To accomplish this we introduce some further categories of variables, m–n–k *operator* variables. These take k m–n unsaturated expressions into an m–n unsaturated expression, for m, k $\geqslant$ 1 and n $\geqslant$ 0. For example, the operation 'plus' would fall into the 1–1–2 category, because it takes 2 1–1 unsaturated expressions into a 1–1 unsaturated expression.

In the category of 1–1–1 operators we shall have two constants, *n* and *S*. The first we shall use as a flag on quantifiers to identify them as numerals 'representing' the *natural* numbers. The second will symbolise the successor function. These two constants allow us to define the numerals symbolising natural numbers, so we can do away with '0', '1', '2', . . ., as primitive quantifier constants.

Identity for the new categories can now be defined. Let o_1 and o_2 be m–n–k operator expressions, let $q_1, \ldots, q_k$ be m–n unsaturated variables and let s be an m–n saturated variable. We have:

$$\text{'}(o_1 = o_2)\text{'} =_{df} \text{'}(\forall q_1) \ldots (\forall q_k)(\forall s)(o_1 q_1 \ldots q_k s = o_2 q_1 \ldots q_k s)\text{'}.$$

Letting $o_1, q_1, \ldots, q_k$, s be as above, and letting A be a wff in which o_1 does not occur free, the comprehension axiom for operators is

$$(\exists o_1)(\forall q_1) \ldots (\forall q_k)(\forall s)(o_1 q_1 \ldots q_k s = A).$$

Let o be a 1–1–1 operator variable, q be a 1–1 unsaturated expression, p be a 1–0 saturated variable and s be a 1–1 saturated variable. We then have the following definitions:

$$\text{'}F\text{'} = \text{'}\forall pp\text{'}.$$
$$\text{'}(Num\ q)\text{'} =_{df} \text{'}(\exists s)(\exists p)(q = \alpha(s, p))\text{'}.$$
$$\text{'}0\text{'} =_{df} \text{'}\alpha(\langle\langle \sim \exists pp \rangle, \langle p \rangle\rangle, \exists pp)\text{'}.$$
$$\text{'}(Nat\ q)\text{'} =_{df} \text{'}((Num\ q) \wedge (nq = 0))\text{'}.$$
$$\text{'}(N+1)\text{'} =_{df} \text{'}\alpha(\langle\langle\langle((q = 0) \vee \ldots \vee (q = N))\rangle, \langle q \rangle\rangle, \exists pp)\text{'}.$$

To *AxN1–AxN5* and *Axa1–Axa9* of section 4, we need add one more AxN axiom and five axioms for our new operator constants *n* and *S*. Let o be a 1–1–1 operator variable, q, q_1, q_2 be 1–1 unsaturated variables and s be a 1–1 saturated variable. We then have:

AxN6. $(\forall s)(\forall q_1)(\forall q_2)([(Num\ q_1) \wedge (Num\ q_2) \wedge ((q_1 s \wedge q_2 s) \neq F)] \rightarrow [q_1 = q_2])$.

AxnS1. $(\forall q_1)([Nat\ q_1] \leftrightarrow (\forall o)(\forall s)[o0s \wedge (\forall q_2)((oq_2 s \wedge (Nat\ q_2))$
             $\rightarrow oSq_2 s)) \rightarrow oq_1 s])$.

AxnS2. $(\forall q)((Nat\ q) \rightarrow (Nat\ Sq))$.

AxnS3. $\sim(\exists q)(0 = Sq)$.
AxnS4. $SN = (N+1)$.
AxnS5. $(\forall q_1)(\forall q_2)((Sq_1 = Sq_2) \rightarrow (q_1 = q_2))$.

We have presented a system with arithmetical content. Numbers are treated as values of quantifier variables. Via the various comprehension axioms and our acceptance of the dictum 'to be is to be the value of a bound variable', we are committed to there being numbers and operations on numbers. We have shown the means of indicating the ordinary natural numbers, and of indicating when one number is the successor of another. However, we shall not have shown that our system is a genuine quantifier arithmetic until we make it clear that Peano's postulates are theorems of it. Informally, Peano's postulates are the following five statements:

p1. 0 is a natural number.
p2. The successor of a natural number is itself a natural number.
p3. No two natural numbers have the same successor.
p4. 0 is not the successor of any natural number.
p5. If P is a property that holds of 0 and furthermore holds of the successor of any
    natural number whenever it is true of that number, then P holds of all natural
    numbers.[12]

In our formalism, these statements are rendered as follows, where o is a 1–1–1 operator variable, q and r are 1–1 unsaturated variables and s is a 1–1 saturated variable:

P1. Nat 0.
P2. $(\forall q)((\mathrm{Nat}\,q) \rightarrow (\mathrm{Nat}\,Sq))$.
P3. $(\forall q)(\forall r)([(\mathrm{Nat}\,q) \wedge (\mathrm{Nat}\,r) \wedge (q \neq r)] \rightarrow [Sq \neq Sr])$.
P4. $\sim(\exists q)((\mathrm{Nat}\,q) \wedge (0 = Sq))$.
P5. $(\forall o)(\forall s)([o0s \wedge (\forall q)(((\mathrm{Nat}\,q) \wedge oqs) \rightarrow oSqs)] \rightarrow (\forall r)[(\mathrm{Nat}\,r) \rightarrow ors])$.

That P1 is a theorem is immediate from *AxnS1*. P2 is just *AxnS2*. P3 is immediate from *AxnS5*. P4 comes by *AxnS3*. Finally P5 comes directly from *AxnS1*.

Section 7
Summary

By way of review, let us take the simplest and most familiar case—1–1 quantifiers like '$\forall$' and '$\exists$'—ignoring the generalisation to m–n quantifiers. The ontological requirements we operate under demand that these constants not be syncategorematic. Thus we must do away with them, or include a class of variables to range over what they stand for. We provide a class of 1–1 *unsaturated* variables to range over what they stand for.

The ontological requirements further demand that a notion of identity be defined for the category of 1–1 unsaturated variables. We are led, then, to incorporate a class of 1–1 *saturated* variables into our language. Where 'A' is a wff, 'v' is a variable of any sort and '∀Av' is a wff, the 1–1 saturated variables go in place of what is left of a wff when the quantifier is removed, i.e., 'Av'.

Now the ontological demands that a notion of identity and that a full comprehension principle be provided for every category of the language can be met.

We introduce a class of 1–1 application *functors*, including the application constant 'α' in order to go beyond the quantifiers '∀' and '∃' and be able to express numerical quantifiers in our language—in particular, to express the number that a 1–1 saturated expression, a variable or a complex like 'Av', assigns to a particular proposition. If 'P' and 'Av' are 1–1 saturated expressions and 'B' is a 1–0 saturated expression (a wff), we may have 'α(P,B) = N' or 'α(Av, B) = N' which, in the latter case, says that there are N v's that A when A expresses what B does. Of course since A contains the free variable v, A may express things beyond what B says.

Finally, we introduce the class of 1–1–1 *operator* variables in order to capture Peano arithmetic in the language—to say such things as: if two natural numbers are different, their successors are different, zero is not the successor of any natural number and the successor of a natural number is itself a natural number.

The language we have described meets all the requirements we set down in Chapter 1 for an ontological ideal language. In addition the Peano postulates are included as theorems. We have thereby fulfilled our promise to provide an ideal language which displays an ontology of number.

3

Mind

Section 1
Thought as a ternary relation

What kind of thing is thought?

Belief is thought's paradigm, and it is a widespread and, indeed, natural view that belief, knowledge and other forms of thought like them relate three things: (1) the person or mind that is their subject, (2) the time at which the subject has them and (3) the proposition, object or content, the truth or falsehood that is 'in' or 'on' the subject's mind at that time.

For instance, a person may believe that Sydney is the capital of Australia, and at the same time another person may or may not have this belief. He may believe that Sydney is the capital of Australia at one time and may or may not believe it at another. He may believe that Sydney is the capital of Australia, while at the same time he may or may not believe that Toronto is the capital of Canada.

There are problems with this view.[1]

Section 2
Indiscernibility of identicals

The idea just put forward, that belief is a ternary relation among people, times and propositions, seems to be incompatible with an equally plausible and widely held principle, the indiscernibility of identicals: if X and Y are identical, then X and Y do not differ in qualities or relations; or if X and Y are identical, what is true of X is true of Y, and vice versa.

Consider the case of the vacationing archaeologist who buys a ticket to Crete and happens to believe in the indiscernibility of identicals. After a brief period of ship-board introspection—inspection, that is, of the contents of his mind, knowing quite well that neither he nor any of his colleagues have a clue where Atlantis really is, he reasons as follows: 'I believe I am going to Crete. I do not believe I am going to Atlantis. Thus something is true of Crete that is not true of Atlantis. Therefore, by the indiscernibility of identicals, Crete and Atlantis are not identical. I must announce this important discovery at once!'

Or consider the case of the mathematician who is not very good at his sums. In the middle of filling out his income tax return, he stops and thinks to himself: 'I do not believe that $1 = 2$. I do believe that $24 - 675 + 857 - 205 = 2$. Therefore, by the indiscernibility of identicals, $1 \neq 24 - 675 + 857 - 205$.' He then rechecks his figures and comes to the conclusion that $1 = 24 - 675 + 857 - 205$ after all. Since he knows that one thing is true of 1 that is not true of $24 - 675 + 857 - 205$, namely, that he did not believe it to be identical to 2 earlier, he concludes, again by the indiscernibility of identicals, that $1 \neq 24 - 675 + 857 - 205$. Since the indiscernibility of identicals is far more fundamental than the consistency of arithmetic, he concludes from the contradiction that arithmetic is inconsistent.

It may be argued, of course, that the indiscernibility of identicals should be restricted, that not absolutely *everything* true of X need be true of Y when X and Y are identical. A restriction on the indiscernibility of identicals would help circumvent the problems raised by belief and other forms of thought.

There is a cost to be paid for restricting the principle, though. Given the reflexivity of identity, i.e., that we always have X identical to X, such a restriction has as a consequence that identity is not the strongest relation a thing can have to itself. Given that *one* thing true of X is that X is identical to X, and given that Y *is* indiscernible from X, we have it also true of Y that Y is identical to X, i.e., the identity of indiscernibles holds.

So we can conclude that indiscernibility is not only a different, but an even stronger relation than identity that a thing can have to itself. And since for *all* X, X *is* indiscernible from X, we are left wondering what the nature is of those things that are not only identical to themselves, but indiscernible from themselves as well.

Furthermore, when it is argued that the indiscernibility of identicals should be restricted—that not *everything* that holds of X need hold of Y when X and Y are identical—the door is opened to a whole host of possible restrictions.

Suppose, for instance, that there is a relation R that X has to Y if and only if for a certain limited range of properties X has one from the range when Y does and vice versa. Suppose that there is a second relation R' that X has to Y if and only if for a different limited range of properties X has one of these when Y does and vice versa. Indeed, there will be a whole host of such relations. Now which of these many relations is the identity relation? And why?

When one defines identity as indiscernibility, the range of relevant properties is not limited. *All* properties are relevant, including even the property of *being indiscernible from X*. There is no problem now about making a selection within the total range of properties and justifying one's choice against others'.

Or having granted the indiscernibility of identicals it might be said that people are simply not good judges of what they don't believe. Our archaeologist, despite what he says to himself, does believe that he's going to Atlantis.

How does one explain his reluctance to say to himself that he's going to Atlantis? He's reluctant to say this to himself because he erroneously believes that he *doesn't* believe that he's going to Atlantis. Indeed, he believes that he doesn't have any beliefs about whether or not he's going to Atlantis.

This won't do. If the archaeologist believes that he doesn't believe that he's going to Atlantis, we have, by the indiscernibility of identicals and the identity of Crete and Atlantis, that he believes that he doesn't believe that he's going to Crete. But if this is so, why is it, then, that he's not equally reluctant to say to himself that he's going to Crete? After all, since, by hypothesis, he believes that he doesn't have any beliefs about whether or not he's going to Atlantis, he therefore believes that he doesn't have any beliefs about whether or not he's going to Crete.

Section 3
Indexicals

A second problem with analysing belief as a ternary relation arises because of the indexical elements that often occur in them. If the objects of belief are propositions, propositions certainly cannot be identified with the sentences we use in expressing them.

I believe that I will win the bet. My opponent believes that he will win the bet. One and only one of us will win. So the belief of one of us is true, the other false. Thus we believe distinct propositions. Yet both my opponent and I would express what we each believe by using the *same* sentence, 'I will win the bet'.

Moreover, there seems to be no indexical-free way of expressing these beliefs. For suppose there were and it took the form 'A will win the bet'. I can fail to believe what I would express by saying 'A will win the bet', while *still* believing that I will win the bet, since I can always, it seems, fail to believe what I would express by saying 'I am A'.[2] Thus what I express by saying 'A will win the bet' is not what I express by saying 'I will win the bet'.

We conclude here (1) that at least some propositions, truths and falsehoods that are objects of belief, have an essential indexical element and (2) that propositions cannot be identified with the sentences we use to express them. These conclusions should give rise to a sense of how very odd 'propositions' are on the view we are now considering.

Yet another difficulty arises to plague an attempt to solve the last. Suppose an analysis of indexical statements is offered that does allow us to express what others believe—in terms of indexical statements of our own. In trying to express what my opponent believes about his winning our bet. I can say 'He will win the bet' or 'You will win the bet'. Indeed this is how I can go about contradicting the proposition he believes. I say 'He won't win the bet' or 'You won't win the bet'.

Yet a case can be made that on the view that belief relates three things, a mind, a time and a proposition, there are some propositions, some truths and falsehoods, others can have in their minds that we cannot even *have* in our minds, much less express, and vice versa.

God, consequently, cannot possibly be omniscient, for even He cannot know all true propositions, owing to the fact that there are propositions, and true ones at that, which I can have in my mind, that He cannot even *have* in His mind, much less believe or know.

If this conclusion holds, the ternary analysis of belief brings with it a commitment to some really strange entities.

In the following it is assumed, for the sake of the argument, that at times two people *can* have the same proposition in mind—for example, when two people think regarding a third '*He* won't win the bet'. If this assumption is not granted, of course, we immediately do have the conclusion already indicated, i.e., that there are some truths and falsehoods others can believe that we cannot even have in our minds, and vice versa.

Now let us put ourselves into a very phenomenological and introspective frame of mind. We have drunk a bit too much at the party and are seated on the floor opposite a mirror, flanking a man and woman who are otherwise engaged. You have forgotten that you put on your Tony Curtis mask instead of your Ronald Reagan mask. And unbeknownst to you, your ex-wife has, at some time during the festivities, mischievously painted a scarlet 'A' upon the forehead of your mask.

You look across the room, not realising that a mirror is there, and spy a figure in a Tony Curtis mask looking at you. You think to yourself, 'My *you've* got a spot on your mask'. At the same time I look across the room and think to myself, 'My, *you've* got a spot on your mask'.

If there are cases in which you and I have the same belief, believe the same proposition, here's one—albeit a case in which indexicality seems to play an essential role. Yet in this situation, one belief you do *not* have is a belief that you would express by saying '*I've* got a spot on my mask'. You do not know that your mask has been written upon, nor do you know that it is you yourself you see in the mirror.

So, given that the proposition I believe is the one you believe, the proposition I believe is not the same as the one you *do not* believe—namely, the one you would express by saying '*I've* got a spot on my mask'.

The question arises of whether I am ever in a better position to believe the proposition you don't believe, the one you would express by saying '*I've* got a spot on my mask', than you are now concerning the figure across the room that, as it happens, is yourself. You might be surprised to learn who the figure across the room is, and you might make this discovery by having a sudden insight which you express to yourself by saying '*You're me!*'.

I might have an insight as well. The couple might have moved on, giving me a chance first to look at the mirror and then at you and think to myself '*You're you!*'. But you yourself might have *my* insight in a situation where you happened to be sitting where I was and an arrangement of mirrors made you appear in the two places I see you in. Yet this latter insight can occur without it happening that you realise that one of the figures is you yourself—what you would want to express by using the first-person pronoun.

It seems that when you think of someone in the second- or third-person way, you do not normally think of that person as yourself. I may, of course, say to myself something like 'Daniels, you idiot!', in full possession of the belief that I am Daniels. Despite appearances, I do not count this kind of case as thinking of myself in a second- or third-person way. It is more like thinking of myself with the royal 'we'. When I focus upon the content of what I have in mind, it is clear that I am not open to the discovery 'I'm Daniels!'. The content of my thought, 'Daniels, you idiot!', itself incorporates my thought 'I'm an idiot!'.

Nor does thinking of someone in a second- or third-person way imply that he is someone other than oneself. If it did, the insight you express to yourself by thinking '*You're me!*' would be self-contradictory and not true.

If these points are correct, then you and I can always think of someone in the second- or third-person way and think the same (or very similar) things about him. But, as a matter of fact, it turns out that the person we are having these same thoughts about is you. You don't, however, believe that you yourself have, in this instance, a spot on your mask. Indeed, you and I may even come to believe what each of us would express by saying 'You don't believe that you yourself have a spot on your mask'. Again we believe the same thing. Yet you still do not have a belief that you would express by saying '*I've* got a spot on my mask'.

The point of this is to make it clear that every second- and third-person belief I can have about you, you can have about yourself in a second- and third-person way without believing it to be you yourself your beliefs are about. If so, then those *additional* beliefs you have about yourself in the first-person way turn out to be beliefs I cannot have. They are beliefs I cannot even have in mind, since whenever I try to entertain one of them, I succeed only in entertaining beliefs you can have in the second- or third-person way without having the first-person belief I was originally trying to get at.

But can this really be true? Can't I have access to the first-person contents of your mind in the following way?

Suppose I believe that you believe that you yourself[3] don't have a spot on your mask and, in addition, that your belief is false. If you were to express the proposition I believe you to believe, you would do so in a first-person way, by saying 'I don't have a spot on my mask'. Now when I believe here that your belief is false, don't I have in my mind one of the propositions that allegedly no one but you could have in your mind?

No. For you, too, can believe (of the figure we both see in the Tony Curtis mask) what you would express by saying 'You believe that you yourself don't have a spot on your mask; your belief is false', while at the same time *not* believing what you would express by saying 'I have a spot on my mask'—since whether or not you yourself have a spot on your mask is something that hasn't even crossed your mind.

So to believe what you would express by saying 'Your belief is false' is not to believe what you would express by saying 'I have a spot on my mask', even though the reference of the phrase 'your belief' is to what you would express by saying 'I don't have a spot on my mask'.

If the results of this effort at introspection are correct, the view that belief is a relation between just three things: a mind, a time and a proposition, drives one to the conclusion that there are propositions that just one person can entertain.[4] Thus we *can* conclude that God isn't omniscient, not being able even to entertain all truths, much less know them—owing to the fact that there are true first-person propositions which I can entertain, that God cannot.[5]

Now what is the source of these very very odd conclusions?

It lies in the duality of the roles the 'objects' of belief must play, given the ternary analysis of belief. The third relatum of a belief must both be a truth or falsehood and a mental content. The content may be the same or very similar when two people think 'I will win the bet'. Yet the thought of one may be true, that of the other false. So there must be different objects in such a case.

On the other hand, even when there are same truth values, indeed, the same object of truth, different contents may be present—as when one person thinks, for example, 'I've got a spot on my mask' and the other looking at him thinks 'You've got a spot on your mask'. So again there must be different objects of belief.

As the result of treating truths and falsehoods as being contents, and contents as being truths and falsehoods, diversity in one respect or the other always prevails. Diversity of content makes for difference in the 'object' of belief, and so does possible diversity in truth value. While your thought 'I will win the bet' and my thought 'I will win the bet' may both be true (when we're not betting against each other), we still want to distinguish what is believed because of a difference of referent and possible truth value.

The view that belief is a ternary relation is a very difficult one to settle down in comfort with.

Section 4
Belief as quaternary

We have seen the difficulties that accompany the view that belief is a ternary relation among minds, times and propositions. Fortunately there is an easy way around this which consists in prising apart the two roles propositions must play in the ternary analysis. We can simply take belief to relate four, not three things: minds, times, truths and falsehoods (propositions) and what might be called 'meanings', 'guises' or 'appearances'.[6]

The proposition is what is true or false. The meaning is the content via which we think truths and falsehoods. In themselves meanings need be neither true nor false.

The vacationing archaeologist mentioned earlier *does* believe he is going to Atlantis, provided, to be sure, that Crete and Atlantis are identical. He believes this via the meaning of the sentence 'I'm going to Crete'. He does not believe it via the meaning of the sentence 'I'm going to Atlantis'. These two sentences have *different* meanings. The mental attitude of belief relates him, the time, the proposition that he is, at that time, going to Crete (which because Crete and Atlantis are identical is the proposition that he is, at that time, going to Atlantis[7]), and the meaning of the sentence 'I'm going to Crete'. Belief does not, in this case, relate the first three and a quite different meaning, the meaning of 'I'm going to Atlantis'.

Our mathematician friend is simply wrong if, when he says he does not believe $1 = 2$, he means that he does not believe the proposition that $1 = 2$. He does indeed believe that $1 = 2$. He believes it via the meaning of the sentence '$24 - 675 + 857 - 205 = 2$', although he does not believe it via a meaning which is quite different, the meaning of the sentence '$1 = 2$'.

Given the fourth element that appears in a mental attitude, it is easy to see how to deal with indexicals. Truths and falsehoods can be kept indexical-free. Meanings are what bring in indexical features. I believe the proposition that there is a bet between Charles B Daniels and Richard J Powers to be settled at time t by it being the case that p (in Daniels' favour) or by it being the case that not-p (in Powers' favour) and p, via the exact same meaning, the meaning of the sentence 'I will win the bet', that my opponent, Richard J Powers, believes quite a different proposition, one that entails that not-p.

Also, there is now no need to grapple with the problem of truths and falsehoods that only one mind can entertain. You can believe the exact same proposition I believe when I believe what I would express by saying 'I've got a spot on my mask'. God too! Needless to say, we believe this proposition via different meanings, you via the meaning of the sentence 'You've got a spot on your mask', I via the meaning of 'I've got a spot on my mask'. But now this difference between us is anything but puzzling. Of course you cannot believe that I, who am not you, have a spot on my mask via the meaning of the sentence 'I've got a spot on my mask'. You cannot *state* that I have a spot on my mask by saying 'I've got a spot on my mask' either.

Sentences such as 'Richard J Powers believes that he himself will win the bet' provide grave difficulties for the view that beliefs are ternary relations. To analyse such statements seems to demand that we, who are not Powers, be able to entertain or to state the proposition he believes. This we could not do since on the ternary view the proposition is a first-person one particular to Powers.

On the present view there is no such difficulty. The proposition that Powers believes is indexical-free and can be believed by anybody. And the meaning via which he believes it also seems perfectly clear and accessible to others. It is the meaning of the sentence 'I will win the bet'. What others cannot do is to put the two together the way Powers does, to believe what Powers believes via the meaning he believes it.

Finally, the introduction of meanings as a fourth relatum of beliefs brings with it a bonus, it furnishes a general way of treating appetitive and erotetic[8] attitudes as propositional.

Not only indicative sentences have meanings. So do sentences in the imperative and interrogative moods. It seems appropriate to say that epistemic forms of thought like belief are those propositional attitudes that have indicative meanings as components.

Imperative meanings will allow appetitive forms of thought to be treated as propositional. Wanting, for example, may be treated as a relation takes a mind, a time, a proposition (the proposition that has to be true for the want to be satisfied) and an imperative meaning as relata.

Suppose I want to win this afternoon's bet. The proposition involved is that there is a bet to be settled at t between Charles B Daniels and Richard J Powers . . .; the meaning involved is the meaning of the sentence 'Let me win my bet this afternoon!'.

Interrogative meanings will allow erotetic attitudes to be treated as propositional too. More will be said about the distinction of epistemic from appetitive and erotetic attitudes in the following.

It may be suggested that the third relatum of a belief, the proposition—the truth or falsehood—has now become superfluous, since in analysing belief we seem to have all we need with the subject, time and content.

This suggestion should be resisted. Belief, unlike supposition, we value because we trust there to be a connection between what's believed and what's true. It is this connection between mind and world that the third relatum of belief is designed to capture. After all, the same meaning—that of 'I will win the bet', for instance—may be related by belief to different truth values.

Both Russell and Wittgenstein were exercised by the problem of how thoughts can connect with reality. Indeed, Russell [1] held the view that the true components of a thought *were* elements of reality. His analysis of definite descriptions is designed to show how we can avoid taking what they purport to refer to as true components of thought; rather definite descriptions are analysed as incomplete symbols. In this way we preserve our thoughts intact, rather than having, so to speak, a thought with a gap or hole in it due to failure of reference. It is only those things with which we are *acquainted* that comprise the real components of our thoughts. Indeed, acquaintance gives every appearance of being Russell's ontological touchstone.

Wittgenstein, too, wrestled with this problem in the *Tractatus*. Thoughts can be false. That is, there may be nothing in reality corresponding to them. What ties thought—true *or* false—to reality is the relationship between the non-propositional elements or components of thoughts, 'names', and those components of reality that names stand for which must be there *whatever the facts*, i.e., 'objects'.

For us, the propositional component of a belief is what makes the belief be *about* reality. The 'meaning', so to speak, lies on the side of mind; the proposition on the side of reality.[9]

Section 5
Meanings

What is the ontological status of this fourth kind of relatum which seems to be needed in an analysis of belief? What kind of things are 'meanings'?

First, as noted in Daniels [2], not all of the entities that serve as contents of belief are meanings, in the strict sense of meanings of sentences of a language understood by the subjects of those beliefs.

Certain lower animals may well have beliefs without having languages. It is the wish of some moral philosophers, for example, to distinguish between an animal that is merely sentient and an animal that besides sentience has a concept of its own continuing self.

The claim of these philosophers is that while the aversion to pain of the first sort of animal is *prima facie* reason to refrain from torturing it, there is no such reason to refrain from killing it painlessly—inasmuch as this sort of animal has no aversion to death, no aversion to having no future life, since it has no concept of its own future. The beliefs of this sort of animal will, on the proposed analysis, have no meanings that are first-personal and truly future.

Furthermore, those of us who have mastered English have no claim to have exhausted, through the meanings of the sentences of our language, all meanings. The presence in English of such words as 'this' and 'that', 'these' and 'those', make English ambiguous not only with respect to the things denoted, but also with respect to the fourth sort of relata of beliefs.

I may on two occasions say 'I want that, that and that, and two of those', once when looking at the crown jewels and another time at a bakery window. Meanings come in many varieties. Insomuch as the sentence I utter can be said to be synonymous with itself—have the same meaning as itself—we have but one 'meaning' here. But with respect to the fourth relata of belief, the sort of guise or sense in which you believed (of yourself in the mirror) what you would then have expressed by saying 'My, *you've* got a spot on your mask', there are two guises or 'meanings' involved on the two occasions as well as different sets of referents. Indeed, the referents might be the same. The crown jewels might be disguised as bakery goods.

Where English has the two demonstratives 'this' and 'that', Spanish has three: 'éste', 'ése' and 'aquél'. It is hard to believe that Spaniards are making a bogus distinction when trying to convey the contents of their minds.

Also, an artist may convey to us in a portrait how a person, whom we have not seen, appears—the guise under which part of the truth about the subject appeared to him. But it is doubtful whether in any practical sense the information conveyed by the portrait can be conveyed by utterance of a string of English sentences that does not itself rely upon a demonstrative connection with what the sentences describe, with pictures, or with samples.

Secondly, it seems natural to take 'meanings' or 'guises' as appearances to minds. When you and I were looking at the figure in the Tony Curtis mask and both thinking 'My, *you've* got a spot on your mask', things appeared the same way (or at least very similarly) to us.

To be sure, the word 'appearance' will not do either to capture all of the entities that stand as fourth relata in beliefs. It does not seem appropriate to use the word 'appearance' in some cases in which you have a belief which you would express by saying 'I've got a spot on my mask'—since you need not appear one way rather than another to yourself to believe this.

To return to the original question: What kinds of things are these? One way to proceed would be to take them as primitive in an ontological category of their own, or as lumped in the ontological category of individuals with the rest of us. Indeed, lack of time (and inspiration) forces us to treat times as primitive entities in an ontological niche of their own. To do so with meanings, however, is certainly neither desirable nor satisfactory—especially when ontology of mind is the subject under investigation.

We should therefore like to suggest that these items—appearances, guises, meanings, or what have you—be taken to be *properties*, properties of minds at times.

When you believe what you would express by saying 'My, *you've* got a spot on your mask', the appearance involved is an appearance to you, a property you have.[10] When you hope that the next card will be the ace of spades, the guise involved, which you might represent by saying 'Let the next card be the ace of spades!', is a property of you.

Thus on the analysis proposed here, properties have two distinct roles *vis-à-vis* individuals. A property, which is a guise, a time and a mind may be three of the four relata of a propositional attitude; and the property may at that time also hold of that mind.

Treating guises this way brings with it a bonus. It allows us to mark a distinction that cuts across the three sorts of thought that have been mentioned—the epistemic, appetitive and erotetic. Some particular mental attitudes seem to be 'fictional', some not.

The family of the 'fictional' is meant to include such epistemic attitudes as supposing, making believe, proceeding under a hypothesis, entertaining an idea, as well as assuming, considering, making a guess, imagining and granting (in cases, for instance, in which these latter are done at another's invitation).

Propositional attitudes will be fictional when the property or guise that is the fourth relatum of the attitude *need not hold* of the mind that is the first relatum. When you believe what you would express by saying 'You've got a spot on your mask', the guise must be a property you have. When you merely suppose this, without believing it, this same guise is the fourth relatum of the propositional attitude, but it is not a property you have. And when, under this supposition, you at the same time hope the person involved is not your son-in-law, the mayor, you might do so via a guise that you might express by saying 'Let it be the case that you are not Lillian's husband!'; and this guise would not be a property you have either. In this way we can analyse desires that are held in pretence, conditionally, on supposition.

These should be distinguished from conditional preferences, preferences one has that one might express by saying 'I prefer it to be the case that p to it being the case that q'. The latter are propositional attitudes which can be either fictional or not.

Section 6
Believing, wanting, wondering

What distinguishes the basic epistemic, appetitive and erotetic attitudes? It is old hat to say that meanings come in three varieties, distinguished by mood. Can they be distinguished in any deeper way?

One basic difference between belief and wanting, on the one hand, and wondering, on the other, is that more than one proposition may be involved in wondering, while just one is involved in belief and wanting.

Suppose I wonder which US capitals aren't on rivers. That is, I wonder via the meaning of 'Which of the US capitals aren't on rivers?'. The relation of wondering relates me, the time, this meaning and a proposition that asserts that Olympia, Washington, isn't on a river; it relates me, the time, this meaning and a proposition that asserts that Sacramento, California, isn't on a river; it relates me, the time, this meaning and a proposition that asserts that Albany, New York, isn't on a river; and so on.

Thus wondering may relate me, a time, one meaning and more than one proposition.

The erotetic attitude of wondering must be distinguished from *wondering that*, as when I wonder that John arrived at all. *Wondering that* is not an erotetic attitude. It is an epistemic attitude, a kind of *being surprised that*.

The *erotetic* attitude of wondering seems to reduce to *wondering which*. When one wonders when someone will arrive, one wonders at which time he or she will arrive. When one wonders whether or not it will rain, one wonders which of two propositions will be the case. When one wonders how high a building is, one wonders which height it has. When one wonders how to do something, one wonders which method will work.

A third feature of wondering is that it has what might be called a presuppositional aspect. To wonder which face cards in a deck are missing is not to wonder which things *are* face cards in the deck *and* missing.

When one wonders which face cards in the deck are missing, one presupposes, believes, that certain things are face cards in the deck. Possible answers to the question one has in mind concern all and only the items that are face cards in the deck, not other things as well. But when one wonders which things are face cards in the deck and missing, one's presupposition is not so narrow. One may come from another culture where cards are not played. One has trouble perhaps determining what things count as face cards and cards in the deck. Are aces face cards? Are the Jokers left behind in the box, face cards in the deck?

The meaning that is the third relatum of wondering can be represented as the meaning of two open sentences that share exactly the same free variable or variables. The meaning of 'Which face cards in the deck are missing?' can be understood to be the meaning of 'x is a face card in the deck, x is missing from the deck'. The meaning of 'Which things are face cards in the deck and missing?' might be represented as one of: 'x originally came in the box that held the deck, x is a face card and missing', 'x is a card in the deck, x is a face card and missing' or even 'x is a thing (x = x), x is a face card in the deck and missing'. The meaning of 'Is it raining?' can be understood to be the meaning of '(p = it is raining) or (not-p = it is raining),p'.

A fourth feature of wondering has already been remarked upon, i.e., that when one wonders which F's are G, one believes that something F's.[11] The presupposition of wondering one believes to be satisfied by something. This feature allows a neat distinction to be drawn between belief and wanting. Belief is that attitude that always accompanies wondering and concerns its presuppositions in the way just described.

Thus we can identify two basic sorts of guises or meanings: those of . wondering and those of belief and wanting. The latter can be represented as meanings of closed sentences; the former are as described above. And because of the handy distinction just made between the propositional attitude that serves as presuppositional to wondering and the sort that doesn't, we can hold that belief, which does serve as presuppositional to wondering, and wanting, which does not, can have the same meanings as relata and succeed nonetheless in distinguishing them.

Rather than distinguishing among belief, wanting and wondering by the mood of the meanings that are their relata, we distinguish two basic 'moods', that of wondering and that of belief and wanting, and distinguish between the latter by the presuppositional relation belief has to wondering that wanting does not.

It is of interest to note how questions like 'Which F G's?' and 'Which card did he lead?', are related to our standard 'Which F's G?' questions, 'Which cards has he led?'. Both have the form 'x is a card in the deck we're now using, . . .'. The former, however, has the form 'x is a card in the deck we're now using, *there is a unique* y such that he led y during this hand and y = x'.

This kind of 'Which?' question seems to carry with it the presupposed belief that at least *two* things F. The latter has the form 'x is a card in the deck we're now using, he led x during this hand'; and the only presupposition involved here is the belief that at least *one* thing F's. We can cite the non-redundancy of the complex question 'Are there any cards missing from the deck, and if so which?', i.e., '((p = at least one card is missing from the deck) or (not-p = at least one card is missing from the deck)) and x is a card in the deck, p and (if at least one card is missing from the deck, x is missing from the deck)', as evidence that 'Which?' questions have at least the latter kind of presupposed belief.

A fifth feature of wondering arises from the fourth and may give us a clue as to the nature of variables and quantification *vis-à-vis* meanings, or the logic of synonymy.

If the meaning of 'Which face cards in the deck are missing?' can be thought of as the meaning of 'x is a face card in the deck, x is missing from the deck', then the latter will have the *same* meaning as 'y is a face card in the deck, y is missing from the deck'. In a sense the free variables in such a meaning are transparent. And if when one wonders via this meaning, one has a belief via the meaning of 'For some x, x is a face card in the deck', then it seems plausible to hold that the last meaning is the meaning of 'For some y, y is a face card in the deck'. In short, relettering with variables foreign to a sentence preserves meaning.

Furthermore, if the meaning of the complex question 'Which men are married to which women?' can be thought of as the meaning of 'x is a man and y is a woman, x is married to y', the presupposed belief will have the meaning of 'For some x and some y, x is a man and y is a woman'. But there seems no reason to say that the presupposed belief doesn't also have the meaning of 'For some y and some x, x is a man and y is a woman' as well. In short, interchange of adjacent 'for some' quantifiers preserves meaning.

To summarise, we have made the following points concerning belief, wanting and wondering:

(1)   There is exactly one proposition that one believes via a particular meaning at a particular time. The same is true of wanting. But this need not be true of wondering. Wondering may relate a particular mind, time and meaning to more than one proposition.

(2)   The erotetic attitude of wondering reduces to *wondering which.*

(3) *Wondering which* carries with it a presuppositional belief that some candidate 'fills the bill'.

(4) The meaning involved in wondering can be represented by two open sentences that share exactly the same free variable or variables, one sentence to mark out the presupposed domain, the other to point toward the propositions that provide an answer, right or wrong, to what's wondered.

(5) Where 'A' and 'B' are open sentences each of which contain all and only the free variables $v_1, \ldots, v_n$, and one wonders on an occasion via the meaning of 'A,B', one believes on that occasion via the meaning of '$(\exists v_1)\ldots(\exists v_n)A$'.

(6) Where 'A' and 'B' are as above and $u_1, \ldots, u_n$ are variables of the same sort as, respectively, $v_1, \ldots, v_n$, 'A*' and 'B*' are, respectively, the results of substituting u_1 for $v_1, \ldots, u_n$ for v_n in 'A' and 'B'. If no u_i is a v_k, $1 \leqslant i,k \leqslant n$, and in the substitution no u_i, $1 \leqslant i \leqslant n$, becomes bound where v_i was free, then the meaning of 'A*,B*' is that of 'A,B'.

(7) Where 'Q' represents some reordering of the string '$(\exists v_1)\ldots(\exists v_n)$', the meaning of 'QA' is that of '$(\exists v_1)\ldots(\exists v_n)A$'.

(8) Meanings are properties of minds at times.

(9) Finally and most controversially, if belief, wanting and wondering are considered to be, respectively, the *basic* quaternary epistemic, appetitive and erotetic attitudes, in that all other such attitudes are compounded from them, we need consider just two basic kinds of meanings—because we will be able to distinguish belief from wanting by its presuppositional role *vis-à-vis* wondering.

The reader is reminded that we've already settled on a way to mark the distinction between those attitudes that are 'fictional' and those that are not.

Section 7
A language of mind

We have made a case for taking belief, wanting and wondering to be relations with four relata: (1) minds, (2) times, (3) propositions (i.e., truths and falsehoods) and (4) meanings, appearances or guises. We now describe a language which displays these ontological categories, is faithful to the points about believing, wanting and wondering we have made in earlier sections and satisfies the constraints set out in Chapter 1 for an ontologically ideal language—save for the syncategorematic constant '$\forall$', which we have already shown how to treat.

This language contains three basic *kinds*, x, t and p, of variables that range over individuals (including minds), times and propositions respectively. Let 'x_1','x_2',... be variables of the kind x, 't_1','t_2',... be variables of the kind t, and 'p_1','p_2', ... be variables of kind p. Where K_1, ...,K_n are (not necessarily distinct) kinds of variables, this language will also contain variables 'f_1','f_2', ... of kind $\langle K_1, ..., K_n \rangle$.

Meanings (appearances, guises) were earlier said to be properties of minds at times. These, therefore, will be among the things in the range of variables of kind $\langle x,t \rangle$.

Besides variables, each kind may contain constants—as well as other complex expressions in the cases of kinds $\langle x,t \rangle$ and p.

A well-formed formula (wff) is one of the following: (1) a variable or constant in kind p, (2) an expression '$fu_1 \ldots u_n$', where 'f' is in kind $\langle K_1,..., K_n \rangle$, and '$u_1$',..., '$u_n$' are expressions in kinds $K_1,..., K_n$ respectively, and (3) '$\forall$Av' ['($\forall$v)A'] where v is any variable and A is a wff. All wffs fall into kind p.

The project would become unnecessarily complex were we to continue to treat '$\forall$' as categorematic. But that this can be done has already been shown. Besides the syncategorematic '$\forall$', the language will contain the constant '$\rightarrow$' in kind $\langle p,p \rangle$ and constants 'B', 'L' and 'W' in kind $\langle x,t,p,\langle x,t \rangle \rangle$, which represent believing, wanting and wondering.

'F' can be defined as '$\forall$pp', '$\sim$A' as '$\rightarrow$AF' and the other truth functional connectives accordingly. We shall use parentheses and write '$\rightarrow$AB' as '(A $\rightarrow$ B)' and '$\forall$Av' as '($\forall$v)A' for ease in reading. 'T' can be defined as '$\sim$F', '(A = B)' as '($\forall$f)(fA $\leftrightarrow$ fB)' where 'f' is a variable in kind $\langle p \rangle$ and A and B are wffs in which 'f' does not occur free, '$\square$A' as '(T = A)', '(A ent[ails] B)' as '$\square$(A $\rightarrow$ B)' and other modal connectives accordingly.

The language will also contain the indexicals 'i_x' and 'i_t'—'I' and 'now'— in kinds x and t respectively. We have written 'the meaning of "I've got a spot on my mask"', since this we hold to represent one of the four relata of a particular belief. To display the logic of these indexicals, the language will be equipped with a category of quotation symbols, in which 'q' is a quotation constant.

Let 'q' be a quotation symbol. Let A* be the result of replacing all the free variables in a wff A by constants or indexicals of the appropriate kinds. Then 'qA*A*' is in kind $\langle x,t \rangle$. We shall often write 'qA*' for simplicity. Let B* and C* be the results, respectively, of replacing some, but not all, of the free variables in wffs B and C by appropriate constants or indexicals so that B* and C* share the free variables that remain. Then 'qB*C*' is also in kind $\langle x,t \rangle$. We call 'A*A*' and 'B*C*' 'wlffs'. Intuitively 'qA*A*' can be read 'the meaning of "A*"', and 'qB*C*' can be read 'the meaning of "B*,C*"'. The latter designates an erotetic meaning; the former a non-erotetic meaning.

Indexicals appear in wlffs only, always 'within' quotes. No quantifier can reach in from outside a quotation and bind a variable within the quoted wlff.

Identity within kind p (of wffs) has already been defined. Identity within the various other kinds can be defined as follows: where U_1 and U_2 are expressions in kind K and 'f' is a variable in kind $\langle K \rangle$ that is not free in U_1 or U_2,

$$\text{`}(U_1 = U_2)\text{'} =_{df} \text{`}(\forall f)(fU_1 = fU_2)\text{'}.$$

To define identity for quotation symbols requires a further category of variables. Letting 'q' be a quotation variable and 'q_1' and 'q_2' be quotation symbols, and letting 'e' be a variable and 'e_1' and 'e_2' be variables or constants in this further category, 'qe' will be an expression in kind $\langle x,t \rangle$,

$$\text{`}(q_1 = q_2)\text{'} =_{df} \text{`}(\forall e)(q_1 e = q_2 e)\text{'},$$
$$\text{`}(e_1 = e_2)\text{'} =_{df} \text{`}(\forall q)(q e_1 = q e_2)\text{'},$$

and where U_1 and U_2 are both erotetic or non-erotetic wlffs,

$$\text{`}(U_1 = U_2)\text{'} =_{df} \text{`}(\forall q)(qU_1 = qU_2)\text{'}.$$

The comprehension axioms for the various categories are as one might expect:

$$(\exists u)(u = v),$$

where u and v are both in p, $\langle x,t \rangle$, quotation symbols or the category of the variables e, and u is not free in v.

$$(\exists f)(\forall v_1) \ldots (\forall v_n)(f v_1 \ldots v_n = A),$$

where $v_1, \ldots, v_n$ are distinct variables in kinds $K_1, \ldots, K_n$ respectively, f is in kind $\langle K_1, \ldots, K_n \rangle$, A is a wff and f is not free in A.

Section 8
Ideal language and mind

In an ideal language, quantified variables, their kinds and their order are what mirror the things there are in reality and their categories and connections. The constants and indexicals of a language, however, signal the distinctions there are in thought. It is natural, then, that an ideal language for an ontology of mind sentences differing in constants, or indexicals in their order or in their number, should represent different thoughts, different meanings or guises—though not necessarily different truths or falsehoods.

The considerations concerning variables mentioned earlier in connection with 'Which?' questions, with wondering and with the presuppositions of wondering seem to lead easily to the following principles for sameness and difference of meaning or guise:

(1) Where u and v are variables of the same sort, where v does not occur in a wlff A and where A* is the result of replacing all bound occurrences of u in A by v, A and A* should have the same meaning.
(2) The wlffs '(∀u)(∀v)A' and '(∀v)(∀u)A' should mean the same, as should '(∃u)(∃v)A' and '(∃v)(∃u)A'.
(3) Where C and D are open wlffs which contain the same free variables, u and v are variables of the same sort, v does not occur in C or D and 'C*D*' is the result of replacing all free occurrences of u in 'CD' by v, then 'CD' and 'C*D*' should mean the same.
(4) The sameness of meaning relation should be transitive.
(5) In all other cases, different wlffs should have different meanings in an ontologically ideal language, since all other wlffs will differ in constants or indexicals, in their order or in their number.

Section 9
Some simple theorems

In this section we list and discuss certain theorems a logic of belief, wanting and wondering ought to have. In what follows 'f' will be a variable in kind $\langle x,t \rangle$.

First, if meanings are to be treated as properties of minds at times, then that there *is* such a property should be guaranteed for every meaning. Thus

(1) $(\forall e)(\exists f)(f = qe)$,

where 'q' is the quotation constant and 'e' a variable of the special sort described in section 7. From (1) we have by instantiation:

(2) $(\exists f)(f = qCD)$,

where 'CD' is a wlff. It was taking meanings as properties of minds at times that allowed us to distinguish in a simple way between fictional and non-fictional belief, wanting and wondering.

If 'B', 'L' and 'W' represent non-fictional belief, wanting and wondering, then we should have the following:

(3) $(\forall f)(\forall x)(\forall t)(\forall p)(Gxtpf \rightarrow fxt)$,

where G is 'B', 'L' or 'W'. On the other hand, in the fictional case we ought to have

(4) $(\forall f)(\forall x)(\forall t)(\forall p)(\Diamond Gxtpf \rightarrow [\Diamond(Gxtpf \wedge fxt) \wedge \Diamond(Gxtpf \wedge \sim fxt)])$.

Whether one has a property that is a meaning ought to be independent of whether anyone else has it at that or any other time and whether one has it oneself at any other time. This we guarantee by

(5) $(\forall f)(\Diamond(\exists x)(\exists t)(\exists p)[Bxtpf \vee Lxtpf \vee Wxtpf]$
      $\rightarrow (\forall x)(\forall x')(\forall t)(\forall t')[((x \neq x') \vee (t \neq t'))$
      $\rightarrow (\Diamond(fxt \wedge fx't') \wedge \Diamond(fxt \wedge \sim fx't'))])$.

Meanings of wlffs ought to obey the special requirements set out at the end of section 8 for an ontology of mind. Thus we will have

(6) $CD = C'D'$,

where CD and C'D' are wlffs that meet the requirements for sameness of meaning set out at the end of section 8 and

(7) $CD \neq C'D'$,

where CD and C'D' meet the requirements for difference of meaning set out there.

Finally, erotetic meanings should not figure in believing and wanting, and non-erotetic meanings should not figure in wondering. Thus

(8) $(\forall f)(\Diamond(\exists x)(\exists t)(\exists p)Wxtpf \rightarrow [\sim \Diamond(\exists x)(\exists t)(\exists p)Bxtpf$
      $\wedge \sim \Diamond(\exists x)(\exists t)(\exists p)Lxtpf])$,

(9) $(\forall f)([\Diamond(\exists x)(\exists t)(\exists p)Bxtpf \vee \Diamond(\exists x)(\exists t)(\exists p)Lxtpf]$
      $\rightarrow \sim \Diamond(\exists x)(\exists t)(\exists p)Wxtpf)$,

and in particular

(10) $(\forall x)(\forall t)(\forall p) \sim \text{W}xtpq\text{AA}$,

where 'AA' is a non-erotetic wlff; and

(11) $(\forall x)(\forall t)(\forall p) \sim \text{B}xtpq\text{CD}$,

(12) $(\forall x)(\forall t)(\forall p) \sim \text{L}xtpq\text{CD}$,

where 'CD' is an erotetic wlff.
    Belief, we have argued, is presuppositional to wondering. So we want to
have:

(13) $(\forall x)(\forall t)((\exists p)\text{W}xtpq\text{A*C*} \rightarrow (\exists p)\text{B}xtpq(\exists v_1) \ldots (\exists v_n)\text{A})$,

where 'A*C*' is an erotetic wlff, $v_1, \ldots, v_n$ are exactly the variables occurring
free in A*, x and t are not among $v_1, \ldots, v_n$ and A* differs from A only in that
all unquoted occurrences of the indexicals i_x and i_t in A* are replaced in A by
occurrences of x and t respectively.
    In the simplest case, when we wonder something via the meaning of
'Which A's C?', we believe something via the meaning of 'At least one thing
A's'. Not only do we believe this, we *are sure* of it, i.e., we do *not* wonder
something via the meaning of 'Does anything A?'. Thus we ought to have

(14) $(\forall x)(\forall t)((\exists p)\text{W}xtpq\text{AC} \rightarrow \sim (\exists p)\text{W}xtpq((p' = (\exists v_1) \ldots (\exists v_n)\text{A})$
$\vee (\sim p' = (\exists v_1) \ldots (\exists v_n)\text{A}),p'))$,

where $v_1, \ldots, v_n$ are the variables free in A, AC is an erotetic wlff and p' is a
propositional variable.
    Indexicals and the relation between meanings which may contain
indexical elements and propositions may be handled quite intuitively as
follows:

(15) $(\forall x)(\forall t)(\forall p)(\text{G}xtpq\text{A*A*} \rightarrow (p = \text{A}))$,

where A*A* is a non-erotetic wlff, A differs from A* only in that all
unquoted occurrences of i_x and i_t in A* are replaced in A by occurrences of x
and t respectively and G is either 'B' or 'L'. The proposition that a person x
believes at time t via the meaning of 'I now f' is that x f's at t.

Wondering is treated similarly:

$$(16)\quad (\forall x)(\forall t)((\exists v_1) \ldots (\exists v_n)A \to (\forall p)[WxtpqA^*C^*$$
$$\to (\exists v_1) \ldots (\exists v_n)(A \wedge (p = C))]),$$

where A^*C^* is an erotetic wlff, $v_1, \ldots, v_n$ are exactly the variables occurring free in A^*, x, t and p are not among $v_1, \ldots, v_n$ and A^* and C^* differ from A and C respectively only in that all unquoted occurrences of i_x and i_t in A^* and C^* are replaced in A and C by occurrences of x and t respectively. Again, in the easiest case, the propositions wondered via the meaning of 'Which US capital cities are not on rivers?' are: Olympia, Washington, is not on a river; Albany, New York, is not on a river; and so on. Among these propositions is not: Scottsdale, Arizona, is not on a river.

It remains to identify the proposition(s) wondered when one's presupposed belief fails to be true. What proposition, for instance, does one wonder when one wonders via the meaning of, say, 'Which unicorns have won the Kentucky Derby?' or 'Which even prime number greater than five is the number of children of Pierre Trudeau?'?

We take it to be the impossible proposition that is wondered:

$$(17)\quad (\forall x)(\forall t)(\sim(\exists v_1) \ldots (\exists v_n)A \to (\forall p)[WxtpqA^*C^* \to (p = F)]),$$

where A^*C^* is as above, $v_1, \ldots, v_n$ are exactly the variables occurring free in A^* and x and t are not among $v_1, \ldots, v_n$.

At a given time, one may wonder different propositions via a single meaning. But one may not on a particular occasion believe or want different propositions via a single meaning. Hence

$$(18)\quad (\forall x)(\forall t)(\forall p_1)(\forall p_2)(\forall f)([Gxtp_1f \wedge Gxtp_2f] \to [p_1 = p_2]),$$

where G is 'B' or 'L'.

A person can wonder *almost* anything—'Are there five primes between zero and ten?', 'Is there any zinc on the moon?', 'Are triangles trilateral?'. There seems to be just one thing that can't be wondered, 'Are triangles triangles?'. Thus we have

$$(19)\quad \sim(\exists p)WxtpqCC.$$

where C is a wlff with at least one free variable.

We conclude with two minor housekeeping points:

$$(20)\quad (\forall x)(\forall t)(\forall p_1)(\forall p_2)(\forall f)([Wxtp_1f \wedge Wxtp_2f] \to [Wxtp_1f = Wxtp_2f]),$$

i.e., there is just one wondering done via a given meaning at a given time, even though more than one proposition may be wondered via that meaning by a person at that time.

$$(21) \quad (\forall e_1)(\forall e_2)((qe_1 = qe_2) \rightarrow (e_1 = e_2)),$$

i.e., the quotation constant used in our theorems does not allow more synonymy than is called for by an ontologically ideal language.

Section 10
Other mental attitudes

Besides fictional and non-fictional believing, wanting and wondering, there are myriad other quaternary mental attitudes that may or may not be characterised in terms of these one way or another.

It seems to be an impossible task to show that every quaternary mental attitude can be represented by a constant in kind $\langle x,t,p,\langle x,t\rangle\rangle$ and an axiomatic characterisation in our language in terms of its relations to these six mental attitudes. But certain mental attitudes can assuredly be characterised this way.

To *have some doubts* whether p via a meaning A, for example, is to wonder whether A, i.e., to wonder via the meaning of '$((p = A) \vee (\sim p = A))$,p'.

To *be certain* or *sure* that p via A is to believe that p via A and not have any doubts whether p via A. As was indicated in the preceding section, it seems reasonable to hold that the presuppositions of wondering are not merely believed, but believed without doubt, with certainty.

To *be glad* that p via A is to be certain that p via A, wanting that p via A, but having wondered via the meaning of '$((p = A^*) \vee (\sim p = A^*))$,p', where A^* has a future tense instead of present or 'later' instead of 'now'.

Spinoza in Book III of his *Ethics* provides a nice example for philosophers of this kind of analysis. But there remain many many difficult cases. We shall address a few of these.

Section 11
Intending

What is intending?

First, to intend to do A is not merely to intend to try to do A. 'Are you going to make Tung Po pork for the banquet?' a friend may ask—to which the answer may be 'Well, if good side pork is available I shall'. Here, because of doubts about whether success is possible given the circumstances, there is not a categorical intention to make Tung Po pork. So one condition of intending is a lack of doubts as to whether one will succeed. That the road to Hell is paved with good intentions is as much a comment upon the ease with which we are free of doubts about our prowess, as it is about our virtuous aspirations or the steadiness of our resolve.

Secondly, we can intend only what we see ourselves as having a free choice in doing. The man falling past the 42nd floor of the Hancock Building can intend to hit the ground with a splat only if he views himself as having some choice in the matter. And because we normally believe ourselves to have no choice about changing what's already happened, we do not intend to make the past other than it is.

An attempt to analyse intention as a species of doubt-free belief was presented in Daniels [3]. The contents of these particular beliefs were meanings of sentences of the form 'I am bringing [shall bring] it about freely that A'. The conjecture was that intentions can be analysed as doubt-free beliefs with meanings like these. But a counter-example was then offered that shows the analysis to fail. It is instructive to repeat it here.

Dr Jekyll, the analytic man of science, comes to realise, on the basis of the evidence his trained eye detects around him, that he is the nefarious Hyde.

One day Mr. Hyde forms an intention to commit a murder on the following night and writes in his diary 'Tomorrow night I shall commit a murder'. A short time later he changes his mind. This bit of information does not find its way into his diary. That evening Dr. Jekyll reads Hyde's diary entry and on the basis of it and his experience of Hyde's character forms the belief that he will commit a murder, i.e., Jekyll believes *via* the meaning of 'I shall freely bring it about that someone is killed' that Jekyll will freely bring it about that someone is killed. Jekyll has no doubts about the firmness of Hyde's supposed resolve or about Hyde's ability to carry it through if he is not stopped. . . .

. . . [Jekyll] knows that he is strapped to a chair by bands that will spring open at the stroke of midnight. He knows that at the stroke of midnight he will, as always, turn into Hyde. Can he commit suicide by stopping his breath by sheer will-power and thus thwart Hyde's plot? No. He discovers that an automatic breathing device has been clamped to his face. He tries his best to escape from his bonds, but he cannot.

Jekyll then sits back, grows calm, and takes stock. He doesn't rationalize by thinking of Hyde as *him*. He knows that Hyde's actions are as free as his own. And he believes, having no grounds for doubt, *via* the meaning of 'I shall freely bring it about that someone is killed tonight' that he will freely bring it about that someone is killed that night. Yet Jekyll does not intend to kill someone that night, and neither, for that matter, does Hyde.

. . . What seems to be lacking in Jekyll that prevents his belief from being an intention is an overriding desire to kill someone that night. Jekyll believes that

Hyde wants to kill someone; and in the same calm lucid frame of mind in which Jekyll believes that he himself will kill someone that night, Jekyll believes that he himself has an overriding desire to kill someone that night, since he believes that Hyde has such a desire and that he himself is Hyde. Jekyll is wrong about his desiring to kill someone. He doesn't have such a desire, since Hyde doesn't.[12]

Taking the suggestion offered in the last paragraph, what seems to be required to complete the analysis of intending is to provide an analysis of an overriding desire to bring it about freely that A.

We offer the following: one has an overriding desire to bring it about freely that A if (1) one wants via the meaning of 'I am bringing [shall bring] it about freely that A' and (2) one has a further want via the meaning of 'For every proposition p such that my bringing it about freely that p is incompatible, given my circumstances, with my bringing it about freely that A, if it were the case that I bring it about freely that A or I bring it about freely that p, it would be the case that I bring it about freely that A'. Alternately, (2) might read: one has a preference for anything with the meaning 'I am bringing [shall bring] it about freely that A' to anything with the meaning 'I am bringing [shall bring] it about freely that p', where one has a belief via the meaning of 'My bringing it about freely that A is incompatible, given my circumstances, with my bringing it about freely that p'.

Thus to intend to do A is to be certain via the meaning of 'I am bringing [shall bring] it about freely that A' and to have an overriding desire to bring it about freely that A.

Section 12
Knowing

Knowing that is even more difficult and puzzling than intending. Peter Klein [1] offers the following analysis:

S knows that A iff

(1) S believes that A.
(2) the set of S's beliefs provides no grounds for doubt as to whether A, and
(3) there is no truth B such that if B were added to the set of S's beliefs, the resulting set would provide grounds for doubt as to whether A.

Klein's analysis is in terms of the notions of believing and of a set's providing grounds for doubt—in other words, wondering. Clause (2) prevents the very reasonable belief one has before a lottery draw that one's ticket is a loser from being knowledge that it is. The background beliefs that the lottery is fair and that the ticket has at least some chance of winning provide grounds for doubt as to whether the ticket is in fact a loser.

Clause (3) operates in the following sort of case: My watch is very reliable. I look at it and see that it says 11:43. I have no doubts as to the reliability of the watch. I have no doubts as to what time it is. And incidentally, the time is indeed 11:43. Do I know that it's 11:43?

Not in this example. The watch, it turns out, stopped running at 11:43 last night. If I were to believe the true proposition that the watch stopped at 11:43 last night and hasn't been restarted since, in addition to what I already believe, the resulting set of beliefs would provide grounds for doubt as to whether it's now 11:43.

To some, Klein's analysis has seemed too strong. It can be weakened by replacing (3) by any of the following:

(3a)   the set consisting of S's beliefs plus the negations of S's false beliefs does not provide grounds for doubt as to whether A.
(3b)   there is no falsehood B such that if B were removed from the set of S's beliefs, the resulting set would leave room for doubt as to whether A.
(3c)   the set consisting of all S's true beliefs does not leave room for doubt as to whether A.

In (3b) and (3c), the notion of a set of beliefs leaving room for doubt is the key one. A set of beliefs may provide grounds for doubt when in some sense its members are in conflict. But a set of beliefs may also leave room for doubt when its membership is insufficient to settle a matter. My present set of beliefs is insufficient concerning the exact whereabouts this moment of the Archbishop of Canterbury.

In the case described above, I have a false belief that my watch has been running continuously since I last checked it. Without this belief, I might well wonder whether it is 11:43, despite what the watch says. In Gettier's [1] notorious Ford case, the removal of the false belief that Jones owns a Ford would leave Smith room for doubt as to his belief that either Jones owns a Ford or Brown is in Boston. In the Gettier case, Smith has no beliefs concerning Brown's location and so no reason to settle on Boston rather than Palo Alto.

The key to these analyses of knowledge lies in the notion of a set of beliefs providing grounds, or leaving room, for doubt concerning a belief. Can we analyse any of these notions in terms of the limited stock of mental attitudes we have at hand: believing, wanting and wondering?

Clearly this cannot be done in terms of just the *propositions* involved in these mental attitudes. The man who believes that Hesperus is not Phosphorus believes the proposition that Hesperus is not Hesperus, the necessarily false proposition, by virtue of the indiscernibility of identicals— at least in classical logic. When a man believes that he is himself, he believes the necessarily true proposition, the denial of the necessarily false proposition. So the set of *propositions* he believes contains both a proposition and its denial and would, one would think, provide grounds for doubt concerning both—if, that is, propositions were all that counted. The man, in consequence, would not know that he is himself. If we are to stick to classical logic and avoid this kind of result, meanings *must* enter into the analysis.

Furthermore, dogmatic, overly confident people do not have doubts, do not wonder, where they really ought to; and timid, insecure people often have doubts where they ought to have none. Suppose we try to analyse the second clause of Klein's definition as follows:

(2a) S does not wonder whether A via the meaning of '$((p = A) \lor (\sim p = A)),p$',

i.e., via the meaning of 'Which is the case: A or not-A?'. Difficulties surface immediately in that Klein's notion of a set providing grounds for doubt is collapsed to merely doubting whether A. The dogmatic individual doesn't doubt, the insecure one does. Are we to say, then, that the former knows and the latter doesn't? This seems implausible.

At least part of what appears to be required is the notion of an *erotetic ideal*. What, given a set of beliefs, *ought* one to wonder, to have some doubts, about? We propose the following as truths that would hold of a mind x at a time t if things were erotetically ideal. We abbreviate both 'qAA' and '$q((p = A) \lor (\sim p = A))p$' by writing '$qA$', letting context sort out which is which.

EI1. $(\exists p)Bxtpq\square(A \leftrightarrow C) \rightarrow [(\exists p)WxtpqA \leftrightarrow (\exists p)WxtpqC]$.

EI2. $[(\exists p)Bxtpq\square(A \rightarrow (C \leftrightarrow D)) \land (\exists p)BxtpqA] \rightarrow [(\exists p)WxtpqC \leftrightarrow (\exists p)WxtpqD]$.

EI3. $[(\exists p)BxtpqA \land (\exists p)Bxtpq \sim A] \rightarrow (\exists p)WxtpqA$.

EI4. $[\sim (\exists p)BxtpqA \land \sim (\exists p)Bxtpq \sim A \land (\exists f)(\exists p)Bxtpf] \rightarrow (\exists p)WxtpqA$.

EI5. $[(\exists p)Bxtpq\square(A \rightarrow C) \land (\exists p)BxtpqA \land (\exists p)WxtpqC] \rightarrow (\exists p)WxtpqA$.

EI3 will be helpful if (3) of Klein's analysis or alternative (3a) is used, and EI4 if alternative (3b) or (3c) is used.

EI5 is of partial help with the watch example. I believe that the time is

11:43. Why? Because I believe that the watch says 11:43, that the watch is running and that the watch is reliable when running. I also believe that these jointly entail that the watch is running. Under any of the analyses mentioned above, if things were erotetically ideal, I would wonder whether the watch is running, either because on (3) or (3a) I believe both that it is running and that it is not running by EI3, or because on (3b) or (3c) I have no beliefs as to whether it is or isn't running by EI4. Thus, by EI5, if things were erotetically ideal, I would have some doubts about any conjunction I believe, one of whose conjuncts is 'The watch is running'. So I ought to have some doubts about my belief that the watch says 11:43 *and* the watch is running *and* the watch is reliable when running.

EI1 through EI5 will not get us all the way however. They do not suffice to make it ideal that I have at least some doubts concerning my belief that my lottery ticket is a loser.

Suppose that I am a dogmatic, yet benevolent pessimist. I buy the ticket from benevolent motives. I believe part of the proceeds of the lottery will go to support the needy. Yet because I am a dogmatic pessimist, I am dead sure, absolutely certain, that my ticket will lose—even though I also believe the lottery to be fair and above board. Indeed, acting on the certainty of my belief, I throw the ticket away.

Here, provided in fact that the ticket will lose, there seems to be no truth I can add to my set of beliefs, as per (3) or (3a), or falsehood I can subtract, as per (3b) or (3c), that will generate the appropriate wondering via EI1 through EI5—if, owing to some quirk of character on my part, it's not there in the first place.

To resolve this difficulty we must ask why, in the first place, I even *have* the belief that my ticket is a loser. I have this belief *because* I have other beliefs which provide grounds or reasons for it.

It is the same in the watch example. I have the belief that the time is 11:43 because I have the belief that my watch says 11:43, the watch is running and the watch is reliable when running. It seems, then, that to analyse knowledge we need to appeal to a notion of one belief providing grounds or reason for another, in addition to belief and wondering.

Let us represent this further notion by a constant 'H' in kind $\langle x,t,p,\langle x,t\rangle,p,\langle x,t\rangle\rangle$. 'Hxtp$_1f_1p_2f_2$' will say that x's belief at t that p$_1$ via f$_1$ is a ground or reason for x's belief at t that p$_2$ via f$_2$.

What will characterise 'H' axiomatically in the first place and under erotetically ideal circumstances in the second? The following suffice for the purposes at hand. As an axiom we might have:

H1. $(\forall x)(\forall t)(\forall p_1)(\forall f_1)(\forall p_2)(\forall f_2)(Hxtp_1f_1p_2f_2 \rightarrow [Bxtp_1f_1 \land Bxtp_2f_2])$.

And in erotetically ideal circumstances, we should have

EI6. $[(a)(\exists p_1)(\exists p_2)Hxtp_1qAp_2qC \;\wedge\; (b)[\sim(\exists p)Bxtpq\square(A \to C)$
$\vee\;(\exists p)Bxtpq \sim \square(A \to C) \vee (\exists p)Wxtpq\square(A \to C)] \;\wedge\; (c)$
$\sim(\exists f)((f \neq qA) \wedge (\exists p_1)(\exists p_2)Hxtp_1fp_2qC)] \to (\exists p)WxtpqC$

EI7. $[(\exists p_1)(\exists p_2)Hxtp_1qAp_2qC \;\wedge\; (\exists p)WxtpqA \;\wedge\; \sim(\exists f)((f \neq qA)$
$\wedge\;(\exists p_1)(\exists p_2)Hxtp_1fp_2qC)] \to (\exists p)WxtpqC.$

In EI6 condition (a) says that x's belief via the meaning of 'A' forms a reason for x's belief at t via the meaning of 'C'. Condition (b) says that, either epistemologically or erotetically this reason falls short of logical sufficiency. And condition (c) says that x at t has *no other* reason for believing something via the meaning of 'C'. And if these conditions are satisfied, then EI6 says that one ideally will wonder whether C.

One may, of course, have more than one basis for a certain belief. I may believe a certain complex arithmetical truth because an eminent mathematician friend has told me that it's true and because with great effort I've worked through his proof myself. Whether there are any ungrounded beliefs is a question that we need not settle.

The force of EI7 is to say that if one wonders about the basis for one's belief, then ideally one will wonder about the belief itself.

EI6 takes care of the lottery case. My belief that the lottery is fair and the odds are very very much against my ticket being a winner *is* my reason for believing that my ticket is a loser. It is because of the former belief that I have the latter belief. And, dogmatic as I am, I do not believe that the former belief entails the latter, or if I do believe this, I'm wrong, and clause (b) will be satisfied via (3), (3a), (3b) or (3c) of the analysis of knowledge. Nor do I have some other reason for believing my ticket to be a loser. If things are erotetically ideal, I will wonder whether my ticket is a loser.

EI7 resolves what remains of the watch example. By EI5 I have some doubts, when things are erotetically ideal, concerning my grounds for believing that the time is 11:43. My grounds consist of my belief that the watch says 11:43 and the watch is running and the watch is reliable when running. I have no other grounds for believing the time to be 11:43. So I ought to have some doubts as to whether the time is 11:43.

What remains is to explicate the notion of an erotetic ideal for an individual x at a time t. Informally, an erotetically ideal world is one in which x at t has the beliefs he does in the actual world plus or minus those selected by one of (3), (3a), (3b) or (3c), in which EI1–EI7 hold, and in which as far as possible x's beliefs at t are grounded no more than the ways they are in the actual world.

Our language of mental attitudes contains the wherewithal to express this. We can define a maximal or world proposition[13] as follows:

$$\text{`(Max p)'} =_{df} \text{`}(\lozenge p \wedge (\forall p')[(p \text{ ent } p') \vee (p \text{ ent } \sim p')])\text{'}.$$

As axioms we should have:

Max1. $(\exists p)(p \wedge (\text{Max } p))$
Max2. $(\forall p)[(\forall p')((\text{Max } p') \rightarrow (p' \text{ ent } p)) \rightarrow (p = T)].$

Relative to a maximal proposition p, a maximal proposition p' will be erotetically ideal for x at t, if p' entails that x at t believes everything p entails x does at t, minimally adjusted in light of one of (3), (3a), (3b) or (3c), if p' entails EI1–EI7, and if p' entails that x's beliefs at t are grounded in a certain way, p entails that x's beliefs at t are grounded in that way.

Finally, a maximal proposition p_1 will entail that x knows that p via the meaning of 'A' just when there is an erotetically ideal p_2 such that p_2 entails that x believes that p via the meaning of 'A', p_2 entails that x's belief that p via the meaning of 'A' is grounded in the way that p_1 entails that it is, and p_2 entails that x does not wonder whether p via the meaning of '$((p_3 = A) \vee (\sim p_3 = A)),p_3$'.

Section 13
Knowing which

Given an analysis of *knowing that*, how is one to analyse *knowing which*? Indeed, *knowing which* seems one of a whole family of attitudes that contains, for example, understanding which, remembering which and having an idea as to which.

First, when one knows which F's G one does not wonder via the meaning of 'Which F's G?' (i.e., the meaning of 'Fx,Gx').

Secondly, the extremes of *knowing which* are easy: when one knows that *all* F's G or that *none* do, one knows which F's G. So when one knows something via the meaning of 'All F's G' or 'No F's G', one knows which F's G.

We are left, then, with the intermediate cases in which one knows that some F's G and some don't. One may know which numbers between two and twelve are prime by knowing that all and only those written on the right-hand side of the blackboard are, or by knowing that a number is between two and twelve and prime if and only if it is three, five, seven or eleven.

This suggests an analysis of the intermediate cases. In these cases one knows which F's G when there is some proposition one knows via the meaning of '$(\forall x)((Fx \wedge Gx) \leftrightarrow A)$', where 'A' is a wff in which 'x' and no other variable occurs free and it is possible to wonder via the meaning of 'Fx $\wedge$ Gx,A' or 'A,Fx $\wedge$ Gx'. That is, it should be possible to wonder which of the prime numbers between two and twelve are on the right-hand side of the blackboard or which of the numbers on the right-hand side of the blackboard are primes between two and twelve.

More generally then, one knows which via qCD, where 'C' and 'D' are open wffs that share the same free variables, when

(1)   one doesn't wonder via qCD, and

(2a)   one knows something via $q(\forall v_1) \ldots (\forall v_n)(C \rightarrow D)$, where $v_1, \ldots, v_n$ are the free variables in C, or

(2b)   one knows something via $q \sim (\exists v_1) \ldots (\exists v_n)(C \wedge D)$, where the variables are as above or

(2c)   one knows something via $q(\forall v_1) \ldots (\forall v_n)((C \wedge D) \leftrightarrow E)$ and it is possible to wonder something via qC $\wedge$ DE or qEC $\wedge$ D, where the variables are as above and are just those free in E.

Section 14
Iterations

We have not yet touched upon iterations of mental attitudes. One person may, for instance, have desires about the beliefs of others, or beliefs about what others desire, or puzzlement as to what they do believe.

God, of course, would be in a position not merely to know which *propositions* the rest of us believe, want and wonder, but also to know in each case the exact *guise* involved in our doing so. But we mortals are normally not in this knowledgeable position regarding the mental attitudes of others—although at times we may think we are.

Suppose, on viewing a snapshot, John and I both realise that the woman in it is his wife. I also realise that John has realised this. I may think to myself via the meaning of 'John just realised that the woman in the photo is his wife via the meaning of "The woman in the photo is my wife"'. Yet perhaps I'm wrong about the guise under which he believes it.

Perhaps the meaning involved in John's realisation is the meaning of 'The woman in the photo is *our* wife'. John may, unbeknownst to me, secretly think of himself as Henry VIII and use the royal 'we'. Or he and the men I know as his lodgers may come originally from Tibet and have been polyandrously married to the woman there.

I may be mistaken in pinning a guise on John so precisely, and I may not.

But in what is probably the normal run of cases, I am not that fine and precise. I may, for example, realise that John has realised that *I* recognise the woman in the photo. Here I do not commit myself in my thoughts to a particular meaning that John has in mind. I'm not thinking of the exact meaning John has in his mind when he thinks about me.

Yet in the normal course of events I do commit myself to some degree concerning the guises involved in other's beliefs. I am not merely thinking via the meaning of 'There is some meaning f such that John realises via f that I realise that the woman in the photo is John's wife'. I would rule out, for example, the meanings of all the following as candidates for the meaning I believe to be in John's mind: 'Two plus two equals four', 'That tree's an oak', 'The grandson of the dentist Charles L Daniels from Aurora, Illinois, and the railway postal worker Clinton E Berger from Oak Park, Illinois, realises that the woman in the photograph taken from a negative exposed on the 3rd of July, 1977, in Topeka, Kansas, with an Olympus Pen camera is the wife of the Tibetan who twice fell off the roof of his house and broke his right little finger in two places and his big toe in one'.

Generally in cases like this, what is in the mind of a person, S, about what is in the mind of another person, S′, is not a meaning of the form 'There is an f such that S′ believes that A via f', but is rather one of the form 'There is an f such that O(f) and S′ believes that A via f', where O represents a particular condition on the meaning f that records and delimits the sort of meanings S thinks may be on the mind of S′. O may be a disjunction of particular candidate meanings, a constant or take a host of other forms.

Then, too, S may not be willing to be precise about the particular proposition S′ has an attitude toward either. S may think about S′ via meanings of the form 'There is an f and a p such that O(f) and P(p) and S′ believes that p via f', where O is as above and P records and delimits what sort of proposition S thinks may be on the mind of S′.

In brief, when I have a realisation via the meaning of 'I realise that John realises that I recognise the woman in the photo', the indexical 'I' here figures in the meaning *I* have in mind, not in the meaning I believe John to have in *his* mind.

Section 15
Non-quaternary attitudes

We have already seen the need for one non-quaternary feature of thought in connection with knowledge—the relation of dependence of one belief upon another. There are 'relations' among propositions, like that represented by the $\langle p,p \rangle$ constant '$\rightarrow$' and there are 'relations' among mental contents. The history of philosophy is full of debates as to whether, say, causation is an 'objective' feature of the world or whether it is 'mind-dependent'.

Fortunately we do not have to take sides firmly on issues like these. But *vis-à-vis* 'relations' among propositions and 'relations' among beliefs and desires we can propose at least one test to help sort out candidates. It might be argued that what makes one belief grounds or reason for another is, like what is represented by '→', a relation between propositions.

Our test is simple. Where such a connection is proposed, let us represent it by a sentence connective # in kind $\langle p,p \rangle$. Then for sentences A and B, it should make sense to write '$(\exists v)(A \# B)$'. In short, since the constant '#' makes one sentence out of two, we then proceed to quantify the result.

But if we are dealing with a mental relation between *two* mental contents, like that represented in section 12 by 'H', the contents remain separate. And a single '$(\exists v)$' cannot be added to *two* sentences to make a sentence. We *can* write, say, '$(\exists v)HxtAqABqB$' in which the 'H' occurs within the scope of '$(\exists v)$'. But we cannot write '$Hxt(\exists v)Aq(\exists v)ABqB$' and have an occurrence of a variable 'v' in 'B' get bound by the '$(\exists v)$' that stands at the beginning of the wff '$(\exists v)A$'.

Suppose the grounds for my believing that my lottery ticket is a loser is my belief that the lottery is fair and the odds of it losing are well over 100,000 to 1. This state of affairs can be thought of in two ways: (1) as a relation between two mental contents and (2) as a relation between two propositions.

(1) was the approach adopted in section 12, where the constant 'H' represented a mental relation between a proposition and meaning and *another* proposition and meaning.

Under view (2) the analysis would go as follows: I have two beliefs: (a) that the lottery is fair and the odds for my ticket losing are well over 100,000 to 1 and (b) that it's being the case that the lottery is fair and the odds for my ticket losing are well over 100,000 to 1 *provides good support for* its being the case that my ticket is a loser. I put beliefs (a) and (b) together in a rational way and by virtue of the inductive statistical warrant evident in belief (b) I believe that (c) my ticket is a loser.

Now in case (1) what connects (c) and (a) *is* the mental attitude represented by 'H'. Any single quantifier reaching into both (a) and (c) also has within its scope my mental attitude that connects the two. In case (2), however, since (b) is a single belief I have, a single quantifier can reach into both (a) and (c) without having within its scope any mental attitudes or relations. Letting '#' symbolise the connective 'its being the case that . . . provides good support for its being the case that . . .', we can have '$(\exists v)(A \# B)$'.

We must ask ourselves whether we wish to hold, say, that it makes sense to say 'there are at least two things x and y such that its being the case xRy *provides good support for* it's being the case xR'y'—in the way it makes sense to say 'there are at least two things x and y such that xRy *only if* xR'y'.

The alternative is the view that *providing good support for* is not an objective item ontologically and that a complex mental attitude is what ties what has support to what provides the support.

A case in point is *preference.* One view would be that there is an appetitive attitude that takes as its objects two propositions and their correlative meanings. One might prefer one state of affairs to another without actually liking or disliking either, or anything—in just the way that one might hold that one state of affairs is more likely to obtain than another without having a belief that either obtains. Indeed, when A, B, C and D are alternative competing states of affairs, one might hold A to be more likely to obtain than B, C or D and yet have no belief as to which of A, B, C or D does in fact obtain.

The alternative is to make preference into something objective. There would be a proposition p such that one would want that p via a complex meaning, a meaning, say, of the following sort : if it were the case that p or it were the case that q, let it be the case that p. Then the proposition, if it were the case that p or it were the case that q, it would most likely be the case that p, would connect the propositions p and q in a way that does not make p *that* much more likely than q, even when p and q are exhaustive alternatives. The 'relation' here between p and q would be an objective one. Letting '!' symbolise the relation of being a competing alternative and '#' symbolise the relation of most likelihood, it would then be possible to have, say, '($\exists$v)(q # p)' or '($\exists$v)((p ! q) # p)' and, indeed, this proposition could then be the object of an epistemic or appetitive attitude. Analysing what the connectives '!' and '#' represent would be a formidable task.

To adopt the mentalistic alternative seems to accord more with views already in place. Have we not decided that indexicals belong only in meanings? The same might be said for evidential support and preferences, except that the latter belong *between* meanings. This option would block any awkwardnesses that might arise in attempts to make quantifiers include both the support and the supported, and the preferred and the less preferred within their scope—save, of course, as connected within some mental attitude.

4

Sign

Section 1
Introduction

The foregoing discussion of mind, mental contents and propositions does not even begin to furnish an outline of how the signs we use to communicate relate to our mental contents and to propositions. There has been no hint, thus far, as to what ontological status signs have.

In contexts of communication, symbolisation can be complex and take many forms. To get a fix on the ontological parameters of signs and their use we shall describe three kinds of situation in which signs occur.

Section 2
Natural signs

Case 1. Imagine a family of highly intelligent apes, the kind of apes that human beings must once have been. They migrate frequently in search of food. When they do, a few scouts proceed in advance of the main group. For those who follow it is important the scouts leave signs to tell the way they've gone.

The terrain becomes barren and rocky. There's difficulty finding the wherewithal to make signs. Finally one of the scouts spies a patch of bare earth a short distance from the path of ascent. He makes a footprint in the dirt that accords with his belief concerning the direction he's going. Later a member of the following group discovers the footprint, realises the scout went out of his way to put it where he did and comes to a belief concerning the direction the scouts went—the same belief that the scout had when he left the footprint.

Here the scout has made use of a known correlation: that between a footprint and the direction the creature that left it was travelling, i.e., toward the toe-end. Like charred wood for fire, the sign is a natural sign, although the scout left it intentionally and that he did so is recognised by those who come along to 'read' it later.

Let us retell the story, giving the apes a little more in the way of equipment—bows and arrows. There's no patch of bare earth handy. So the scout places an arrow on the ground. He has a belief about the way the scouting party is heading, he knows which way arrows characteristically travel when shot and he lays the point of the arrow in the right direction. Those who follow come to have the same belief he had by reading the sign he's left.

In this retelling a slight step has been taken away from the purely natural sign. While it is true that humans characteristically travel in the direction their footprints point, it is not true they characteristically travel in the direction their unretrieved arrows point.

The scout is saying something in both cases. But what kind of relations does the scout enter into when he does so? What are the parameters of these acts of communication?

As components we seem to have: (1) the scout (an individual, the sayer), (2) the time, (3) the proposition (the truth or falsehood that is the third relatum of the scout's belief about the direction he'll head), (4) the guise (the fourth relatum of his belief), (5) the location or setting, (6) what the scout does to communicate (a property of (1), placing a footprint or arrow on the ground oriented in a certain way), (7) the footprint or arrow (another individual) and (8) a property of (7) (the property that makes (7) a sign, here the property of *being a footprint oriented in* so-and-so *direction* or *being an arrow oriented in* so-and-so *direction*).

One feature of this kind of case is that the symbol-type is a property. The apes that follow recognise the sign to be a sign because of a property it has. It is a sign because it has the property of *being a footprint (an arrow) oriented in* so-and-so *direction*. It is the recognition of this property in the token that leads the 'readers' of the sign to understand the meaning and proposition its 'writer' had in mind.

The scout's act is one of assertion, or perhaps instruction. In the case described, the scout has both a belief about which way his party is headed and a desire that the following party go in a certain direction. It does not seem important here to differentiate between asserting and giving instructions.

There is another, much more important feature of the act that deserves mention. By using a particular footprint or arrow to convey his particular message, the scout shows a mastery not only of one symbol-type, the one actually involved in his communicative act, but others as well. After all, had he believed himself to be headed in a different direction, or wished the following party to proceed in a different direction, he could have put his footprint or arrow down with a different orientation and have conveyed a different message.

So at the time of his act, there is also a further relation of assert*ability* (or ability to issue instructions) having the following relata: (1) him, (2) the time, (3) one of a set of propositions (a truth or falsehood he *could* have conveyed), (4) a meaning (by which he could believe that truth or falsehood), (5) a setting, (6) what the scout might have done to communicate (place a footprint or arrow on the ground with a different orientation) and (7) a property (a symbol-type—the property that would make a thing having it a sign representing (3) and (4)).

Section 3
Metaphorical signs

Case 2. The same scout. No handy patch of bare earth. No arrows. Just smooth rock. The scout spies a piece of chalk, takes it, squats down, places his foot in the right direction, and draws a chalk outline of his foot.

Or he has an arrow, but does not wish to part with it. Arrows are difficult to make and prized. He spies a piece of chalk, takes it, and on the rock draws an arrow-shape pointing in the right direction.

Here, what is to count as the symbol-type is the same as in Case 1, namely, the property of *being a footprint (an arrow) oriented in* so-and-so *direction*. But the scout has left neither a footprint nor an arrow. He's made some marks with chalk. This is the token 'readers' find.

In Case 1, the property that is the symbol-type makes a thing possessing it *be* a token of that type. In Case 2, these two functions get separated. The symbol-type is one property; what makes a thing be a token of that symbol-type is another.

To the eight relata in Case 1, Case 2 adds two. (1) through (8) are as before. (7) is an individual, the token and (8) is a property, the property that makes (7) a token. But in Case 2, this property is *being a* such-and-such *shape oriented in* so-and-so *direction*. The property in (8) is not that of *being a footprint (an arrow) oriented in* so-and-so *direction*, because the token is not a footprint (an arrow). Yet as in Case 1, *being a footprint (an arrow) oriented in* so-and-so *direction* is the symbol-type, the property that leads the 'readers' of the sign to understand the meaning and proposition the 'writer' wishes to convey. So relatum (9) in Case 2, the symbol-type, is this property, *being a footprint (an arrow) oriented in* so-and-so *direction*. Relatum (10) is a second-order relation, the relata of which are (8) and (9).

This second-order relation, perhaps a conventional one, between the property of *being a* such-and-such *shape oriented in* so-and-so *direction* and the property of *being a footprint (an arrow) oriented in* so-and-so *direction* is recorded in our willingness to think of the chalk shape on the rock as *being a* footprint (an arrow), even though it's literally not one. Since we call such chalk shapes 'footprints' ('arrows') even when they are not ones literally, it is not too far amiss to use the word 'metaphor' to describe such cases.

Consider the following signs:

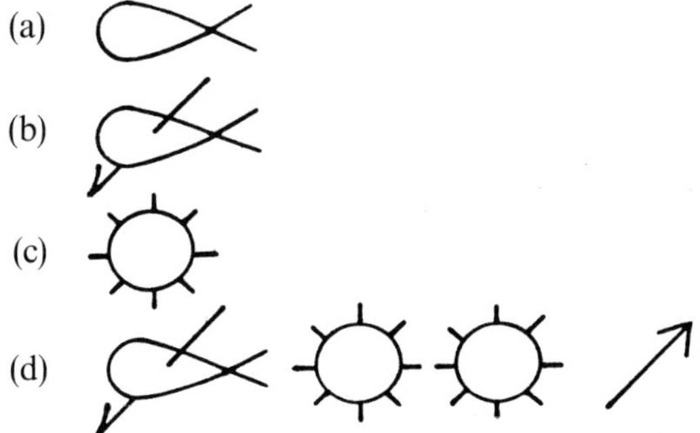

(a) is (metaphorically) a fish, (b) (metaphorically) a speared fish, (c) (metaphorically) the sun—despite the fact that each may be a shape drawn in chalk that is neither a fish, nor a speared fish, nor the sun. What makes, say, (b) a speared fish is a second-order relation between a property that the chalk inscription does have literally and a property that it does not have literally.

The same sort of second-order relation between a property that certain parts of Michelangelo's *Creation* have and a property they do not have leads us to say, when looking at the painting, 'That's an old bearded man touching a young man', or 'That's God creating Adam'. The figures on the wall of the Sistine Chapel aren't men at all, much less an old bearded man and a young man, or God and Adam.[1]

'Metaphorically', if these non-literal cases be construed as metaphor, is not an operator to be cashed out as truth or falsehood in some member or members of a set of possible worlds. We hardly want to say that a chalk token like that in (c) is literally the sun in any possible world. To say that (c) is the sun is more a *façon de parler* we employ because we recognise certain customary second-order relations between token-making properties and properties we take as symbol-types.

The further connection between, say, the symbol-type *being a speared fish* of (b) and the meaning and proposition in the 'writer's' mind is like that in the case in which a real arrow is used to convey the scout's belief. The scout conveyed his belief about the direction people were travelling by using an arrow—despite the fact that people do not normally go in the directions their unretrieved arrows point. Here the scout uses the speared fish sign to convey his belief that there is good fishing nearby—despite the fact that one speared fish does not good fishing make.

In (d) signs are used in both Case 1 and Case 2 ways. The arrow is a Case 2 use, provided that it's chalk. A chalk sun does not represent the scout's beliefs about the sun, but rather it is a sign for a length of time. The number of chalk suns is two; that is, the symbol-type *being a pair* holds literally of the chalk suns. So the number of days is conveyed in a Case 1 way. The suns individually and the speared fish are Case 2 examples.

In sum, the scout is trying to convey his belief that there is good fishing two days' journey in the direction indicated by the arrow.

Implicit in Case 2, as in Case 1, is a relation of assertability, over and beyond the particular assertion. And by chalking a footprint on the rock, the scout shows not just mastery of a whole vocabulary of symbol-types, but that he knows how to produce tokens of these types, to write them down. Assertability, then, will be a relation that holds among: (1) the scout, (2) the time, (3) one of a set of propositions, (4) an appropriate meaning, (5) a setting, (6) a property (creating a token), (7) a token-making property, (8) a property that is a symbol-type, and (9) the second-order relation that makes (7) a token-making property for (8).

Section 4
Conventional signs

Case 3. During the depression, a tramp chalks

on a fence. He has just had a difficult time trying to get a handout from the people who live within. A second tramp passes and does not bother to try his story on the householders.

A tramp emerges running from the yard. Later that night he returns and chalks

on a fence at the edge of the farm. A second tramp is about to take the road past the farm, but changes his mind on seeing the sign and takes a road that does not pass it.

In the one case the tramp is conveying his judgement that temperamental people live in the house, cause for some caution. In the other, he is saying the people who live there will harm beggars, to visit the farm is downright dangerous.

Once more we have the eight relata of Case 1. (7) is the individual token, (8) the token-making property *being a circle with a dot in its centre* or *being a square*. But, as in Case 2, the token-making property (8) is not the symbol-type. There is no natural or associative inferential connection, among those not familiar with the symbolism itself, between *being a circle with a dot in its centre* or *being a square* and the behaviour of people, as there is between *being a footprint oriented in* so-and-so *direction* and the direction its maker has gone.

In the latter kind of case, we can easily understand why people would choose *these* properties to convey what's in their minds. But why should a tramp choose *squareness* or *being a circle with a dot in its centre* rather than anything else that's fairly easy to draw to convey his particular message?

In Case 3 whatever connection there is between token-making properties and the meanings and propositions to be conveyed is conventional in a twofold way: first, the relation that ties the token-making property to the symbol-type is conventional; second, the symbol-type seems itself to be a conventional entity.

It does not seem right to take the token-making property to *be* the symbol-type—even though the relation of the symbol-type to meanings and propositions is conventional. For in the 'language' of tramps, putting a

on a fence is the same as putting

there. We have *two* token-making properties, *being a square* and *being a circle with two dots side by side in its centre*, that are alternate ways to 'spell out' or 'write down' *the same* symbol.

It might be suggested that the real token-making property is disjunctive, *being a square or a circle with two dots side by side in its centre*.

But a tramp might recognise and understand a square without having in mind the disjunctive property, not being familiar with the alternate 'writing down' convention.

Secondly, the matter of how a symbol is written down, spelled or spoken out is altogether *too* conventional (albeit habitual) to make such an idea plausible. When Morse invented his code, was the one disjunctive token-making property for the word 'wife' abandoned in favour of a wider, more liberal disjunctive token-making property, or did Morse simply introduce a new convention for writing symbol-types down—a *new* set of token-making properties for symbol-types already in use, a new second-order relation between token-making properties and symbol-types? The latter seems the more plausible story.

One conventional aspect of Case 3 examples is the second-order relation that records the connection between token-making properties and the symbol-types instantiations of these properties 'write down'. In Case 2 the second-order relation is not entirely conventional. In performances of plays, for example, many kinds of things serve as props. *Hamlet* calls for a flute, and many things will symbolise one. *But not everything will.* A rubber band won't do. Neither will an elephant.

In Case 2 the token-making properties and the properties that are symbol-types are plaintly different. The possibility of alternate 'spellings' of *the same* symbol-type, as in 'color', 'colour' and '_._ ___ ._.. ___ ._.', or 'wife', '.__ ..._. .' and perhaps 'trouble-and-strife', alternate ways of writing it down or saying it (as in pig-Latinised English), leads us in Case 3 to distinguish token-making properties, item (8) among the relata of communicative acts, from symbol-types. As in Case 2 the symbol-type will be relatum (9), and relatum (10) will be the relation that makes (8) a token-making property for (9).

In Case 2, relatum (10) was a relation between first-order properties; and individual possessing the first was said to possess the second, even though it literally didn't. We *are* willing to call a chalk figure 'an arrow'. In the present case, (10) is a relation between a first-order property and a symbol-type. Here, however, an individual possessing the first property is not said metaphorically to be the possessor of the second—if, indeed, the Case 3 symbol-type even qualifies as a property.

We do not say that an 'M' painted on a toilet door is a man, or a chalk inscription of the English phrase 'footprint oriented toward the northeast' is a footprint oriented toward the northeast. In the earlier cases, there was good reason to hold that the symbol-type was a property. In the present case no such reason seems to exist.

There is reason to hold the symbol-type to be a conventional entity. One convention writes the word '_._ .__.. __ ___ ... _', another 'almost'. We have two token-making properties for one symbol-type. But it also seems to be conventional that the *two* words 'almost' and 'nearly' *are found* in English—as nearly synonymous a pair as one gets in a natural language. Why should English contain *two* such words, rather than one? Why, on the other hand, shouldn't English have a third synonym? Indeed, why not?

Word-strings, as entities, do seem to have a conventional status. Words can be called into existence by being coined. 'Stagflation' was probably coined within our lifetimes. Case 2 symbol-types, like the property, *being the sun*, are not coined, although innovative metaphorical symbolic use may be made of old familiar properties. It does not seem plausible to hold that properties themselves are brought into existence in the way words are.

Thus we are led to posit an ontological category of *word-strings*. Symbol-types of the Case 3 variety will be among the word-strings. The simple sort of symbol-types that tramps wrote on fences in England during the depression can be viewed as word-strings of length 1, like the English word-string 'Fire!'.

In Case 3, then, the communicative act relates (1) the sayer, (2) the time, (3) the proposition, (4) the meaning, (5) the setting, (6) what the sayer does to communicate, (7) the token, (8) the token-making property, (9) the word-string (the symbol-type) and (10) the relation between (8) and (9) that makes a possessor of (8) an inscription or utterance of (9).

The relation of assertability will relate (1)–(6), (7) a token-making property, (8) a symbol-type and (9) a relation between (7) and (8).

By placing an arrow on the ground to convey a particular message, the scout showed that he could convey other messages by making other signs. Other things were assertable by him at that time in other ways. But the fact that a tramp demonstrates mastery of the sign

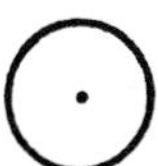

doesn't seem to show that he can assert other things as well by other signs, e.g., what writing

conveys. So the relation of assertability *may* not extend beyond the symbol-type involved in the actual assertion itself.

One further sort of communicative act must be mentioned. A shake of the head can be used *to deny*. In denial, the entitles related are the same as in assertion, but the stance *vis-à-vis* them is different. Normally, a sentence asserted represents a meaning and a proposition that are components of a belief of the person making the assertion. In denial, a meaning and a proposition are represented, but we normally take it that the person making the denial does not believe the meaning and proposition represented and furthermore that he *does* believe the negation of the proposition represented via some other (unspecified) meaning. As Wittgenstein somewhere suggested, we might signify denial by writing exactly the same words we would write in assertion, but writing them, say, in red or upside down. The important point is that *the same* meaning and proposition are represented in either case.

What we have just characterised and called 'denial' is not the same as what we do when we question a speaker's reliability, or accuse him of making a category mistake or no sense.

To deny what a speaker says is not the same thing as to question that *he* is saying it. Normally we expect others not to lie, not to assert things they don't believe. But when we know that another believes what he asserts, we still want the fact of his belief to provide good reason for *us* to believe what he asserts.

If my beliefs about a subject are notoriously unreliable, if the fact that I have a belief about it is not believed by others to be a reliable indication that the belief is true, then others may reject my talk about the subject. They aren't denying *what* I say. They may have no opinions about that. They object to me putting my beliefs on display as a source of truth.

Should I make a category mistake, a person objecting denies that what I'm saying makes sense. Here the person points out that there can be no belief behind what I'm asserting.

The Case 1 arrow language, as described, does not have denial in it. Nor does it have an interrogative aspect. But there might develop head-shakes. Or a scout might introduce the use of a broken arrow to say 'Not that way!'. Denial, then, might well appear in a Case 1, 2 or 3 guise.

Besides the act of denial, there will also be deni*ability*, the mastery of a vocabulary of denial. Just as assertability is shown by assertion, deniability will be shown by denial.

Section 5
Communication

In a single act of communication several sorts of signs are often employed. A policeman, for instance, may point to a sketch while uttering the words 'Was that the man?'. This combines the features of Cases 2 and 3.

Case 2 distinguishes between token-making properties and properties that are symbol-types. In Case 1 the token-making properties *are* symbol-types. This can be viewed as limiting—the Case 2 relation (10) between (8), the token-making property, and (9), the symbol-type, being identity.

Case 3, however, demands separate treatment, since its symbol-types do not fall into the same ontological category as Case 2 symbol-types. In Case 3 the symbol-type is a *word-string*, not a property.

A communicative act can thus be viewed as a complex relation, the relata of which are (1) the sayer, (2) the time, (3) the proposition, (4) the meaning, (5) the setting, (6) what the sayer does (to communicate), (7) the (Case 2) token, (8) the (Case 2) token-making property, (9) the (Case 2) property that is the symbol-type, (10) the relation that makes a possessor of (8) an inscription or utterance of (9), (11) the (Case 3) token, (12) the (Case 3) token-making property, (13) the (Case 3) word-string that is the symbol-type and (14) the relation that makes a possessor of (12) an inscription or utterance of (13).[2]

Not all acts of communication need be mixed. A pure Case 2 communicative act can be represented in this extended scheme by making items (7) and (11) the same and by making items (12) and (13) trivial (the trivial property and a string that is not a sentence).

The assert-(deni-, etc.)*ability* relation can be extended similarly.

Section 6
Word-strings

Words can be coined, come into existence. There are individuals that don't exist—Santa Claus and Pegasus, for example. And there are words that don't exist. 'Glombone' is one. This, of course, is not to say that individuals and word-strings need fall into the same ontological category.

In the following we shall not attempt to extend the language of propositional attitudes by adding a kind s of word-string variables and constants (as well as a category c of setting variables and constants), so that the various communicative acts which tie sentences, meanings and propositions together can be represented. Just attempting to represent word-strings, *their* properties and relations, is complicated enough. Nor shall we attempt to distinguish an existence quantifier from the more basic quantifier that ranges over word-strings both existent and non-existent, coined and uncoined. Here we repeat our endorsement of Cocchiarella's analysis in which existence comes by the possession of certain existence-entailing attributes. Doubtless *being coined by someone existing* is one of them.

To represent word-strings, we shall need a language with the basic *kinds* p and s of variables and constants, the kind p consisting of sentential variables and constants, $p_1, p_2, \ldots$, and the kind s word-string variables and constants, $s_1, s_2, \ldots$. As before, where $K_1, \ldots, K_n$ are kinds, so is $\langle K_1, \ldots, K_n \rangle$.

A crucial feature of word-strings is their structure. Some are included in others. Indeed, one word-string may appear a number of times in another. In this word-strings are like sequences.

To help convey their structure we introduce a category Qs of word-string quotation marks, variables and constants, $q_1, q_2, \ldots$. But symbols in such a category may themselves appear in word-strings; and we cannot allow a quotation mark q to appear in a word-string it quotes.

Consider the following English string:

man"man""man"man""man

If we use double quotes to quote it, it can be parsed in the following ways:

"man"man""man"man""man"
"man"man""man"man"/"man"
"man"man"/"man"man""man"
"man"man"/"man"man"/"man"

The crucial issues that arise are whether it is appropriate to use a one-place, two-place or a three-place predicate in front of this string and if a two-place predicate is used, which of two interpretations is intended. The same problems arise if single quotes instead of double are used to quote the fragment.

If we resolve the problem by not allowing q to be used to quote a string that contains it or by specifying that the scope of a quotation mark is, say, the least scope possible, we must have infinitely many quotation marks—or there are going to be word-strings that are unquotable. We want all word-strings to be quotable, so we opt for infinitely many quotation marks.

Defining identity for the various kinds raises no new problems. Where a and b are expressions of kind K and f is a variable of kind $\langle K \rangle$ which is not free in a or b.

$$'(a = b)' =_{df} '(\forall f)(fa = fb)'.$$

How, then, do we define identity for the category Qs? We were able to define identity for meaning quotations earlier as

$$'(q_1 = q_2)' =_{df} '(\forall e)(q_1 e = q_2 e)'.$$

Let us introduce a similar device for word-string quotations, a category Es having infinitely many variables $e_1, e_2, \ldots$, and perhaps some constants as well.

Where q_1 and q_2 are in Qs, if we define '$(q_1 = q_2)$' as '$(\forall e_1)$ $(q_1e_1q_1 = q_2e_1q_2)$', a problem arises. How do we quote the simple word-string 'e_1' in our language? In the definiens of our proposed definition, 'e_1', occurs bound by the initial '$(\forall e_1)$', free in '$(q_1e_1q_1 = q_2e_1q_2)$' and hence free and not quoted in '$q_1e_1q_1$'. How, then, *are* we to quote it?

We introduce the notion of *type*. In Es and Qs there will be a denumerably infinite number of variables (and perhaps some constants) of every finite type greater than one. '$\forall$' and the variables and constants of all the kinds will be of type one.

We are now in a position to define identity for each type in Qs. Where 'q' and 'q^*' are of type i in Qs and 'e' is a variable of type i in Es, $1 \leqslant i$,

$$\text{'}(q = q^*)\text{'} =_{df} \text{'}(\forall e)(qeq = q^*eq^*)\text{'}$$

and 'qeq' is in kind s. Where S and S* are word-strings in Es of a type less than or equal to type i and 'q' is of type i in Qs, $1 \leqslant i$,

$$\text{'}(S =_i S^*)\text{'} =_{df} \text{'}(\forall q)(qSq = qS^*q)\text{'}.$$

The type of a word-string will be the type of the variable or constant in it with the highest type. In 'qeq' the variable 'e' is quoted if the type of 'e' is less than the type of 'q'. 'e' is free and unquoted if the type of 'e' is the type of 'q'. If the type of 'e' is greater than that of 'q', 'qeq' is not a well-formed expression in kind s.

We can now give more details about how word-strings can be given order and treated like sequences. We do this with the help of some constants.

The numeral 'n' we define as '$q^*e_nq^*$', where 'q^*' is a special quotation constant in type 3 and 'e_n' is the nth variable in Es of type 2.

The constant 'S' in kind $\langle s,s \rangle$ represents a successor relation for which we have such theorems as '$Sn(n+1)$', '$\sim(\exists s)(Ss1)$', '$\sim(\exists s)(Sns \wedge Ss(n+1)$', '$\sim(\exists s)(\exists s_1)(Sss_1 \wedge Ss_1s)$', etc.

Finally, the constant 'C' in kind $\langle s,s,s \rangle$ represents 'the word-string _____ has word-string _____ as its _____ atomic component'. For instance, where 'q' is of type $i > 1$, 'q^*' is of type 3 and 'e_3' is the 3rd variable in Es of type 2,

$$Cq\forall f\forall qq\forall qq^*e_3q^*$$

says 'Word-string "$\forall f\forall$" has word-string "$\forall$" as its 3rd atomic component'. A characteristic theorem schema is

$$Cqa_1 \ldots a_nqqa_hqh,$$

where $1 \leqslant h \leqslant n$, all a_h are atomic and of lower type than i and 'q' is of type i. Here, as before with meaning quotes, we have as a theorem

$$(A \neq_i B),$$

where A and B are distinct word-strings of a type less than i.

The form the various comprehension axioms should take is obvious.

5

Conclusion

We began by setting out requirements for an ontologically ideal language. We then described a language meeting these requirements in which numbers are values of quantifier variables and Peano arithmetic can be developed. Next we showed how an ontology of mind would be reflected in an ontologically ideal language. Finally, we turned to signs themselves to sketch out very briefly how they might be accommodated too.

We hope we have shown how these three ontologies—of number, mind and sign—can be treated given the constraints with which we began.

The reader is invited to peruse the technical discussions in the Appendices where we provide more formal characterisations of our ideal languages.

Appendix 1

Number

Section 1
The language of quantifier arithmetic

In the language LQ of quantifier arithmetic developed here, there are four categories of expressions.

(1) By an *m–n saturated expression letter* we mean an expression of the form p[m,n], where m $\geqslant$ 1 and n $\geqslant$ 0. For each m,n, S[m,n] is a denumerable set of m–n saturated expression letters. S[m,n] has two mutually exclusive denumerable subsets: the m–n saturated expression variables, and the m–n saturated expression constants. The latter set is denoted by SC[m,n].

(2) By an *m–n unsaturated expression letter* we mean an expression of the form f[m,n], where again m $\geqslant$ 1 and n $\geqslant$ 0. For each m,n, U[m,n] is a denumerable set of m–n unsaturated expression letters, divided also into denumerable subsets of m–n unsaturated expression variables and constants. The latter set is similarly denoted by UC[m,n].

(3) By an *m–n functorial letter* we mean an expression of the form a[m,n], m,n $\geqslant$ 1. For each m,n, F[m,n] is a denumerable set of m–n functorial variables and constants. The latter set is denoted by FC[m,n].

(4) By an *m–n–k operation letter* we mean an expression of the form o[m,n,k], where m,k $\geqslant$ 1 and n $\geqslant$ 0. Syntactically o[m,n,k] takes k m–n quantifiers into an m–n quantifier. We let m–n–k range widely for generality. Ordinarily, we shall be interested in 1–1–1 operation letters. For each m,n,k, O[m,n,k] is a denumerable set of m–n–k operation letters, divided into denumerable sets of m–n–k operation variables and constants. The latter set is denoted by OC[m,n,k].

All of these sets of expressions are pairwise disjoint.

We use special symbols for certain constants. →[2,0] in UC[2,0] symbolises the material conditional, ∀[1,1] and ∃[1,1] in UC[1,1] the universal and existential quantifiers, α[m,n] in FC[m,n] special functorial constants and n and s in OC[1,1,1]. The various signs '[m,n]' attached to the variables and constants of LQ are simply flags that aid in identifying the syntactic category to which they belong and are in no way essential. For convenience we shall write $\rightarrow$ instead of $\rightarrow$[2,0], $\forall$ instead of $\forall$[1,1], etc. We shall also omit the '[1,0]' on 1–0 saturated variables and constants. s will symbolise the successor function. n is a flag on quantifiers; we shall let n identify the natural numbers by defining '(Nat f[1,1])' as '((Num f[1,1]) $\wedge$ (nf[1,1] = 0))'.

By a *primitive symbol* of LQ we mean any variable or constant of LQ. By an *expression* we mean any non-empty finite string of primitive symbols of LQ. Let us consider triplets of the form $\langle c,\underline{C},F \rangle$, where c is an expression, $\underline{C}$ a category of expression and F a set (the free variables in c).

Formation axioms

(FA1) $\langle c,\underline{E},\varnothing \rangle$, where c is a constant such that $c \in E$ and E is S[m,n], U[m,n], F[m,n] or O[m,n,k].

(FA2) $\langle c,\underline{E},\{c\} \rangle$, where c is a variable such that $c \in E$ and E is as above.

Formation rules

(FR1) $\langle c_1,F[m,n],F_0 \rangle$, $\langle c_2,\underline{S}[m,n],F_1 \rangle$, $\langle c_3,\underline{S}[m,0],F_2 \rangle$
      $\Rightarrow \langle c_1c_2c_3,\underline{U}[m,n], F_0 \cup F_1 \cup F_2 \rangle$, m,n $\geqslant$ 1.

(FR2) $\langle c_1,\underline{F}[m,n],F_0 \rangle$, $\langle A_1,\underline{S}[1,0],F_1 \rangle$, . . ., $\langle A_m,\underline{S}[1,0],F_m \rangle$,
      $\langle c_3,\underline{S}\langle m,0\rangle, F_{m+1} \rangle \Rightarrow \langle c_1A_1 \ldots A_m v_1 \ldots v_n c_3,\underline{U}[m,n],F_0$
      $\cup F_{m+1} \cup ((F_1 \cup \ldots \cup F_m) - \{v_1, . . ., v_n\})\rangle$,
      where $v_1, . . ., v_n$ are variables and m,n $\geqslant$ 1.

(FR3) $\langle c_1,\underline{F}[m,n],F_0 \rangle$, $\langle c_2,\underline{S}[m,n],F_{m+1} \rangle$, $\langle A_1,\underline{S}[1,0],F_1 \rangle$, . . .,
      $\langle A_m,\underline{S}[1,0],F_m \rangle \Rightarrow \langle c_1c_2A_1 \ldots A_m,\underline{U}[m,n],F_0$
      $\cup F_{m+1} \cup F_1 \cup \ldots \cup F_m \rangle$, m $\geqslant$ 2, n $\geqslant$ 1.

(FR4) $\langle c_1,\underline{F}[m,n],F_0 \rangle$, $\langle A_1,\underline{S}[1,0],F_1 \rangle$, . . ., $\langle A_m,\underline{S}[1,0],F_m \rangle$,
      $\langle B_1,\underline{S}[1,0],G_1 \rangle$, . . ., $\langle B_m,\underline{S}[1,0],G_m \rangle$
      $\Rightarrow \langle c_1A_1 \ldots A_m v_1 \ldots v_n B_1 \ldots B_m,\underline{U}[m,n],F_0 \cup G_1 \cup \ldots \cup G_m$
      $\cup ((F_1 \cup \ldots \cup F_m) - \{v_1, . . ., v_n\})\rangle$,
      where $v_1, . . ., v_n$ are variables, n $\geqslant$ 1, and m $\geqslant$ 2.

(FR5) $\langle c_0,O[m,n,k],F_0 \rangle$, $\langle c_1,\underline{U}[m,n],F_1 \rangle$, . . ., $\langle c_k,\underline{U}[m,n],F_k \rangle$
      $\Rightarrow \langle c_0c_1 \ldots c_k,\underline{U}[m,n],F_0 \cup F_1 \cup \ldots \cup F_k \rangle$.

(FR6) $\langle c_0,\underline{U}[m,n],F_0 \rangle$, $\langle A_1,\underline{S}[1,0],F_1 \rangle$, . . ., $\langle A_m,\underline{S}[1,0],F_m \rangle$
      $\Rightarrow \langle c_0A_1 \ldots A_m v_1 \ldots v_n,\underline{S}[1,0],F_0 \cup ((F_1 \cup \ldots \cup F_m)$
      $- \{v_1, . . ., v_n\})\rangle$,
      where $v_1, . . ., v_n$ are variables (n may be 0).

(FR7) $\langle c_0,\underline{U}[m,n],F_0 \rangle$, $\langle c_1,\underline{S}[m,n],F_1 \rangle \Rightarrow \langle c_0c_1,\underline{S}[1,0],F_0 \cup F_1 \rangle$, n $\geqslant$ 1.

A *formation derivation* (FD) is a finite tree-like array of triplets such that every triplet is either a formation axiom or follows by one of the formation rules from the triplets above it. Where d is an FD, the triplet in d which is not a rule premise is called *the conclusion* of d. The premises of the conclusion of d are also called *the* premises of d. The first element of the conclusion of d is also called the conclusion of d, letting context disambiguate.

d is a *wff-derivation* iff the conclusion of d is $\langle A, \underline{S}[1,0], F \rangle$ for some A and F; and in such a case, A is called a *wff*. If $F = \emptyset$, A is called a *sentence*. v *occurs free* in a wff A iff there is a derivation with the conclusion $\langle A, \underline{S}[1,0], F \rangle$, where $v \in F$.

Section 2
Sentences without punctuation

The language LQ contains no punctuation marks. To show that the notions of wff and sentence are well defined, the following must be established:

Lemma F1. Each expression can be the conclusion of at most one derivation.

Where $c'_1 \ldots c'_n$ is an expression of length n (i.e., each c'_i is a primitive expression, $1 \leqslant i \leqslant n$) and $c_1 \ldots c_m$ is an expression of length m, $m < n$, the latter is an *initial part* of the former iff for all i, $1 \leqslant i \leqslant m$, c'_i is c_i.

Lemma F2. No two derivations are such that $\langle A_1, \underline{E}, G \rangle$ is the conclusion of one and $\langle A_2, \underline{E}, G \rangle$ is the conclusion of the other, and A_2 is an initial part of A_1.

The following are all obvious from inspection of the formation rules:

Lemma 1. There is no derivation with conclusion $\langle c, \underline{S}[1,0], F \rangle$, where c is not itself a primitive expression in $S[1,0]$ and yet the initial primitive expression in c is a member of $S[1,0]$.

Lemma 2. If $n \geqslant 1$, all members of $S[m,n]$ are primitive expressions.

Lemma 3. All members of $F[m,n]$ are primitive expressions.

Lemma 4. If $m > 1$, all members of $S[m,n]$ are primitive expressions.

Lemma 5. All members of $O[m,n,k]$ are primitive expressions.

Lemma 6. There is no derivation with a conclusion $\langle A, \underline{S}[1,0], F \rangle$, where the initial letter of A is a member of $S[m,n]$, and $n \geqslant 1$ or $m \geqslant 2$.

Lemma 7. If $c \in U[m,n]$ and the initial letter a of c is in $F[x,z]$ or $O[x,z,k]$, then $x = m$ and $z = n$.

Lemma 8. No members of $U[m,n]$ are complex and yet begin with a member of $U[x,z]$.

Lemmas F1 and F2 can be proved by induction on the length of expressions with the help of Lemmas 1 through 8.

Proof of Lemmas F1 and F2
BASIS CASE
Expressions of length 1. The derivations concerned can only be axioms (establishing F1), and there are no initial parts of the first member of an axiom (establishing F2).

INDUCTION HYPOTHESIS (IH)
F1 and F2 hold for all expressions of length less than or equal to i.

Let $c_1{}^*$ be $c_1 \ldots c_{i+1}$, where each c_h, $1 \leqslant h \leqslant i+1$ is a primitive expression, and suppose that d_1 and d_2 are distinct derivations with conclusions $c_1{}^*$ and $c_2{}^*$, respectively, where $c_2{}^*$ is $c_1{}^*$ or an initial part of it or $c_1{}^*$ is an initial part of $c_2{}^*$. Consider cases according to which rule is applied last in d_1 and d_2.

Clearly d_1 cannot be an axiom, since $i+1 > 1$. But the only case in which d_2 could be an axiom is where $c_2{}^*$ is in $U[m,n]$ or $S[1,0]$, since the formation rules only allow $c_1{}^*$ to be in $U[m,n]$ or $S[1,0]$. Yet none of FR1–FR5 has a primitive expression in $U[m,n]$ as its left-hand premise so $c_2{}^*$ can't be in $U[m,n]$, nor can $c_2{}^*$ be a primitive expression in $S[1,0]$ by Lemma 1. So d_2 cannot be an axiom either.

Case FR1-FR1 (Rule FR1 is the final rule applied in d_1 and d_2). Let the premises of d_1 be a_1, a_2, a_3 and of d_2 be b_1, b_2, b_3. By Lemma 3, $a_1 = b_1$. Since $n \geqslant 1$, $a_2 = b_2$ by Lemma 2. If $m > 1$, a_3 and b_3 are (the same) primitive expressions in $S[m,0]$ by Lemma 4. If $m = 1$, IH applies to the premises used in d_1 and d_2 that contain a_3 and b_3. Thus $d_1 = d_2$.

Case FR1-FR2 (d_1 ends by FR1, d_2 by FR2). Let the premises of d_1 be as above and of d_2 be $b_1, B_1, \ldots, B_m, b_3$, $a_1 = b_1$ by Lemma 3. Since $n \geqslant 1$, the first letter of B_1 is a_2 by Lemma 2. But this is contrary to Lemma 6.

Case FR1-FR3. Let the premises of d_1 be as above and of d_2 be $b_1, b_2, B_1, \ldots, B_m$. $a_1 = b_1$ as above. $a_2 = b_2$ by Lemma 2. By Lemma 4, a_3 is the first letter of B_1, but this contradicts Lemma 6.

Case FR1-FR4. Let the premises of d_1 be as above and of d_2 be $b_1,B_1,\ldots,$ $B_m,B'_1,\ldots,$ B'_m with variables $v_1,\ldots,v_n$. $a_1 = b_1$ as above. By Lemma 2, a_2 is the first letter of B_1, but this contradicts Lemma 6.

Case FR1-FR5. Let the premises of d_1 be as above and of d_2 be $b_0,b_1,\ldots,$ b_k. By Lemmas 3 and 5 both a_1 and b_0 are primitive expressions; so $a_1 = b_0$. But $a_1 \neq b_0$, since $O[x,y,z] \cap F[m,n] = \emptyset$.

Case FR1-FR6. Let the premises of d_1 be as above and of d_2 be $b_0,B_1,\ldots,$ B_x, with variables $v_1,\ldots,v_z$. Since the conclusion of d_1 is in $U[m,n]$ and that of d_2 is in $S[1,0]$, we only have to worry about the case in which $c_1{}^* = c_2{}^*$. a_1 is the first letter of b_0 by Lemma 3. a_2 can't be the first letter of B_1 by Lemma 6. So a_2 is the second letter of b_0. Thus a_3 must be complex. Hence $m = 1$, by Lemma 4. $a_3 \in S[1,0]$. Let b_0 be a_1a_2C. $a_1 \in F[1,n]$; $a_2 \in S[1,n]$. Thus b_0 is the result of FR1. Then $C \in S[1,0]$ and $a_3 \in S[1,0]$. But then C is an initial part of a_3, contrary to IH.

Case FR1-FR7. Let the premises of d_1 be as above and of d_2 be b_1,b_2. $c_1{}^* = c_2{}^*$ as above. a_1 is then the initial letter of b_1, since $b_1 \notin F[m,n]$. Since $n \geqslant 1$, a_2 is a primitive expression by Lemma 2, and so is b_2. Let b_1 be $a_1a_2A[m,0]$ as per FR1. Suppose that $a_3 \neq A[m,0]$. Then a_3 is an initial part of $A[m,0]$ or vice versa, contrary to IH. So $a_3 = A[m,0]$. So b_2 is an additional letter making the conclusion of FR7 longer than that of FR1. So $c_1{}^* \neq c_2{}^*$. Let b_1 be $a_1a_2A_1[1,0] \ldots A_m[1,0]$ as in FR3. Thus $m = 1$, if $a_1a_2a_3$ is not to be shorter than b_1b_2, since if $m > 1$, a_3 is a primitive expression by Lemma 4. So $c_2{}^*$ is $a_1a_2A_1[1,0]b_2$, and $A_1[1,0]$ is an initial part of a_3, contrary to IH.

Case FR2-FR2. Let the premises of d_1 be $a_1,A_1,\ldots,A_m,a_3$ with variables $v_1,\ldots,v_n$ and of d_2 be $b_1,B_1,\ldots,B_x,b_3$ with variables $u_1,\ldots,u_z$. $a_1 = b_1$ by Lemma 3, and $m = x$ and $n = z$ by Lemma 7. Suppose that $A_1 \neq B_1$. Then A_1 is an initial part of B_1, or vice versa, contrary to IH. So $A_1 = B_1$. Similarly $A_i = B_i$, $1 \leqslant i \leqslant m$. And $v_i = u_i$, $1 \leqslant i \leqslant n$. And $a_3 = b_3$ by the same reasoning.

Case FR2-FR3. Let the premises of d_1 be as above and of d_2 be $b_1,$ $b_2,B_1,\ldots,B_m$. $a_1 = b_1$ as before. b_2 is a primitive expression in $S[m,n]$ by Lemma 4. Thus b_2 is the first letter in A_1, which contradicts Lemma 6.

Case FR2-FR4. Let the premises of d_1 be as above and of d_2 be $b_1,B_1,\ldots,$ $B_x,B'_1,\ldots,$ B'_x, with variables $u_1,\ldots,u_z$. $a_1 = b_1$ by Lemma 3 and, $m = x$ and $n = z$ by Lemma 7. Suppose $A_1 \neq B_1$. Then A_1 is an initial part of B_1, or vice versa, contradicting IH. So $A_1 = B_1$. Similarly $A_i = B_i$, $1 \leqslant i \leqslant m$. $v_i = u_i$, $1 \leqslant i \leqslant n$. Suppose $m > 1$. Then by Lemma 4, a_3 is a primitive expression, and B'_1 begins with a_3, contrary to Lemma 6. So $m = 1$. But then FR4 does not apply.

Case FR2-FR5. See Case FR1-FR5.

Case FR2-FR6. Let the premises of d_1 be as above and of d_2 be $b_0,B_1,\ldots,$

B_x, with variables $u_1, \ldots, u_z$. $c_1{}^* = c_2{}^*$ as in Case FR1-FR6. a_1 is the first letter of b_0 by Lemma 3 and $b_0 \in U[x,z]$. $x = m$, and $z = n$ by Lemma 7. b_0 is the result of one of FR1–FR4. Lemmas 1, 2 and 6 rule out FR1 and FR3. If FR2 or FR4, then b_0 is $a_1 C_1 \ldots C_m u_1' \ldots u_n' Z$, where $C_1, \ldots, C_m \in S[1,0]$, $u_1', \ldots, u_n'$ are variables, $Z \in S[m,0]$ or Z is $C_1' \ldots C_m'$, $C_i' \in S[1,0]$, $1 \leqslant i \leqslant m$. Suppose $C_1 \neq A_1$. Then C_1 is an initial part of A_1, or vice versa, contrary to IH. So $C_1 = A_1$. Similarly $C_h = A_h$, $1 \leqslant h \leqslant m$. And $v_h = u_h'$, $1 \leqslant h \leqslant n$. If $m > 1$, a_3 is a primitive expression by Lemma 4. Hence $c_1{}^* \neq c_2{}^*$, since $c_2{}^*$ is longer than $c_1{}^*$ by $B_1, \ldots, B_x$. So $m = 1$ and FR4 is ruled out. $Z, a_3 \in S[1,n]$, and by IH, $Z = a_3$. So once again $c_1{}^* \neq c_2{}^*$, since $c_2{}^*$ is longer by $B_1, \ldots, B_x$.

Case FR2-FR7. Let the premises of d_1 be as above and of d_2 be b_0, b_1, where $b_0 \in U[x,z]$ and $b_1 \in S[x,z]$. $c_1{}^* = c_2{}^*$ as above. Clearly a_1 is the initial letter of b_0. So $x = m$ and $z = n$ by Lemma 7. b_0 is the result of one of FR1–FR4. If FR1 or FR3, b_0 is $a_1 c_1 Z$, where Z is either in $S[m,0]$ or $C_1' \ldots C_m'$, $C_i' \in S[1,0]$, $1 \leqslant i \leqslant m$. By Lemma 2, c_1 is a primitive expression, and consequently the first letter of A_1, which contradicts Lemma 6. So b_0 is the result of FR2 or FR4 and is $a_1 C_1 \ldots C_m u_1' \ldots u_n' Z$, where Z is as above. $C_h = A_h$, $1 \leqslant h \leqslant m$, by IH. $u_h' = v_h$, $1 \leqslant h \leqslant n$. If $m > 1$, a_3 is a primitive expression by Lemma 4, and $c_2{}^*$ is longer than $c_1{}^*$ by at least b_1. If $m = 1$, $Z, a_3 \in S[1,0]$. $Z = a_3$ by IH. So $c_2{}^*$ is still longer than $c_1{}^*$ by b_1.

Case FR3-FR3. Let the premises of d_1 be $a_1, a_2, A_1, \ldots, A_m$ and of d_2 be $b_1, b_2, B_1, \ldots, B_m$. $a_1 = b_1$ by Lemma 3. $a_2 = b_2$ by Lemma 2. $A_h = B_h$, $1 \leqslant h \leqslant n$, by IH. Hence $d_1 = d_2$.

Case FR3-FR4. Let the premises of d_1 be as above and of d_2 be $b_1, B_1, \ldots, B_x, B_1', \ldots, B_x'$, with variables $v_1, \ldots, v_z$. $a_1 = b_1$. a_2 is a primitive expression by Lemma 2. Hence a_2 is the first letter of B_1, which contradicts Lemma 6.

Case FR3-FR5. See Case FR1-FR5.

Case FR3-FR6. Let the premises of d_1 be as above and of d_2 be $b_0, B_1, \ldots, B_x$, with variables $u_1, \ldots, u_z$. $c_1{}^* = c_2{}^*$ as in Case FR1-FR6. a_1 is the first letter of b_0 by Lemma 3. $x = m$ and $z = n$ by Lemma 7. $b_0 \in U[x,z]$, and b_0 is the result of one of FR1-FR4. a_2 is a primitive expression by Lemma 2. So Lemma 6 rules out FR2 and FR4. So b_0 is $a_1 a_2 Z$, where $Z \in S[m,0]$ or Z is $C_1 \ldots C_m$, where $C_1, \ldots, C_m \in S[1,0]$. If FR1, Z is a primitive expression by Lemma 4, since $m \geqslant 2$. But then Z is the first letter of A_1, contrary to Lemma 6. So b_0 results by FR3 and is $a_1 a_2 C_1 \ldots C_m$. But then $A_h = C_h$, $1 \leqslant h \leqslant m$, by IH, and $c_2{}^*$ is longer than $c_1{}^*$ by $B_1, \ldots, B_x, u_1, \ldots, u_z$.

Case FR3-FR7. Let the premises of d_1 be as above and of d_2 be b_0, b_1, where $b_0 \in U[x,z]$ and $b_1 \in S[x,z]$, $c_1{}^* = c_2{}^*$ as above. Clearly a_1 is the initial letter of b_0. So $x = m$ and $z = n$ by Lemma 7. b_0 is the result of FR1-FR4. a_2 is a primitive expression by Lemma 2. So Lemma 6 rules out FR2 and FR4. b_0 is $a_1 a_2 Z$, where Z is in $S[m,0]$ or is $C_1 \ldots C_m$, $C_i \in S[1,0]$,

$1 \leqslant i \leqslant m$. If $Z \in S[m,0]$, Z is a primitive expression by Lemma 4, since $m > 1$. But then Z is the first letter of A_1, contrary to Lemma 6. So b_0 results by FR3 and is $a_1 a_2 C_1 \ldots C_m$. But then $A_h = C_h$, $1 \leqslant h \leqslant m$, by IH, and c_2^* is longer than c_1^* by b_1.

Case FR4-FR4. Let the premises of d_1 be $a_1 A_1 \ldots A_m v_1 \ldots v_n A_1' \ldots A_m'$ and of d_2 be $b_1 B_1 \ldots B_x u_1 \ldots u_z B_1' \ldots B_x'$. $a_1 = b_1$ by Lemma 3. $m = x$ and $n = z$ by Lemma 7. $A_h = B_h$, $1 \leqslant h \leqslant m$, by IH. $v_h = u_h$, $1 \leqslant h \leqslant n$. $A_h' = B_h'$, $1 \leqslant h \leqslant m$ by IH. So $d_1 = d_2$.

Case FR4-FR5. See Case FR1-FR5.

Case FR4-FR6. Let the premises of d_1 be as above and of d_2 be $b_0, B_1, \ldots, B_x$, with variables $u_1, \ldots, u_z$. $c_1^* = c_2^*$ as in Case FR1-FR6. a_1 is the first letter of b_0 by Lemma 3. $x = m$ and $z = n$ by Lemma 7. b_0 is the result of one of FR1–FR4. Since $m > 1$, Lemmas 4 and 6 rule out FR1 and FR3; the second letter of b_0 would be the initial letter of A_1 otherwise. So b_0 is $a_1 C_1 \ldots C_m u' \ldots u_n' Z$, where $C_1, \ldots, C_m \in S[1,0]$, $u_1', \ldots, u_n'$ are variables, and $Z \in S[m,0]$ or Z is $C_1' \ldots C_m'$, where $C_1', \ldots, C_m' \in S[1,0]$. $C_h = A_h$, $1 \leqslant h \leqslant m$, by IH. $v_h = u_h'$, $1 \leqslant h \leqslant n$. Since $m > 1$, Z is a primitive expression, if $Z \in S[m,0]$, by Lemma 4. But then Z is the initial letter of A_1'', contrary to Lemma 6. So b_0 must result by FR4, and Z is $C_1' \ldots C_m'$, $C_i' \in S[1,0]$, $1 \leqslant i \leqslant m$. But then $C_h' = A_h$, $1 \leqslant h \leqslant m$, by IH, and c_2^* is longer than c_1^* by $B_1, \ldots, B_m, u_1, \ldots, u_m$.

Case FR4-FR7. Let the premises of d_1 be as above and of d_2 be b_0, b_1, where $b_0 \in U[x,z]$ and $b_1 \in S[x,z]$. $c_1^* = c_2^*$ as above. Clearly a_1 is the initial letter of b_0. So $x = m$ and $z = n$ by Lemma 7. b_0 is the result of one of FR1–FR4. Since $m > 1$, Lemmas 4 and 6 rule out FR1 and FR3; the second letter of b_0 would be the initial letter of A_1 otherwise. So b_0 is as described in the preceding case. The argument proceeds similarly to the conclusion that c_2^* is longer than c_1^* by b_1.

Case FR5-FR5. Let the premises of d_1 be $a_0, a_1, \ldots, a_k$ and of d_2 be $b_0, b_1, \ldots, b_k$. $a_0 = b_0$ by Lemma 5. Suppose $a_1 \neq b_1$. Then a_1 is an initial part of b_1, or vice versa, which contradicts IH. So $a_1 = b_1$. Similarly $a_h = b_h$, $1 \leqslant h \leqslant k$. So $d_1 = d_2$.

Case FR5-FR6. Let the premises of d_1 be as above and of d_2 be $b_0, B_1, \ldots, B_x$, with variables $v_1, \ldots, v_z$. $c_1^* = c_2^*$ as in Case FR1-FR6. $b_0 \in U[x,z]$. a_0 is the first letter of b_0 by Lemma 5. $x = m$ and $z = n$ by Lemma 7. b_0 results by an application of FR5. Let b_0 be $a_0 Q_1[m,n] \ldots Q_k[m,n]$. $a_h = Q_h[m,n]$, $1 \leqslant h \leqslant k$, by IH. So c_2^* is longer than c_1^* by $B_1, \ldots, B_x, v_1, \ldots, v_z$.

Case FR5-FR7. Let the premises of d_1 be as above and of d_2 be b_0, b_1, where $b_0 \in U[x,z]$ and $b_1 \in S[x,z]$. $c_1^* = c_2^*$ as above. a_0 is the first letter of b_0 by Lemma 5. $x = m$ and $z = n$ by Lemma 7. b_0 results by an application of FR5. Let b_0 be $a_0 Q_1[m,n] \ldots Q_k[m,n]$. The argument proceeds as in the preceding case to the conclusion that c_2^* is longer than c_1^* by b_1.

Case FR6-FR6. Let the premises of d_1 be $a_0, A_1, \ldots, A_m$, with variables $v_1, \ldots, v_n$, and of d_2 be $b_0, B_1, \ldots, B_x$, with variables $u_1, \ldots, u_z$. If a_0 is a primitive expression in $U[m,n]$, so is b_0, and vice versa, by Lemma 8. The initial letter of a_0 is the initial letter of b_0 if not. $x = m$ and $z = n$, by Lemmas 3, 5, 7, and 8. Hence by IH, $a_0 = b_0$, $A_h = B_h$ ($1 \leqslant h \leqslant m$), and $v_h = u_h$ ($1 \leqslant h \leqslant n$). Thus $d_1 = d_2$.

Case FR6-FR7. Let the premises of d_1 be as above and of d_2 be b_0, b_1, where $b_0 \in U[x,z]$ and $b_1 \in S[x,z]$. By the argument of the preceding case $x = m$, $z = n$, and $a_0 = b_0$. Since $n \geqslant 1$, b_1 is a primitive expression by Lemma 2. So b_1 is the initial letter of A_1, which contradicts Lemma 6.

Case FR7-FR7. Let the premises of d_1 be a_0, a_1 and of d_2 be b_0, b_1, where $a_0 \in U[m,n]$, $a_1 \in S[m,n]$, $b_0 \in U[x,z]$, and $b_1 \in S[x,z]$. By the argument of Case FR6-FR6, $x = m$, $z = n$, and $a_0 = b_0$. But then by IH $a_1 = b_1$, and $d_1 = d_2$.

This completes the proof of Lemmas F1 and F2.

Section 3
Definitions

A 1–0 saturated expression letter is a propositional letter. m–0 unsaturated expression letters are m-ary propositional connectives and symbolise m-ary modalities. For $m \geqslant 1$, $p[m,0]$ symbolises an ordered m-tuple of propositions. We consider the 1-tuple $\langle p[1,0] \rangle$ to be the same as $p[1,0]$. Where $n \geqslant 1$, $p[m,n]$ syntactically behaves as an m-lengthed sequence or string of wffs followed by an n-lengthed sequence or string of variables. Where $n \geqslant 1$, syntactically $f[m,n]$ takes m wffs and n variables, or a member of $S[m,n]$ into a wff. We shall frequently refer to m–n unsaturated expression letters as quantifiers.

Where $c_0 \in U[m,n]$, $A_1, \ldots, A_m \in S[1,0]$, $v_1, \ldots, v_n$ are variables, and $c_0 A_1 \ldots A_m v_1 \ldots v_n$ is the conclusion of an application of FR6, we write what's left when c_0 is removed from this wff $\langle\langle A_1, \ldots, A_m \rangle, \langle v_1, \ldots, v_n \rangle\rangle$, as explained in section 2, Chapter 2. We also define a general class of m–n *saturated expressions*, denoted by $\Sigma[m,n]$, $\phi[m,n] \in \Sigma[m,n]$ just in case $\phi[m,n] \in S[m,n]$, or for some wffs $A_1, \ldots, A_m$ and variables $v_1, \ldots, v_n$, $\phi[m,n] = \langle\langle A_1, \ldots, A_m \rangle, \langle v_1, \ldots, v_n \rangle\rangle$. If $\phi[1,0] \in \Sigma[1,0]$, $\phi[1,0]$ is a wff. We often write $\langle\langle A_1, \ldots, A_m \rangle, \varnothing \rangle$ as $\langle A_1, \ldots, A_m \rangle$. It will also be convenient to define a general class of m–n *unsaturated expressions*, denoted by $\Gamma[m,n]$, $\delta[m,n] \in \Gamma[m,n]$ just in case $\delta[m,n] \in U[m,n]$.

Wffs are expressions, sequences or strings of symbols. Where $^\frown$ indicates concatenation of expressions, $\phi^\frown \psi^\frown \chi$ may denote a wff. Let $\phi^\frown [\psi/\Delta]^\frown \chi$

$= \phi^\neg \Delta^\neg \chi$. A wff B is a *well-formed subpart* of A iff for some sequences ϕ and χ (perhaps empty), $A = \phi^\neg B^\neg \chi$ and if C is any wff, $\phi^\neg C^\neg \chi$ is also a wff. An m–n saturated expression α is a *well-formed subpart* of a wff A just in case there are sequences of expressions ϕ and χ such that $A = \phi^\neg \alpha^\neg \chi$, and for any m–n saturated expression β, $\phi^\neg \beta^\neg \chi$ is a wff. An m–n unsaturated expression δ is a *well-formed subpart* of a wff A just in case there are sequences of expressions ϕ and χ such that $A = \phi^\neg \delta^\neg \chi$, and for any m–n unsaturated expression γ, $\phi^\neg \gamma^\neg \chi$ is a wff. For example, where A is a wff and p a 1–0 saturated expression letter, $\forall Ap$ is a wff in which A is a well-formed subpart and p is not. In $\forall pp$, the first occurrence of p is a well-formed subpart, the second is not.

Where $v_1, \ldots, v_n$ are variables, for some i, $1 \leqslant i \leqslant n$, a variable $v = v_i$, $\delta \in \Gamma[m,n]$ and $C_1, \ldots, C_m \in \Sigma[1,0]$, an occurrence of v in a wff A is *free* if it does not occur in a well-formed subpart of A of the form $\langle\langle C_1, \ldots, C_m\rangle, \langle v_1, \ldots, v_n\rangle\rangle$, which is in turn a well-formed subpart of $\delta C_1 \ldots C_m v_1 \ldots v_n$, which is in turn a well-formed subpart of A. Where δ occurs in a well-formed subpart of the form $\delta\phi$, $\phi \in S[m,n]$, the *scope* of δ is ϕ. Where δ occurs in a well-formed subpart of A of the form $\delta C_1 \ldots C_m v_1 \ldots v_n$, the *scope* of δ is $\langle\langle C_1, \ldots, C_m\rangle, \langle v_1, \ldots, v_n\rangle\rangle$. Where $a \in F[m,n]$ and A is a wff, if a occurs as the initial letter of a well-formed subpart of A of the form $a\phi\psi\chi$, where $\phi, \chi \in \Sigma[m,n]$ and $\psi \in \Sigma[m,0]$, the *scope* of a at this occurrence is $\langle\phi, \psi, \chi\rangle$. Where $o \in O[m,n,k]$ and A is a wff, if o occurs as the initial letter of a well-formed subpart of A of the form $o\delta_1 \ldots \delta_k \psi$, where $\delta_1, \ldots, \delta_k \in \Gamma[m,n]$ and $\psi \in \Sigma[m,n]$, the *scope* of o at this occurrence is $\langle\delta_1, \ldots, \delta_k, \psi\rangle$.

We shall in the following use parentheses and rearrange wffs into a more standard-looking format, so the reader will have an easier time reading them. We use A,B,C, with or without subscripts, as metavariables ranging over wffs; p,q,r, with or without subscripts, as metavariables ranging over propositional variables; P,Q,R, with or without subscripts, as metavariables ranging over members of $S[m,n]$, f,g, with or without subscripts, as metavariables ranging over members of $U[m,n]$, u,v,w, again with or without subscripts, as metavariables ranging over variables. $\phi[m,n], \psi[m,n], \chi[m,n]$ may range over members of $\Sigma[m,n]$, and $\delta_1[m,n], \delta_2[m,n], \delta_3[m,n], \gamma[m,n]$ over members of $\Gamma[m,n]$. Sometimes the flags '[m,n]' are dropped as well.

We define 'F' as '$\forall pp$', '$(\forall v)A$' and '$(\exists v)A$' as '$\forall Av$' and '$\exists Av$' respectively, '$(A \rightarrow B)$' as '$\rightarrow AB$', '$\sim A$' as '$(A \rightarrow F)$', 'T' as '$\sim F$', '$\square A$' as '$(A = T)$', and '$(A \wedge B)$', '$(A \vee B)$', and '$(A \leftrightarrow B)$' as usual. Where u and v are variables or constants appropriate for one another (both in $S[m,n]$, $U[m,n]$, $F[m,n]$ or $O[m,n,k]$), '$A[v/u]$' denotes the result of replacing all free occurrences of v in A by u.

We define several further symbols:

(D1)   '(A = B)' =$_{df}$ '(∀f)(fA ↔ fB)', where f ∈ U[1,0], A,B ∈ Σ[1,0], and f is not free in A or B.

(D2)   '(P$_1$ = P$_2$)' =$_{df}$ '(∀f)(fP$_1$ ↔ fP$_2$)', where f ∈ U[m,n] and P$_1$,P$_2$ ∈ S[m,n].

(D3)   '(φ = χ)' =$_{df}$ '(∀f)(fφ ↔ fχ)', where f ∈ U[m,n], φ,χ ∈ Σ[m,n], and f is not free in φ or χ.

(D4)   '(f$_1$ = f$_2$)' =$_{df}$ '(∀g)(∀P)(gf$_1$P ↔ gf$_2$P)', where g ∈ U[1,0], f$_1$,f$_2$ ∈ U[m,n], P ∈ S[m,n], and g is distinct from f$_1$ and f$_2$.

(D5)   '(A ent B)' =$_{df}$ '□(A → B)'.

(D6)   '(Max A)' =$_{df}$ '((A ≠ F) ∧ (∀p)((A ent p) ∨ (A ent ∼p)))', where p does not occur free in A.

(D7)   Where v$_1$, . . ., v$_n$ are variables and u$_1$, . . ., u$_n$ are variables or constants such that for 1 ⩽ i ⩽ n, u$_i$ is appropriate for v$_i$, by the notation 'A[v$_1$,..., v$_n$/u$_1$,..., u$_n$]', we indicate the result of replacing each free occurrence of v$_k$ in A by u$_k$, 1 ⩽ k ⩽ n.

(D8)   '(δ$_1$ = δ$_2$)' =$_{df}$ '(∀f)(∀P)(fδ$_1$P ↔ fδ$_2$P)', where δ$_1$,δ$_2$ ∈ Γ[m,n], f ∈ U[1,0], P ∈ S[m,n], f is distinct from δ$_1$ and δ$_2$, and f and P do not occur free in δ$_1$ or δ$_2$.

(D9)   '(a$_1$ = a$_2$)' =$_{df}$ '(∀f)(∀P)(∀R)(∀Q)(fa$_1$PRQ ↔ fa$_2$PRQ)', where f ∈ U[1,0], a$_1$,a$_2$ ∈ F[m,n], P,Q ∈ S[m,n], and R ∈ S[m,0].

(D10) '≠ (v$_1$, . . ., v$_n$)' =$_{df}$ '((v$_1$ ≠ v$_2$) ∧ . . . ∧ (v$_1$ ≠ v$_n$) ∧ (v$_2$ ≠ v$_3$) ∧ . . . ∧ (v$_2$ ≠ v$_n$) ∧ . . . ∧ (v$_{n-1}$ ≠ v$_n$))', where v$_1$, . . ., v$_n$ are expressions all of the same category.

(D11) '[∧ A$_i$, i ⩽ i ⩽ n]' =$_{df}$ '(A$_1$ ∧ . . . ∧ A$_n$)'.

(D12) '[∨ A$_i$, 1 ⩽ i ⩽ n]' =$_{df}$ '(A$_1$ ∨ . . . ∨ A$_n$)'.

(D13) '(o$_1$ = o$_2$)' =$_{df}$ '((∀f)(∀f$_1$) . . . (∀f$_k$)(∀P)(fo$_1$f$_1$ . . . f$_k$P ↔ fo$_2$f$_1$ . . . f$_k$P)', where f,f$_1$, . . ., f$_k$ are all distinct, f ∈ U[1,0], f$_1$, . . .,f$_k$ ∈ U[m,n], P ∈ S[m,n], and o$_1$,o$_2$ ∈ O[m,n,k].

(D14) '(Num f)' =$_{df}$ '(∃P)(∃Q)(f = α[m,n](P,Q))', where f ∈ U[m,n], P ∈ S[m,n], and Q ∈ S[m,0].

(D15) '0' =$_{df}$ 'α[1,1](⟨⟨∼∃pp⟩,⟨p⟩⟩,∃pp)'.

(D16) '(Nat f)' =$_{df}$ '((Num f) ∧ (nf = 0))', where f ∈ U[1,1].

(D17) '(f suc g)' =$_{df}$ '(sf = g)', where f,g ∈ U[1,1].

(D18) '(f suc* g)' =$_{df}$ '((Nat f) ∧ (Nat g) ∧ (∀o)(∀P)([(ogP) ∧ (∀i)(∀j)([(Nat i) ∧ (Nat j) ∧ (oiP) ∧ (j suc i)] → ojP))] → (ofP)) = T)', where f,g,i,j ∈ U[1,1], P ∈ S[1,1], and o ∈ O[1,1,1].

(D19) '(N + 1)' =$_{df}$ 'α[1,1](⟨⟨⟨((f = 0 ∨ . . . ∨ (f = N)))⟩,⟨f⟩⟩,T)', where f ∈ U[1,1].

(D20) '0[m,n]' =$_{df}$ 'α[m,n](⟨⟨∼∃p$_1$p$_1$, . . ., ∼∃p$_m$p$_m$⟩,⟨q$_1$, . . ., q$_n$⟩⟩, ⟨∃p$_1$p$_1$, . . ., ∃p$_m$p$_m$⟩)', where ⟨m,n⟩ ≠ ⟨1,1⟩.

We now turn to the issue of a general notion of substitution and first characterise formally the two ways in which a sequence $\langle\langle C_1, \ldots, C_m\rangle, \langle v_1, \ldots, v_n\rangle\rangle$ may (genuinely) occur in a well-formed subpart of A.

$\langle\langle C_1, \ldots, C_m\rangle, \langle v_1, \ldots, v_m\rangle\rangle$ occurs in a well-formed subpart of A just in case (α) for some unsaturated expression $\delta[m,n] \in \Gamma[m,n]$, $\delta[m,n]C_1 \ldots C_m v_1 \ldots v_n$ is a well-formed subpart of A, or (β) for some $a[m,n] \in F[m,n]$ and $\phi[m,0] \in \Sigma[m,n]$, $a[m,n]C_1 \ldots C_m v_1 \ldots v_n \phi[m,0]$ is a well-formed subpart of A.

Below we shall need notation for substituting expressions of several different categories for free variables within an unsaturated expression. We define the notation in rather more generality than we need, adapting it from similar notation in Daniels and Freeman [1], p. 6. (This in turn is adapted from Church [1].)

Definition. Where $v_1, \ldots, v_k$ are variables (from any category), $e_1, \ldots, e_k$ are expressions in corresponding categories, σ is a wff or an m–n unsaturated expression, by the notation

$$\underline{S}[v_1, \ldots, v_k/e_1, \ldots, e_k]\,\sigma\,|$$

we indicate the result of replacing each free occurrence of v_i in σ by e_i, for $1 \leqslant i \leqslant k$.

Where $P \in S[m,n]$ and $\phi \in \Sigma[m,n]$,

$$\check{S}[P/\phi]\,A\,|$$

shall stand for A unless there is no sequence $\langle\langle C_1, \ldots, C_h\rangle, \langle v_1, \ldots, v_k\rangle\rangle$ in A such that for some $1 \leqslant i \leqslant k$, v_i occurs free in ϕ (or v_i is ϕ), for some $1 \leqslant i \leqslant h$, P occurs free in C_i and either (α) or (β) holds for A. If this condition is satisfied, the notation shall stand for

$$\underline{S}[P/\phi]\,A\,|.$$

Definition. If $f \in U[m,n] - UC[m,n]$, $\delta \in \Gamma[m,n]$, and A is a wff, then the notation

$$\check{S}[f/\delta]\,A\,|$$

shall stand for A unless (1) f does not occur free in δ, and (2) if u is a variable free in δ (or u is δ), then there is no sequence $\langle\langle C_1, \ldots, C_h\rangle, \langle v_1, \ldots, v_k\rangle\rangle$ in A such that for $1 \leqslant i \leqslant k$, $v_i = u$, for $1 \leqslant i \leqslant h$, f occurs free in C_i and either of conditions (α) or (β) holds for A. If this condition is satisfied, then the notation shall stand for

$$\underline{S}[f/\delta]\,A\,|.$$

Definition. Where σ is $a \in F[m,n]$ or $o \in O[m,n,k]$, by an *innermost free occurrence of σ in A*, we mean a free occurrence of σ in A containing no further free occurrence of σ in its scope.

Definition. If $a \in F[m,n] - FC[m,n]$, $P \in S[m,n] - SC[m,n]$, $Q \in S[m,0] - SC[m,0]$, $\delta \in \Gamma[m,n]$ and A is a wff, the notation

$$\check{S}_1[aPQ/\delta]\,A\,|$$

shall stand for A unless the following conditions are satisfied:

(1) a does not occur free in δ,
(2) where for $\phi \in \Sigma[m,n]$ and $\psi \in \Sigma[m,0]$ the occurrence of a in $a\phi\psi$ is an innermost free occurrence of a in A, and u is a variable free in either ϕ or ψ, then there is no sequence $\langle\langle C_1, \ldots, C_h\rangle, \langle v_1, \ldots, v_k\rangle\rangle$ in δ such that
(a) for some $1 \leqslant i \leqslant k$, $v_i = u$,
(b) if u occurs in ϕ, then P occurs in some C_i, $1 \leqslant i \leqslant h$,
(c) if u occurs in ψ, Q occurs in some C_i, $1 \leqslant i \leqslant h$,
(d) there is a quantifier $\delta_1 \in \Gamma[h,k]$, or some $a_1 \in F[h,k]$, $\chi_1 \in \Sigma[h,0]$, and $\chi_2 \in \Sigma[h,k]$, such that $\delta_1 C_1 \ldots C_h v_1 \ldots v_k$ or $a_1 C_1 \ldots C_h v_1 \ldots v_k \chi_1 \chi_2$ is a subsequence of δ, and for any wff D, if δ is a well-formed subpart of D, so is $\delta_1 C_1 \ldots C_h v_1 \ldots v_k$ or $a_1 C_1 \ldots C_h v_1 \ldots v_k \chi_1 \chi_2$,
(3) there is no variable u, other than P or Q, occurring free in δ such that there is a sequence $\langle\langle C_1, \ldots, C_h\rangle, \langle v_1, \ldots, v_k\rangle\rangle$ in A, for some $1 \leqslant i \leqslant k$, $v_i = u$, and either condition (α) or (β) holds for A.

If (1)–(3) are satisfied, then the notation shall stand for what results from replacing $a\phi\psi$ in A by

$$\underline{S}[PQ/\phi\psi]\,\delta\,|$$

at all occurrences where the initial occurrence of a in $a\phi\psi$ is an innermost free occurrence of a in A. This replacement is to be carried out simultaneously for all $\langle\chi_1[m,n], \chi_2[m,0]\rangle$ such that the occurrence of a in $a\chi_1[m,n]\chi_2[m,0]$ in A is an innermost free occurrence of a in A.

Having defined the notion of an innermost free occurrence of a functorial letter and the notation

$$\check{S}_1[aPQ/\delta] A\,|,$$

an inductive definition allows us to proceed from the assumption that

$$\check{S}_k[aPQ/\delta] A\,|$$

is defined to the definition of

$$\check{S}_{k+1}[aPQ/\delta] A\,|.$$

(The reader may wish to refer to Daniels and Freeman [1].)

Definition. If $o \in O[m,n,k] - OC[m,n,k]$, $f_1, \ldots, f_k \in U[m,n] - UC[m,n]$, $\delta \in \Gamma[m,n]$ and A is a wff, the notation

$$\check{S}_1[of_1 \ldots f_k/\delta] A\,|$$

shall stand for A unless the following conditions are satisfied.

(1) o does not occur free in δ,
(2)   where for $\delta_1, \ldots, \delta_k \in \Gamma[m,n]$ the occurrence of o in $o\delta_1 \ldots \delta_k$ is an innermost free occurrence of o in A, there is no sequence $\langle\langle C_1, \ldots, C_x\rangle, \langle v_1, \ldots, v_z\rangle\rangle$ in δ and variable u free in some δ_1, for $1 \leqslant i \leqslant k$, such that
    (a) $u = v_i$, for some $1 \leqslant i \leqslant z$,
    (b) f_i occurs free in some C_s, $1 \leqslant s \leqslant x$ and
    (c)   condition (2)(d) above holds for $\langle\langle C_1, \ldots, C_x\rangle, \langle v_1, \ldots, v_z\rangle\rangle$,
(3)   there is no variable u other than $f_1, \ldots, f_k$, occurring free in δ such that there is a sequence $\langle\langle C_1, \ldots, C_x\rangle, \langle v_1, \ldots, v_z\rangle\rangle$ in A, for some $1 \leqslant i \leqslant z$, $u = v_i$, and either conditions (α) or (β) hold for A.

If (1)–(3) are satisfied, the notation shall stand for what results replacing $o\delta_1 \ldots \delta_k$ in A by

$$\underline{S}[f_1 \ldots f_k/\delta_1 \ldots \delta_k] \delta\,|$$

at all occurrences where the initial occurrence of o in $o\delta_1 \ldots \delta_k$ in A is an innermost free occurrence of o in A. This replacement is to be carried out simultaneously for all $\langle \gamma_1, \ldots, \gamma_k\rangle$, $\gamma_1, \ldots, \gamma_k \in \Gamma[m,n]$, such that the initial occurrence of o in $o\gamma_1 \ldots \gamma_k$ in A is an innermost free occurrence of o in A. As with functorial letters, general substitution is now easily defined.

Section 4
Axiomatisation

In stating the axiom schemes of LQ, it will be convenient to group them into propositional schemes, quantificational schemes and schemes of other sorts. We say that an occurrence of a variable v in a wff A is *free for a variable* (or constant) u just in case there is no free occurrence of v in a well-formed subpart C of A of the form $\delta C_1 \ldots C_m v_1 \ldots v_n$, where $\delta \in \Gamma[m,n]$, $C_1, \ldots, C_m \in \Sigma[1,0]$, $v_1, \ldots, v_n$ are variables, and for some $1 \leqslant i \leqslant n$, $u = v_i$.

AxPC1. $A \rightarrow (B \rightarrow A)$.
AxPC2. $(A \rightarrow (B \rightarrow C)) \rightarrow ((A \rightarrow B) \rightarrow (A \rightarrow C))$.
AxPC3. $\sim \sim A \rightarrow A$.

AxQC1. $(\forall v)A \rightarrow A[v/u]$, where v is free for u in A.
AxQC2. $(\forall v)(A \rightarrow B) \rightarrow (A \rightarrow (\forall v)B)$, where v is not free in A.
AxQC3. $(\exists v)A \leftrightarrow \sim (\forall v) \sim A$.

AxC1. $(\exists P)(P = \phi)$, where $P \in S[m,n]$, $\phi \in \Sigma[m,n]$, $1 \leqslant m$, $0 \leqslant n$, and P does not occur free in ϕ.

AxC2. $(\exists p_1) \ldots (\exists p_m)(\langle p_1, \ldots, p_m \rangle = \phi)$, where $\phi \in \Sigma[m,0]$, and for $1 \leqslant i \leqslant m$, p_i does not occur free in ϕ.

AxC3. $(\exists f)(\forall p_1) \ldots .(\forall p_m)(fp_1 \ldots p_m = A)$, where $f \in U[m,0]$, f does not occur free in A, and $p_1, \ldots, p_m$ are distinct propositional variables.

AxC4. $(\exists f)(\forall P)(fP = A)$, where $f \in U[m,n]$, $P \in S[m,n]$, $1 \leqslant m$, $0 \leqslant n$ and f does not occur free in A.

AxC5. $(\exists a)(\forall P)(\forall Q)(\forall R)(aPQR = A)$, where $a \in F[m,n]$, $P,R \in S[m,n]$, $Q \in S[m,0]$, $1 \leqslant m,n$, a does not occur free in A and P and R are distinct variables.

AxC6. $(\exists o)(\forall f_1) \ldots (\forall f_k)(\forall P)(of_1 \ldots f_k P = A)$, where $o \in O[m,n,k]$, $P \in S[m,n]$, $f_1, \ldots, f_k \in U[m,n]$, $1 \leqslant m,k$, $0 \leqslant n$, o does not occur free in A and $f_1, \ldots, f_k$ are distinct variables.

AxI1. $(\forall v_1) \ldots (\forall v_k)(\phi = \psi) \rightarrow (A \leftrightarrow B)$, where $\phi, \psi \in \Sigma[m,n]$, $0 \leqslant k$ and B is just like A except that B has ψ in exactly one place where A has ϕ, provided that

 (a) if $\phi \in S[m,n] - SC[m,n]$, the occurrence of ϕ replaced by ψ does not lie within a sequence $\langle \langle C_1, \ldots, C_x \rangle, \langle u_1, \ldots, u_z \rangle \rangle$ such that $C_1, \ldots, C_x$ are wffs, $u_1, \ldots, u_z$ are variables, for some h, $1 \leqslant h \leqslant z$, $u_h = \phi$, and that occurrence of the sequence is such that for some $\delta \in \Gamma[x,z]$ or some $a \in F[x,z]$ and $\chi \in \Sigma[x,0]$, $\delta C_1 \ldots C_x u_1 \ldots u_z$ or $aC_1 \ldots C_x u_1 \ldots u_z \chi$ is a well-formed subpart of A, and

(b) if u is a variable free in $(\forall v_1)\ldots(\forall v_k)(\phi = \psi)$, then the occurrence of ϕ in A replaced by ψ in B does not occur within a sequence $\langle\langle C_1,\ldots, C_x\rangle,\langle u_1,\ldots, u_z\rangle\rangle$ such that for some h, $1 \leqslant h \leqslant z$, $u_h = u$ and either for some $\delta \in \Gamma[x,z]$ or for some $a \in F[x,z]$ and $\chi \in \Sigma[x,0]$, $\delta C_1 \ldots C_x u_1 \ldots u_z$ or $aC_1 \ldots C_x u_1 \ldots u_z\chi$ is a well-formed subpart of A.

AxI2. $(\forall v_1)\ldots(\forall v_k)(\delta_1 = \delta_2) \to (A \leftrightarrow B)$, where $\delta_1,\delta_2 \in \Gamma[m,n]$ and B is exactly like A except that one occurrence of δ_1 in A has been replaced by δ_2 in B, provided that

(a) if $\delta_1 \in U[m,n] - UC[m,n]$, the occurrence of δ_1 replaced by δ_2 does not lie within a sequence $\langle\langle C_1,\ldots, C_x\rangle,\langle u_1,\ldots, u_z\rangle\rangle$ such that $C_1,\ldots, C_x$ are wffs, $u_1,\ldots, u_z$ are variables, for some h, $1 \leqslant h \leqslant z$, $u_h = \delta_1$ and that occurrence of the sequence is such that for some $\delta_3 \in \Gamma[x,z]$ or some $a \in F[x,z]$ and $\chi \in \Sigma[x,0]$, $\delta_3 C_1 \ldots C_x u_1 \ldots u_z$ or $aC_1 \ldots C_x u_1 \ldots u_z\chi$ is a well-formed subpart of A,

(b) either there is an $\phi \in \Sigma[m,n]$ such that $\delta_1\phi$ is a well-formed subpart of A, or there is an $o \in O[m,n,h]$ and $\gamma_1,\ldots, \gamma_h \in \Gamma[m,n]$ such that for some $1 \leqslant i \leqslant h$, δ_1 is γ_i and $o\gamma_1 \ldots \gamma_h$ is a well-formed subpart of A and

(c) no variable v occurs free in either δ_1 or δ_2 which is bound at the occurrence of δ_1 replaced by δ_2 other than $v_1, \ldots, v_k$.

AxI3. $(A \neq B) \to \square(A \neq B)$.

AxN1. $(\forall P)(0P \leftrightarrow {\sim}\exists P)$, where $P \in S[1,1]$.

AxN2. $(1v)A \leftrightarrow (\exists v)(A \wedge (\forall v)(A[v/u] \to (v = u)))$, where u does not occur free in A.

AxN3. $(Nv)A \leftrightarrow (\exists v_1) \ldots (\exists v_n)[\neq (v_1, \ldots, v_n) \wedge A[v/v_1] \wedge \ldots \wedge A[v/v_n] \wedge (\forall u)(A[v/u] \to ((u = v_1) \vee \ldots \vee (u = v_n)))]$, where $v_1,\ldots, v_n$ are distinct variables appropriate to v, none of $v_1,\ldots, v_n$ occurs free in A and v is free for $v_1, \ldots, v_n, u$ in A.

AxN4. $(\forall P)(NP \to {\sim}MP)$, where $P \in S[1,1]$ and $N \neq M$.

AxN5. $(\exists P)NP$, for all $N \in \omega$, where $P \in S[1,1]$.

AxN6. $(\forall P)(\forall f)(\forall g)([(\text{Num } f) \wedge (\text{Num } g) \wedge ((fP \wedge gP) \neq F)] \to (f = g))$, where $f,g \in U[m,n]$ and $P \in S[m,n]$.

Ax*ns*1. $(\forall f)((\text{Nat } f) \leftrightarrow (\forall o)(\forall P)([o0P \wedge (\forall g)((ogP \wedge (\text{Nat } g)) \to osgP)] \to ofP))$, where $o \in O[1,1,1]$, $f,g \in U[1,1]$, $P \in S[1,1]$.

Ax*ns*2. $(\forall f)((\text{Nat } f) \to (\text{Nat } sf))$.

Ax*ns*3. ${\sim}(\exists f)(0 = sf)$.

Ax*ns*4. $(sN = (N + 1))$.

Ax*ns*5. $(\forall f)(\forall g)((sf = sg) \to (f = g))$.

Axα1. $(\forall P)(\forall p_1)\ldots(\forall p_k)((\neq (p_1,\ldots, p_k) \wedge [\wedge (\alpha(P,p_i) = M_i), 1 \leqslant i \leqslant k]$

$\wedge\ [\wedge\, p_i, 1 \leqslant i \leqslant k]\ \wedge\ (\forall p_0)(((\alpha(P,p_0) \neq 0)\ \wedge\ p_0) \rightarrow [\vee\, (p_0 = p_i),$
$1 \leqslant i \leqslant k])) \rightarrow NP)$, where $P \in S[1,1]$, $p_0, p_1, \ldots, p_k$ are distinct propositional variables, for $1 \leqslant i \leqslant k$, $M_i \neq 0$ and $N = \Sigma\{M_i :$
$1 \leqslant i \leqslant k\}$.

Axα2. $(\forall P)(NP \rightarrow (\exists p_1)\ \ldots\ (\exists p_n)([\wedge\, (\alpha(P,p_i) \neq 0), 1 \leqslant i \leqslant n]\ \wedge\ [\wedge\, p_i,$
        $1 \leqslant i \leqslant n]\ \wedge\ (\forall p_0)([(\alpha(P,p_0) \neq 0)\ \wedge\ p_0] \rightarrow [\vee\, (p_0 = p_i),$
        $1 \leqslant i \leqslant n])))$, $P \in S[1,1]$.

Axα3. $(\forall P)(\forall P \leftrightarrow (\forall p)((\alpha(P,p) \neq 0) \rightarrow p))$, where $P \in S[1,1]$.

Axα4. $(\forall P)(\exists P \leftrightarrow (\exists p)((\alpha(P,p) \neq 0)\ \wedge\ p))$, where $P \in S[1,1]$.

Axα5. $(\forall P)(\forall Q)((\forall R)(\alpha(P,R) = \alpha(Q,R)) \rightarrow (P = Q))$, where $P,Q \in S[m,n]$
        and $R \in S[m,0]$.

Axα6. $(\forall P)(\forall p)([NP\ \wedge\ (\alpha(P,p) \neq 0)\ \wedge\ p] \rightarrow [(\alpha(P,p) = 1)\ \vee\ \ldots\ \vee$
        $(\alpha(P,p) = N)])$, where $P \in S[1,1]$.

Axα7. $\alpha(\langle\langle A\rangle,\langle v\rangle\rangle,A[v/u]) \neq 0$, where v is free for u in A.

Axα8. $(\forall p)((\exists v_1)\ \ldots\ (\exists v_n)(\neq (v_1, \ldots, v_n)\ \wedge\ [\wedge\, (A[v/v_i] = p), 1 \leqslant i \leqslant n]$
        $\wedge\ (\forall v_0)((A[v/v_0] = p) \rightarrow [\vee\, (v_0 = v_i),\quad 1 \leqslant i \leqslant n])) \leftrightarrow (\alpha(\langle\langle A\rangle,$
        $\langle v\rangle\rangle,p) = N))$, where $v,v_0,v_1, \ldots, v_n$ are distinct variables, $v_0,$
        $v_1, \ldots, v_n$ are appropriate for v, v is free for $v_0,v_1, \ldots, v_n$ in A and at
        most v is free in A.

Axα9. $(\forall p)((\alpha(\langle\langle A\rangle,\langle v\rangle\rangle,p) \neq 0) \rightarrow (\exists v)(p = A))$, where v and p are
        distinct variables.

AxMi. $(\exists p)(p\ \wedge\ \text{Max}\, p))$.[1]

AxM2. $(\forall p)((\forall q)((\text{Max}\, q) \rightarrow (q\ \text{ent}\ p)) \rightarrow \square p)$.

R1.   If $\vdash A$ and $\vdash (A \rightarrow B)$, then $\vdash B$.

R2.   If $\vdash A$, then $\vdash (\forall v)A$.

R3.   If $\vdash (A \leftrightarrow B)$, then $\vdash (fA \leftrightarrow fB)$, where $f \in U[1,0]$.

A's being an LQ theorem, in symbols $\vdash A$, may be understood in the normal inductive way. Where $K \cup \{A\}$ is a set of LQ wffs, K yields A, in symbols $K \vdash A$, if there is a sequence of wffs $A_1, \ldots, A_n$, for some $n \in \omega$, such that $A_n = A$ and for $1 \leqslant i \leqslant n$, either $A_i \in K$, A_i is an LQ theorem or A_i comes from previous members of the sequence by R1 or R2. We understand a wff B's depending on a wff A in a derivation as in Mendelson [1], p. 60.

Section 5
Some theorems of LQ

In this section we present some consequences of these axiom and rule schemes:

Lemma 1.

(1) $\vdash (A = B) \to (A \leftrightarrow B)$.

(2) $\vdash (A = A)$.

(3) $\vdash (\forall v)(A = B) \to ((\forall v)A = (\forall v)B)$.

(4) $\vdash (\forall v)(A \to B) \to ((\forall v)A \to (\forall v)B)$.

(5) $\vdash (\forall v)(A \to B) \to ((\exists v)A \to (\exists v)B)$.

(6) $\vdash (\exists v)(A \leftrightarrow B) \to ((\forall v)A \to B)$, where v is not free in B.

(7) $\vdash (\exists v)(A = T) \to ((\exists v)A = T)$.

(8) $\vdash (F = \sim T)$.

(9) $\vdash (A = T) \to (\sim A = F)$.

(10) $\vdash (A \neq F) = (\sim A \neq T)$.

(11) $\vdash (\forall p)((p \neq F) \to (\exists q)((\text{Max } q) \wedge (q \text{ ent } p)))$.

(12) $\vdash ((A = B) \wedge (C = D)) \to ((A \wedge C) = (B \wedge D))$.

(13) $\vdash (A \text{ ent } B) \to ((A = T) \to (B = T))$.

(14) $\vdash ((A \wedge B) = T) \leftrightarrow ((A = T) \wedge (B = T))$.

(15) $\vdash (A \text{ ent } (B \wedge C)) \leftrightarrow ((A \text{ ent } B) \wedge (A \text{ ent } C))$.

(16) $\vdash ((A \wedge \sim A) = F)$.

(17) $\vdash ((F \to A) = T)$.

(18) $\vdash ((A \text{ ent } B) \wedge (A \text{ ent } \sim B)) \to (A = F)$.

(19) $\vdash ((\text{Max } A) \wedge (A \text{ ent } B)) \to \sim (A \text{ ent } \sim B)$.

(20) $\vdash ((\text{Max } A) \wedge ((A \text{ ent } B) \to (A \text{ ent } C))) \to (A \text{ ent } (B \to C))$.

(21) $\vdash (\forall p)(\forall q)(((p \neq q) \wedge (p \neq F) \wedge (q \neq F)) \to (\exists r)((\text{Max } r) \wedge (((r \text{ ent } p) \wedge \sim (r \text{ ent } q)) \vee ((r \text{ ent } q) \wedge \sim (r \text{ ent } p)))))$.

(22) $\vdash (\text{Max } A) \to ((\text{Max } A) = T)$.

(23) $\vdash (\forall f)(fA_1 \ldots A_m \leftrightarrow fB_1 \ldots B_m) \to (\forall g)(gA_i \leftrightarrow gB_i)$, for $1 \leqslant i \leqslant m$, where $f, g \in U[m,0]$ and neither f nor g occur free in any A_i or B_i, $1 \leqslant i \leqslant m$.

(24) $\vdash (\forall v)(\forall f)(fA_1 \ldots A_m \leftrightarrow fB_1 \ldots B_m) \to (\forall f)(f(\forall v)A_1 \ldots (\forall v)A_m \leftrightarrow f(\forall v)B_1 \ldots (\forall v)B_m)$, where $f \in U[m,0]$, f is distinct from v, and f does not occur free in any A_i or B_i, $1 \leqslant i \leqslant m$.

(25) $\vdash (\forall f)(\forall g)((f = g) \to ((f = g) = T))$, where $f, g \in U[m,n]$.

(26) $\vdash (\forall a_1)(\forall a_2)((a_1 = a_2) \to ((a_1 = a_2) = T))$, where $a_1, a_2 \in F[m,n]$.

(27) $\vdash (\forall o_1)(\forall o_2)((o_1 = o_2) \to ((o_1 = o_2) = T))$, where $o_1, o_2 \in O[m,n,k]$.

(28) $\vdash ([(\forall v_1) \ldots (\forall v_n)A] = T) \to (\forall v_1) \ldots (\forall v_n)(A = T)$.

Lemma 2 (change of bound variables). Where $v_1, \ldots, v_n, u_1, \ldots, u_n$ are variables such that v_i and u_i are of the same sort, $1 \leqslant i \leqslant n$, and

where $A[v_1/u_1] \ldots [v_n/u_n][u_1/v_1] \ldots [u_n/v_n]$ is the same wff as A, $\vdash (\forall v_1) \ldots$
$(\forall v_n)A = (\forall u_1) \ldots (\forall u_n)A[v_1/u_1] \ldots [v_n/u_n]$.

Theorem 3. $(\forall P)A \rightarrow \check{S}[P/\phi] A \,|$, where $P \in S[m,n]$ and $\phi \in \Sigma[m,n]$.
Proof: We may assume, without loss of generality, that P occurs free in A
and

$$\check{S}[P/\phi] A \,| = \underline{S}[P/\phi] A \,|.$$

Let $Q \in S[m,n] - SC[m,n]$ be a variable with no occurrence in either A or ϕ,
and ϕ^* be $\phi[P/Q]$. Clearly if P does not occur free in ϕ, ϕ^* is ϕ. By
hypothesis and AxI1, we have that $\vdash (P = \phi^*) \rightarrow (A \leftrightarrow A_1)$, where A_1 has ϕ^*
in exactly one occurrence where A has a free occurrence of P. Where k is
the total number of free occurrences of P in A and for $1 \leqslant i \leqslant k-1$, A_{i+1}
has ϕ^* in exactly one place where a_i has a free occurrence of P, we have
in general $\vdash (P = \phi^*) \rightarrow (A_i \leftrightarrow A_{i+1})$. But A_k is $\check{S}[P/\phi^*] A \,|$. By R2,
$\vdash (\forall P)((P = \phi^*) \rightarrow (A \leftrightarrow \check{S}[P/\phi] A \,|))$. By Lemma 1.5, $\vdash (\exists P)(P = \phi^*)$
$\rightarrow (\exists P)(A \leftrightarrow \check{S}[P/\phi^*] A \,|)$. Since P is not free in ϕ^*, $\vdash (\exists P)(P = \phi^*)$, by AxC1.
So $\vdash (\exists P)(A \leftrightarrow \check{S}[P/\phi^*] A \,|)$. Since P is not free in $\check{S}[P/\phi^*] A \,|$, $\vdash (\forall P)A$
$\rightarrow \check{S}[P/\phi^*] A \,|$, by Lemma 1.6. By R2 and AxQC2, $\vdash (\forall P)A$
$\rightarrow (\forall Q)\check{S}[P/\phi^*] A \,|$. But since Q is free for P in $\check{S}[P/\phi^*] A \,|$,
$\vdash (\forall Q)\check{S}[P/\phi^*] A \,| \rightarrow \check{S}[P/\phi^*] A \,|[Q/P]$ is an instance of AxQC1. But the
consequent is $\check{S}[P/\phi] A \,|$ and the theorem is established.

Theorem 4. $\vdash (\forall f)A \rightarrow \check{S}[f/\delta] A \,|$, where $f \in U[m,n]$ and $\delta \in \Gamma[m,n]$.
Proof: We may assume that $\check{S}[f/\delta] A \,|$ is a distinct wff from A. By repeated
application of AxI2, we have $\vdash (f = \delta) \rightarrow (A \leftrightarrow \check{S}[f/\delta] A \,|)$. Hence $\vdash (\exists f)(f = \delta)$
$\rightarrow (\exists f)(A \leftrightarrow \check{S}[f/\delta] A \,|)$. By (D8) and (D1), $\vdash (\forall P)(fP = \delta P) \rightarrow (f = \delta)$, where
$P \in S[m,n]$. Hence $\vdash (\exists f)(\forall P)(fP = \delta P) \rightarrow (\exists f)(f = \delta)$. So $\vdash (\forall f)A \rightarrow \check{S}[f/\delta] A \,|$,
by AxC4 and Lemma 1.6.
Corollary. If $\vdash A$, $\vdash \check{S}[f/\delta] A \,|$.

Theorem 5. $\vdash (\forall a)A \rightarrow \check{S}[aPQ/\delta] A \,|$, where $a \in F[m,n]$, $\delta \in \Gamma[m,n]$,
$P \in S[m,n]$ and $Q \in S[m,0]$.
Proof: We may assume that $\check{S}[aPQ/\delta] A \,|$ is a distinct wff from A. Let k be
the total number of free occurrences of a in A and let $A_0, A_1, \ldots, A_k$ be a series
of wffs such that $A_0 = A$ and for $0 \leqslant i \leqslant k-1$, A_{i+1} is exactly like A_i except
that for some $\phi \in \Sigma[m,n]$ and $\psi \in \Sigma[m,0]$ one occurrence of $a\phi\psi$ has been
replaced by $\underline{S}[PQ/\phi\psi] \delta \,|$, where the initial occurrence of a in $a\phi\psi$ is an
innermost free occurrence of a in A_i. (We may assume that all innermost free
occurrences of a in A are removed first, then all innermost free occurrences
of a in the resulting wff, etc.) Clearly $A_k = \check{S}[aPQ/\delta] A \,|$. For $0 \leqslant i \leqslant k-1$,

by AxI2, $\vdash (\forall u_1) \ldots (\forall u_h)(a\phi\psi = \underline{S}[PQ/\phi\psi]\,\delta\,|) \to (A_i = A_{i+1})$, where $u_1, \ldots,$ u_h are all the variables free in $\langle \phi, \psi \rangle$ which are bound at the occurrence of $a\phi\psi$ being replaced. Clearly where C is the conjunction of all the antecedents in this series, by universal instantiation for saturated variables (Theorem 3), $\vdash (\forall P)(\forall Q)(aPQ = \delta) \to C$. Where D is the conjunction of all consequents, $\vdash D \to (A \leftrightarrow \check{S}[aPQ/\delta]\,A\,|)$. So $\vdash (\exists a)(\forall P)(\forall Q)(aPQ = \delta)$ $\to (\exists a)(A \leftrightarrow \check{S}[aPQ/\delta]\,A\,|)$, by R2 and Lemma 1.5. By by AxC5 and (D8), $\vdash (\exists a)(\forall P)(\forall Q)(aPQ = \delta)$. The result now follows by Lemma 1.6.

Theorem 6. $\vdash (\forall o)A \to \check{S}[of_1 \ \ldots \ f_k/\delta]\,A\,|$, where $o \in O[m,n,k] - OC[m,n,k]$, $f_1, \ldots, f_k \in U[m,n] - UC[m,n]$, and $\delta \in \Gamma[m,n]$.

Proof: As previously, we assume that $\check{S}[of_1 \ldots f_k/\delta]\,A\,|$ is a distinct wff from A. By the strategy for proving Theorem 5, we may easily show that $\vdash (\exists o)(\forall f_1) \ldots (\forall f_k)(of_1 \ldots f_k = \delta) \to (\exists o)(A \leftrightarrow \check{S}[of_1 \ldots f_k/\delta]\,A\,|)$. By (D8) and AxC6, $\vdash (\exists o)(\forall f_1) \ldots (\forall f_k)(of_1 \ldots f_k = \delta)$. Again we use Lemma 1.6 to show the theorem.

Lemma 7. $\vdash ((N+1)f)[(\text{Num}\,f) \wedge ((f = 0) \vee \ldots \vee (f = N))]$, where $f \in U[1,1]$.

Proof: The argument divides on whether $N = 0$ or $N > 0$. If $N = 0$, by (D8), (D14), (D15), and Theorem 3, $\vdash ((\text{Num}\,0) \wedge (0 = 0))$. Clearly $\vdash (\forall g)(((\text{Num}\,g) \wedge (g = 0)) \to (0 = g))$. By AxN2, $\vdash (1f)((\text{Num}\,f) \wedge (f = 0))$. If $N > 0$, for $M_1, M_2 < N+1$, if $M_1 \neq M_2$, then by AxN4, $\vdash (\forall P)(M_1 P \to \sim M_2 P)$. By AxI2, $\vdash (M_1 = M_2) \to (\forall P)(M_1 P \to \sim M_1 P)$. Clearly $\vdash (\forall P)(M_1 P \to \sim M_1 P) \to (\forall P) \sim M_1 P$. But by AxN5 and AxQC3, $\vdash \sim (\forall P) \sim M_1 P$. So $\vdash (M_1 \neq M_2)$. Hence $\vdash \neq (0, \ldots, N)$. By (D8), (D14), (D15), (D19), and Theorem 3, $\vdash (((\text{Num}\,0) \wedge [(0 = 0) \vee \ldots \vee (0 = N)]) \wedge \ldots \wedge ((\text{Num}\,N) \wedge [(N = 0) \vee \ldots \vee (N = N)]))$. Clearly $\vdash (\forall g)(((\text{Num}\,g) \wedge [(g = 0) \vee \ldots \vee (g = N)]) \to [(g = 0) \wedge \ldots \wedge (g = N)])$. The result follows by AxN3.

Lemma 8. $\vdash (\exists o)(\exists P)(\forall f_1) \ldots (\forall f_k)(of_1 \ldots f_k P = A)$, where $0 \in O[m,n,k] - OC[m,n,k]$, $P \in U[m,n] - UC[m,n]$, o does not occur free in A, and $f_1, \ldots, f_k$ are distinct members of $U[m,n] - UC[m,n]$.

Proof: The lemma is an easy consequence of AxComp6.

Lemma 9. $\vdash ((N+1)\,\text{suc}\,N)$.

Proof: The lemma follows immediately from Axns4 and (D17).

Lemma 10. $\vdash (\text{Nat}\,N)$, for all $N \in \omega$.

Proof: Clearly by Axns1, $\vdash (n0 = 0)$. By Axns2, Axns4, and AxI2, $\vdash (nN = 0) \to (n(N+1) = 0)$. But from this the lemma readily follows.

Lemma 11. $\vdash (N \neq M)$, where N and M are distinct.

Proof: $\vdash (N = M) \to (\forall P)(NP \to MP)$, where $P \in S[1,1]$, by (D4) and Lemma 1.1. $\vdash (\forall P)(NP \to \sim MP)$, by AxN4. Hence $\vdash (N = M) \to \sim (\forall P)NP$. But by AxN5, $\vdash (\exists P)NP$. So $\vdash (N \neq M)$.

Lemma 12. $\vdash (N \neq M) \to ([(\exists g_1)\ldots(\exists g_k)((N \operatorname{suc} g_1) \wedge \ldots \wedge (g_k \operatorname{suc} M)) \wedge \sim(\exists h_1)\ldots(\exists h_i)((M \operatorname{suc} h_1) \wedge \ldots \wedge (h_i \operatorname{suc} N))] \vee [(\exists g_1)\ldots(\exists g_k)((M \operatorname{suc} g_1) \wedge \ldots \wedge (g_k \operatorname{suc} N)) \wedge \sim(\exists h_1)\ldots(\exists h_i)((N \operatorname{suc} h_1) \wedge \ldots \wedge (h_i \operatorname{suc} M))])$.

Proof: Whichever numerical quantifiers N and M replace the schematic letters in the above schema, we have that for the corresponding natural numbers n and m, if $n \neq m$, either $n > m$ or $m > n$. We may assume that $n > m$ without loss of generality. Hence where $k = (n-m)$, by Axns4, $\vdash (N = X_k M)$, where X_k is s iterated k times. Now assume, *per reductio*, that there is a i such that $\vdash (M = X_i N)$, $m = (i+n)$ and since, by Axns3, $n \neq 0$, $n = (j+1)$, for some $j \in \omega$. Hence $\vdash (M = s \ldots s(J+1))$. Hence $\vdash (s(X_{k+i}J) = sJ)$. By Ax$ns$5, $\vdash (X_{k+i}J = J)$. But this is impossible, by Lemma 11 and (D19). From these considerations and (D17), the lemma readily follows.

Section 6
Semantics

Where W is a non-empty set, $\underline{D}$ *is a structure on* W just in case $\underline{D} = \langle D, M, J, L \rangle$, where $D = \langle D[m,n] \rangle$, $m \in \omega - \{0\}$, $n \in \omega$, $M = \langle M[m,n] \rangle$, $m \in \omega - \{0\}$, $n \in \omega$, $J = \langle J[m,n] \rangle$, $m,n \in \omega - \{0\}$ and $L = \langle L[m,n,k] \rangle$, $n \in \omega$, $m,k \in \omega - \{0\}$, such that

(1) $D[1,0] \subseteq \mathscr{P}(W)$
(2)   for $m > 1$, $D[m,0] = D[1,0]^m$
(3a) $d[1,1] \subseteq \{F: D[1,0] \to \chi[1,1]\}$, where $\omega \subseteq \chi[1,1]$,
(3b)   for $m,n \geqslant 1$, $\langle m,n \rangle \neq \langle 1,1 \rangle$, $D[m,n] \subseteq \{F: D[m,0] \to \chi[m,n]\}$,
(4)   for $m > 0$, $M[m,0] \subseteq D[1,0]^{D[m,0]}$,
(5)   for $m,n > 0$, $M[m,n] \subseteq D[1,0]^{D[m,n]}$,
(6)   for $m,n \in \omega - \{0\}$, $J[m,n] \subseteq M[m,n]^{D[m,n] \times D[m,0]}$,
(7)   for $n \in \omega$, $m,r \in \omega - \{0\}$, $L[m,n,r] \subseteq M[m,n]^{M[m,n]^r}$.

$\underline{S} = \langle W, \underline{D}, O \rangle$ is an *arithmetical second-order generalised model structure*, a $2\overline{AGMS}$ for short, if $\underline{S}$ satisfies

(1) W is a set and $O \in W$,
(2) $\underline{D}$ is a structure on W,
(3) (a) $\varnothing \in D[1,0]$
      (b)   if $X \in D[1,0]$, $\bar{X}(W-X) \in D[1,0]$,

(c)   if $X,Y \in D[1,0]$, $X \cup Y \in D[1,0]$,

(d)   if $F \in D[1,1]$ and $X = \{Y \in D[1,0] : F(Y) \neq 0\}$, $\cup X \in D[1,0]$ and if $X \neq \varnothing$, $\cap X \in D[1,0]$,

(e) $d_\rightarrow \in M[2,0]$, where for all $\langle X,Y \rangle \in D[2,0]$, $d_\rightarrow(\langle X,Y \rangle) = \bar{X} \cup Y$.

(f) $d_\forall \in M[1,1]$, where for all F in $D[1,1]$, if $X = \{Y \in D[1,0] : F(Y) \neq 0)$, $d_\forall(F) = \cap X$, if $X \neq \varnothing$; otherwise $d_\forall(F) = W$,

(g) $d_\exists \in M[1,1]$, where for all $F \in D[1,1]$, if $X = \{Y \in D[1,0] : F(Y) \neq 0\}$, $d_\exists(F) = \cup X$,

(h)   for each $N \in \omega$, $d_N \in M[1,1]$ such that for all $F \in D[1,1]$ and $w \in W$, $w \in d_N(F)$ iff $\Sigma\{F(X) : X \in D[1,0]$ and $w \in X\} = N$,[2]

(i.1) for each $x,y \in \chi[1,1] - \omega$, if there are $F,G \in D[1,1]$ and $X,Y \in D[1,0]$ such that $F(X) = x$, $G(Y) = y$, and $x \neq y$, there are $d_x,d_y \in M[1,1]$ such that $d_x \neq d_y$ and $d_x,d_y \neq N$, for any $N \in \omega$,

(i.2) for each $x,y \in \chi[m,n]$, if there are $F,G \in D[m,n]$ and $X,Y \in D[m,0]$ such that $F(X) = x$, $G(Y) = y$ and $x \neq y$, there are $d_x,d_y \in M[m,n]$ such that $d_x \neq d_y$, where $\langle m,n \rangle \neq \langle 1,1 \rangle$,

(j.1) there is a $j([1,1]) \in J[1,1]$ such that for $F \in D[1,1]$ and $X \in D[1,0]$, $F(X) = N$ for some $N \in \omega$ iff $j(F,X) = d_N$; and $F(X) = x$ for some $x \in \chi[1,1] - \omega$ iff $j(F,X) = d_x$,

(j.2) there is a $j[m,n] \in J[m,n]$ such that for $F \in D[m,n]$ and $X \in D[m,0]$, $F(X) = x$ for some $x \in \chi[m,n]$ iff $j(F,X) = d_x$, where $\langle m,n \rangle \neq \langle 1,1 \rangle$,

(k)   for each $d_x \in M[1,1]$ and $d_N \in M[1,1]$, where $x \in \chi[1,1] - \omega$ and $N \in \omega$, for all $F \in D[1,1]$, $d_x(F) \cap d_N(F) = \varnothing$,

(l.1) for each $d_x,d_y \in M[1,1]$, where $x,y \in \chi[1,1] - \omega$ and $d_x \neq d_y$, for all $F \in D[1,1]$, $d_x(F) \cap d_y(F) = \varnothing$,

(l.2) for each $d_x,d_y \in M[m,n]$, where $\langle m,n \rangle \neq \langle 1,1 \rangle$, $x,y \in \chi[m,n]$, and $d_x \neq d_y$, for all $F \in D[m,n]$, $d_x(F) \cap d_y(F) = \varnothing$.

There are functions v and σ in $L[1,1,1]$ such that

(m)   for all $d \in M[1,1]$, there are $F \in D[1,1]$ and $X \in D[1,0]$ such that $d = j(F,X)$ and $vd = d_0$ if for any $\delta \in L[1,1,1]$ and $F \in D[1,1]$ if $O \in \delta d_0(F)$ and for all $d' \in M[1,1]$, [if (i) $a \in \delta d'(F)$ and (ii) there is a $G \in D[1,1]$ and a $Y \in D[1,0]$ such that $d' = j(G,Y)$ and $vd' = d_0$, then $O \in \delta \sigma d'(F)$], then $O \in \delta d(F)$,

(n)   if there is an $F \in D[1,1]$ and a $X \in D[1,0]$ such that $j(F,X) = d$ and $vd = d_0$, then $v\sigma d = d_0$,

(o) σ is one–one, for all $d \in M[1,1]$, $\sigma(d) \neq d_0$ and $\sigma(d_N) = d_{N+1}$.

$\underline{S}$ is an *atomic 2AGMS* if

(4) for all $w \in W$, $\{w\} \in D[1,0]$.

$\underline{S}$ is a *normal 2AGMS* iff

(5) for all $w \in W$, $\langle m,n \rangle \in (\omega - \{0\}) \times \omega$, $X, Y \in D[m,n]$, if for every $d \in M[m,n]$, $w \in d(X)$ iff $w \in d(Y)$, then $X = Y$.

   $\underline{S}$ is a *hereditary* 2AGMS iff $\underline{S}$ is normal and

(6) for each $n \geqslant 1$, there is a $d_i \in M[m,0]$, $1 \leqslant i \leqslant m$, such that for $\langle X_1, \ldots, X_m \rangle \in D[m,0]$, $d_i(X_1, \ldots, X_m) = X_i$ (that is, M contains all projection functions on sequences of propositions),
(7) for each $X \in D[1,0]$, there is a $d \in M[m,n]$ such that for all $Y \in D[m,n]$, $d(Y) = X$ (that is, for $\langle m,n \rangle \in (\omega - \{0\}) \times \omega$, $M[m,n]$ contains all constant functions for each $X \in D[1,0]$).

   Where $\underline{S}$ is a 2AGMS, by a *value assignment* (or *valuation*) V associated with $\underline{S}$, we mean a mapping such that

(1)   if $P \in S[m,n]$, $V(P) \in D[m,n]$;
(2)   if $f \in U[m,n]$, $V(f) \in M[m,n]$, where $V(\rightarrow) = d_{\rightarrow}$, $V(\forall) = d_\forall$, and $V(\exists) = d_\exists$;
(3) $a \in F[m,n]$, $V(a) \in J[m,n]$, where $V(\alpha[m,n]) = j[m,n]$;
(4)   if $o \in O[m,n,k]$, $V(o) \in L[m,n,k]$, where $V(n) = v$ and $V(s) = \sigma$.

   The notion of a variant V′ of a valuation V is a straightforward adaptation of that of Cresswell [1], pp. 300–1. The following clauses give a partial indication of how a valuation V is extended to assign a value to sequences of expressions $\phi[m,n]$ and wffs A in general. Remember that the expression $\phi[m,n]$ may be the same as the expression $\psi[m+1,n-1]$. ('ppp' can be taken as in $\Sigma[2,1]$ or $\Sigma[1,2]$ or $\Sigma[3,0]$, i.e., as $\langle\langle p,p \rangle,\langle p \rangle\rangle$, $\langle\langle p \rangle,\langle p,p \rangle\rangle$, or $\langle p,p,p \rangle$.) We discuss an arbitrary variant V′ of V.

(5)   Where $A_1, \ldots, A_m$ are wffs such that for $1 \leqslant i \leqslant m$, $V'(A_i) \in D[1,0]$, $V'(\langle A_1, \ldots, A_m \rangle) = \langle V'(A_1), \ldots, V'(A_m) \rangle$. If for any i, $1 \leqslant i \leqslant m$, $V'(A_i) \notin D[1,0]$, $V'(\langle A_1, \ldots, A_m \rangle)$ is undefined.
(6)   Where v is a variable and A a wff such that for any variant V″ of V′ which differs from V′ at most a v, V″ (A) $\in D[1,0]$, $X \in D[1,0]$, and $X = \{V'' : V''$ differs from V′ at most at v and $V''(A) = X\}$, $V'(\langle\langle A \rangle,\langle v \rangle\rangle) = F$ such that $F(X) = \text{card}(X)$ if card(X) is finite and $F(X) = x \in \chi[1,1] - \omega$ otherwise. If for any such V″, $V''(A) \notin D[1,0]$, $V'(\langle\langle A \rangle,\langle v \rangle\rangle)$ is undefined.
(7)   Where $v_1, \ldots, v_n$ are variables, $A_1, \ldots, A_m$ are wffs, $m,n \geqslant 1$, $\langle m,n \rangle \neq \langle 1,1 \rangle$, such that for any variant V″ of V′ which differs from V′ at most at $v_1, \ldots, v_n$, $V''(A_1), \ldots, V''(A_m) \in D[1,0]$, and $X \in D[m,0]$, $V'(\langle\langle A_1, \ldots, A_m \rangle,\langle v_1, \ldots, v_n \rangle\rangle) = F$ such that $F(X) \in \chi[m,n]$. If for

any i, $1 \leqslant i \leqslant m$, and V'' differing from V' at most at $v_1, \ldots, v_n$, $V''(A_i) \notin D[1,0]$, $V'(\langle\langle A_1, \ldots, A_m\rangle,\langle v_1, \ldots, v_n\rangle\rangle)$ shall be undefined.

(8)   Where $a \in F[m,n]$, $V'(\phi[m,n]) \in D[m,n]$, and $V'(\psi[m,0]) \in D[m,0]$, $V'(a\phi\psi) = V'(a)(\langle V'(\phi),V'(\psi)\rangle)$. If either $V'(\phi) \notin D[m,n]$ or $V'(\psi) \notin D[m,0]$, in particular if either is undefined, $V'(a\phi\psi)$ shall be undefined.

(9)   Where $o \in O[m,n,k]$, $V'(\delta_1), \ldots, V'(\delta_k) \in M[m,n]$, $V'(o\delta_1 \ldots \delta_k) = V'(o)(\langle V'(\delta_1), \ldots, V'(\delta_k)\rangle)$. If for some $1 \leqslant i \leqslant k$, $V'(\delta_i) \notin M[m,n]$, in particular if $V'(\delta_i)$ is undefined, $V'(o\delta_1 \ldots \delta_k)$ shall be undefined.

(10)   Where $V'(\delta) \in M[m,n]$ and $V'(\phi) \in D[m,n]$, $V'(\delta\phi) = V'(\delta)(V'(\phi))$. If either $V'(\delta) \notin M[m,n]$ or $V'(\phi) \notin D[m,n]$, in particular if either is undefined, $V'(\delta\phi)$ shall be undefined.

V is a *standard* valuation just in case where V' is any variant of V,

(1)   if u is a set of variables, none of which occur free in $\langle\langle A\rangle,\langle v\rangle\rangle$, V^* differs from V' at most at u, for all V^{**} differing from V^* at most at v, V^{**} is defined, $X \in D[1,0]$ and $\text{card}(X) \notin \omega$, for $X = \{V^{**}: V^{**}$ differs from V^* at most at v and $V^{**}(A) = X\}$, then $V'(\langle\langle A\rangle,\langle v\rangle\rangle)X = V^*(\langle\langle A\rangle,\langle v\rangle\rangle)X$,

(2)   if X is as above, $v_1, \ldots, v_n$ are variables distinct from v, $u_1, \ldots, u_n$ are variables or constants distinct from v, for $1 \leqslant i \leqslant n$, v_i is free for u_i in A, for all V'' differing from V' at most at v, $V''(A[v_1, \ldots, v_n/u_1, \ldots, u_n])$ is defined, for all $V''[v_1/V'(u_1), \ldots, v_n/V'(u_n)]$ differing from $V'[v_1/V'(u_1), \ldots, v_n/V'(u_n)]$ at most at v, $V''[v_1/V'(u_1), \ldots, v_n/V'(u_n)](A)$ is defined and $\text{card}(X) \notin \omega$, $V'(\langle\langle A[v_1, \ldots, v_n/u_1, \ldots, u_n]\rangle,\langle v\rangle\rangle)X = V'[v_1/V'(u_1), \ldots, v_n/V'(u_n)](\langle\langle A\rangle,\langle v\rangle\rangle)X$.

(3)   where $(\forall v_1) \ldots (\forall v_k)(\phi[m,n] = \psi[m,n])$, A and B satisfy the hypotheses of AxI1, $V'(\langle\langle A\rangle,\langle v\rangle\rangle)$ and $V'(\langle\langle B\rangle,\langle v\rangle\rangle)$ are defined, as is $V'((\forall v_1) \ldots (\forall v_k)(\phi[m,n] = \psi[m,n]))$, X is as above, $O \in V'((\forall v_1) \ldots (\forall v_k)(\phi[m,n] = \psi[m,n]))$ and $\text{card}(X) \notin \omega$, $V'(\langle\langle A\rangle,\langle v\rangle\rangle)X = V'(\langle\langle B\rangle,\langle v\rangle\rangle)X$.

(4)   where $(\forall v_1) \ldots (\forall v_k)(\delta_1 = \delta_2)$, A and B satisfy the hypothesis of AxI2, $V'(\langle\langle A\rangle,\langle v\rangle\rangle)$ and $V'(\langle\langle B\rangle,\langle v\rangle\rangle)$ are defined, as is $V'((\forall v_1) \ldots (\forall v_k)(\delta_1 = \delta_2))$, $O \in V'((\forall v_1) \ldots (\forall v_k)(\delta_1 = \delta_2))$, X is as above and $\text{card}(X) \notin \omega$, $V'(\langle\langle A\rangle,\langle v\rangle\rangle)X = V'(\langle\langle B\rangle,\langle v\rangle\rangle)X$.

(5)   if u is a set of variables none of which occur free in $\langle\langle A_1, \ldots, A_m\rangle, \langle v_1, \ldots, v_n\rangle\rangle$, $\langle m,n\rangle \neq \langle 1,1\rangle$, V^* differs from V' at most at u, for all V^{**} differing from V^* at most at $v_1, \ldots, v_n$, $V^{**}(\langle A_1, \ldots, A_m\rangle)$ is defined, and $X \in D[m,0]$, then $V'(\langle\langle A_1, \ldots, A_m\rangle,\langle v_1, \ldots, v_n\rangle\rangle)X = V^*(\langle\langle A_1, \ldots, A_n\rangle,\langle v_1, \ldots, v_n\rangle\rangle)X$,

(6)   if X is as above, $v_1, \ldots, v_n$ are variables distinct from $w_1, \ldots, w_h, u_1, \ldots, u_n$

are variables or constants distinct from $w_1, \ldots, w_h$, $A_1, \ldots, A_m$ are wffs, $\langle m,h \rangle \neq \langle 1,1 \rangle$, v_k is free for u_k in A_i, $1 \leqslant i \leqslant m$ and $1 \leqslant k \leqslant n$, for all V'' differing from V' at most at $w_1, \ldots, w_h$, $V''(\langle A_1[v_1, \ldots, v_n/u_1, \ldots, u_n], \ldots, A_m[v_1, \ldots, v_n/u_1, \ldots, u_n] \rangle)$ is defined, and for all $V''[v_1/V'(u_1), \ldots, v_n/V'(u_n)]$ differing from $V'[v_1/V'(u_1), \ldots, v_n/V'(u_n)]$ at most at $w_1, \ldots, w_h$, $V''[v_1/V'(u_1), \ldots, v_n/V'(u_n)](\langle A_1, \ldots, A_m \rangle)$ is defined, then $V'(\langle \langle A_1[v_1, \ldots, v_n/u_1, \ldots, u_n], \ldots, A_m[v_1, \ldots, v_n/u_1, \ldots, u_n] \rangle, \langle w_1, \ldots, w_h \rangle \rangle)X = V'[v_1/V'(u_1), \ldots, v_n/V'(u_n)](\langle \langle A_1, \ldots, A_m \rangle, \langle w_1, \ldots, w_h \rangle \rangle)X$,

(7) where $\phi_1, \psi_1 \in \Sigma[m_1,n_1], \ldots, \phi_x, \psi_x \in \Sigma[m_x,n_x]$, $(\forall v_1^1) \ldots (\forall v_{k1}^1)(\phi_1 = \psi_1)$, A_1, and $B_1, \ldots, (\forall v_1^x), \ldots, (\forall v_{kx}^x)(\phi_x = \psi_x)$, A_x and B_x satisfy the hypotheses of AxI1, $V'(\langle \langle A_1, \ldots, A_x \rangle, \langle u_1, \ldots, u_z \rangle \rangle)$, $V'(\langle \langle B_1, \ldots, B_x \rangle, \langle u_1, \ldots, u_z \rangle \rangle)$, $V'((\forall v_1^1) \ldots (\forall v_{k1}^1)(\phi_1 = \psi_1)), \ldots, V'((\forall v_1^x) \ldots (\forall v_{kx}^x)(\phi_x = \psi_x))$ are all defined, $O \in V'((\forall v_1^1) \ldots (\forall v_{k1}^1)(\phi_1 = \psi_1)), \ldots, V'((\forall v_1^x) \ldots (\forall v_{kx}^x)(\phi_x = \psi_x))$, $X \in D[x,0]$, and $\langle x,z \rangle \neq \langle 1,1 \rangle$, then $V'(\langle \langle A_1, \ldots, A_x \rangle, \langle u_1, \ldots, u_z \rangle \rangle)X = V'(\langle \langle B_1, \ldots, B_x \rangle, \langle u_1, \ldots, u_z \rangle \rangle)X$,

(8) where $\delta_1, \gamma_1 \in \Gamma[m_1,n_1], \ldots, \delta_x, \gamma_x \in \Gamma[m_x,n_x]$, $(\forall v_1^1) \ldots (\forall v_{k1}^1)(\delta_1 = \gamma_1)$, A_1, and $B_1, \ldots, (\forall v_1^x) \ldots (\forall v_{kx}^x)(\delta_x = \gamma_x)$, A_x, and B_x satisfy the hypotheses of AxI2, $V'(\langle \langle A_1, \ldots, A_x \rangle, \langle u_1, \ldots, u_z \rangle \rangle)$, $V'(\langle \langle B_1, \ldots, B_x \rangle, \langle u_1, \ldots, u_z \rangle \rangle)$, $V'((\forall v_1^1) \ldots (\forall v_{k1}^1)(\delta_1 = \gamma_1)), \ldots, V'((\forall v_1^x) \ldots (\forall v_{kx}^x)(\delta_x = \gamma_x))$ are all defined, $O \in V'((\forall v_1^1) \ldots (\forall v_{k1}^1)(\delta_1 = \gamma_1)), \ldots, V'((\forall v_1^x) \ldots (\forall v_{kx}^x)(\delta_x = \gamma_x))$, $X \in D[x,0]$ and $\langle x,z \rangle \neq \langle 1,1 \rangle$, then $V'(\langle \langle A_1, \ldots, A_x \rangle, \langle u_1, \ldots, u_z \rangle \rangle)X = V'(\langle \langle B_1, \ldots, B_x \rangle, \langle u_1, \ldots, u_z \rangle \rangle)X$.

Henceforth all valuations mentioned will be standard valuations.

By a *model*, we mean a structure $\langle \underline{S}, V \rangle$, where $\underline{S}$ is a 2AGMS and V is a valuation associated with $\underline{S}$, satisfying (1)–(10).

Assume that $\langle \underline{S}, V \rangle$ is a model, where $\underline{S} = \langle W, \underline{D}, a \rangle$. Where v is a variable, an element X of $\underline{D}$ *is appropriate for* v just in case if $v \in S[m,n]$, $X \in D[m,n]$, if $v \in U[m,n]$, $X \in M[m,n]$, if $v \in F[m,n]$, $X \in J[m,n]$, and $v \in O[m,n,k]$, $X \in L[m,n,k]$.

Where $v_1, \ldots, v_n$ are variables and $A_1, \ldots, A_m$ are wffs such that for any $X_1, \ldots, X_n$ in $\underline{D}$, where each X_i is appropriate for v_i, $1 \leqslant i \leqslant n$, $V[v_1/X_1, \ldots, v_n/X_n](\langle A_1, \ldots, A_m \rangle) \in D[m,0]$, the notation $V((\lambda v_1) \ldots (\lambda v_n)(\langle A_1, \ldots, A_m \rangle))$ shall denote that function d such that for the appropriate $X_1, \ldots, X_n$, $d(X_1, \ldots, X_n) = V[v_1/X_1, \ldots, v_n/X_n](\langle A_1, \ldots, A_m \rangle)$. Where $v_1, \ldots, v_n, X_1, \ldots, X_n, A_1, \ldots, A_m$ are as above and $u_1, \ldots, u_k$ are variables such that for any $Y_1, \ldots, Y_k \in \underline{D}$, where each Y_i is appropriate for u_i, $1 \leqslant i \leqslant k$, $V[v_1/X_1, \ldots, v_n/X_n, u_1/Y_1, \ldots, u_k/Y_k](\langle A_1, \ldots, A_m \rangle) \in D[m,0]$, the notation $V((\lambda v_1) \ldots (\lambda v_n))V((\lambda u_1) \ldots (\lambda u_k)(\langle A_1, \ldots, A_m \rangle))$ shall denote that function d such that for appropriate $X_1, \ldots, X_n$, $d(X_1, \ldots, X_n) = V[v_1/X_1, \ldots, v_n/X_n]((\lambda u_1) \ldots (\lambda u_k)(\langle A_1, \ldots, A_m \rangle))$.

If $d = V((\lambda v_1) \ldots (\lambda v_n)(\langle A_1, \ldots, A_m \rangle))$, d *is represented* in $\langle \underline{S}, V \rangle$ by $\langle \langle A_1, \ldots, A_m \rangle, \langle v_1, \ldots, v_n \rangle \rangle$. (Compare Cresswell [1], p. 301.)

We proceed now to define regular models. Where $\underline{S} = \langle W,\underline{D},a\rangle$, a model $\langle \underline{S},V\rangle$ is D-regular just in case

(a) $\underline{S}$ is hereditary,

(b) where V′ is any variant of V, v is a variable, and A a wiff, if for any variant V″ differing from V′ at most at v, $V''(A) \in D[1,0]$, $X = \{V'' : V''$ differs from V′ at most at v and $V''(A) = X\}$, then $F \in D[1,1]$ such that for $X \in D[1,0]$, $F(X) = \mathrm{card}(X)$ if $\mathrm{card}(X) \in \omega$, and $F(X) = x \in \chi[1,1] - \omega$ such that $V'(\langle\langle A\rangle,\langle v\rangle\rangle)X = x$ otherwise,

(c) where $\langle m,n\rangle \neq \langle 1,1\rangle$, $v_1, \ldots, v_n$ are variables, $A_1, \ldots, A_m$ are wffs, and V′ is any variant of V, if for any variant V″ differing from V′ at most at $v_1, \ldots, v_n$, $V''(\langle A_1, \ldots, A_m\rangle) \in D[m,0]$, then $F \in D[m,n]$ such that for $X \in D[m,0]$, $F(X) \in \chi[m,n]$ such that $V'(\langle\langle A_1, \ldots, A_m\rangle,\langle v_1, \ldots, v_n\rangle\rangle)X = F(X)$.

$\langle \underline{S},V\rangle$ is M-regular iff for any variant V′ of V, if d is represented in $\langle \underline{S},V'\rangle$ by $\langle\langle A\rangle,\langle P[m,n]\rangle\rangle$, then $d \in M[m,n]$, and if d is represented in $\langle \underline{S},\overline{V'}\rangle$ by $\langle\langle A\rangle,\langle p_1, \ldots, p_m\rangle\rangle$, then $d \in M[m,0]$.

$\langle \underline{S},V\rangle$ is J-regular iff for any variant V′ of V, if d is represented in $\langle \underline{S},\overline{V'}\rangle$ by $\langle\langle A\rangle,\langle P[m,n],Q[m,0],R[m,n]\rangle\rangle$, there is a $d' \in J[m,n]$ such that for $X,Z \in D[m,n]$ and $Y \in D[m,0]$, $(d'(X,Y))(Z) = d(X,Y,Z)$, i.e., $d'(X,Y) = V'[P[m,n]/X,Q[m,0]/Y]((\lambda R[m,n])A)$.

$\langle \underline{S},V\rangle$ is L-regular iff for any variant V′ of V, if d is represented in $\langle \underline{S},V'\rangle$ by $\langle\langle A\rangle,\langle f_1, \ldots, f_k,P\rangle\rangle$, $f_1, \ldots, f_k \in U[m,n]$ and $P \in S[m,n]$, there is a $d' \in L[m,n,k]$ such that for $M_1, \ldots, M_k \in M[m,n]$ and $X \in D[m,n]$, $(d'(M_1, \ldots, M_k))(X) = d(M_1, \ldots, M_k,X)$, i.e., $d'(M_1, \ldots, M_k) = V'[f_1/M_1, \ldots, f_k/M_k]((\lambda P)A)$.

$\langle \underline{S},V\rangle$ is *regular* iff $\langle \underline{S},V\rangle$ is D, M, J- and L-regular.

A *2AGMS model* is an atomic regular model $\langle \underline{S},V\rangle$. Where $S = \langle W,\underline{D},O\rangle$ and V is an assignment associated with S, A is true in $\langle \underline{S},V\rangle$, in symbols $\langle \underline{S},V\rangle |\vdash A$, iff $O \in V(A)$. A is $\underline{S}$-valid, in symbols $S |\vdash A$, iff for all V associated with $\underline{S}$, $\langle \underline{S},V\rangle |\vdash A$. A is valid, in symbols $|\vdash A$, iff for all $\underline{S}$ such that $\langle \underline{S},V\rangle$ is a 2AGMS model, $\underline{S} |\vdash A$. A is false in $\langle \underline{S},V\rangle$, in symbols $\langle \underline{S},V\rangle |\hspace{-0.4em}/\vdash A$, iff $O \notin V(A)$, $\langle \underline{S},V\rangle$ is a *general model* iff $\langle \underline{S},V\rangle$ is a model, $\underline{S}$ is a normal 2AGMS and if A is an instance of a universal closure of any AxC scheme, $\langle \underline{S},V\rangle |\vdash A$. (Compare Cresswell [1], p. 309.) We shall now show that the classes of regular and general models coincide.

Section 7
Regular and general models

Definition. Where V_1, V_2, V_3 and V_4 are valuations and u is a set of variables, by the notation $\theta(V_1,V_2,V_3,V_4,u)$ we indicate that for any $v \in u$, $V_3(v) = V_4(v)$ and V_3 differs from V_1 and V_4 from V_2 at most at u.

Lemma 1. (1) Where $\langle \underline{S},V \rangle$ is a model, A is a wff, v is a set of variables not occurring free in A and $\underline{V'}$ is a valuation differing from V at most at v, if V(A) is defined, so is V'(A) and V(A) = V'(A).

(2) Where $\langle \underline{S},V \rangle$ is a model, $\phi = \langle\langle A_1,\ldots, A_m \rangle,\langle v_1,\ldots, v_n \rangle\rangle$, v is a set of variables which do not occur free in ϕ and V' is a valuation differing from V at most at v, if $V(\phi)$ is defined, so is $V'(\phi)$ and $V(\phi) = V'(\phi)$.

Proof: ad (1). We induct on the length of formula over all pairs of variants V,V' such that for some set of variables u, $\theta(V,V',\underline{V},\underline{V'},u)$. Notice that any such $\underline{V},\underline{V'}$ differ at most at v. We consider the cases where A is of the form (i) $fB_1 \ldots B_x v_1 \ldots v_z$, (ii) $a\phi\psi\chi$ and (iii) $o\delta_1 \ldots \delta_k \chi$, where $f \in U[x,z]$, $a \in F[x,z]$, $\phi,\chi \in \Sigma[x,z]$, $\psi \in \Sigma[x,0]$, $\delta_1, \ldots, \delta_k \in \Gamma[x,z]$ and $o \in O[x,z,k]$.

(ia) $\langle x,z \rangle = \langle 1,1 \rangle$. If V(A) is defined, so is $\underline{V}(\langle\langle B_1 \rangle,\langle v_1 \rangle\rangle)$ by (10) of the definition of a valuation. If $\underline{V}(\langle\langle B_1 \rangle,\langle v_1 \rangle\rangle)$ is defined, where $\underline{V}$ is any variant of V that differs from V at most at v_1, $\underline{V}(B_1) \in D[1,0]$. Let $\underline{V}$ be as above and $\underline{V'}$ be such that $\theta(\underline{V},\underline{V'},\underline{\underline{V}},\underline{\underline{V'}},\{v_1\})$. Hence $\theta(V,V',\underline{V},\underline{V'},v \cup \{v_1\})$. By inductive hypothesis we have that $\underline{V'}(B_1) = \underline{V}(B_1)$. So by (6) of the definition of a valuation $\underline{V'}(\langle\langle B_1 \rangle,\langle v_1 \rangle\rangle)$ is defined and $\underline{V'}(\langle\langle B_1 \rangle,\langle v_1 \rangle\rangle) = \underline{V}(\langle\langle B_1 \rangle,\langle v_1 \rangle\rangle)$, since all valuations under discussion are standard.

(ib) $\langle x,z \rangle \neq \langle 1,1 \rangle$. If V(A) is defined, so is $\underline{V}(\langle\langle B_1,\ldots, B_x \rangle,\langle v_1,\ldots, v_z \rangle\rangle)$ by (10) of the definition of a valuation. If the latter is defined, where $\underline{V}$ is any variant of V that differs from V at most at $v_1, \ldots, v_z$, $\underline{V}(B_k) \in D[1,0]$, $1 \leqslant k \leqslant x$. Let $\underline{V}$ be as above and $\underline{V'}$ be such that $\theta(\underline{V},\underline{V'},\underline{\underline{V}},\underline{\underline{V'}},\{v_1,\ldots, v_z\})$. Hence $\theta(V,V',\underline{V},\underline{V'},v \cup \{v_1,\ldots, v_z\})$. By inductive hypothesis we have that $\underline{V'}(B_k) = \underline{V}(B_k)$, $1 \leqslant k \leqslant x$. So by (6) of the definition of a valuation, $\underline{V'}(\langle\langle B_1, \ldots, B_x \rangle,\langle v_1, \ldots, v_z \rangle\rangle)$ is defined and $\underline{V'}(\langle\langle B_1, \ldots, B_x \rangle,\langle v_1, \ldots, v_z \rangle\rangle) = \underline{V}(\langle\langle B_1, \ldots, B_x \rangle,\langle v_1, \ldots, v_z \rangle\rangle)$, since all valuations are standard.

(ii) We may assume, without loss of generality, that either $\phi,\chi \notin \Sigma[x,z]$, or $\psi \notin \Sigma[x,0]$. By the argument for (i) or inductive hypothesis, $\underline{V}(\phi) = \underline{V'}(\phi)$, $\underline{V}(\psi) = \underline{V'}(\psi)$ and $\underline{V}(\chi) = \underline{V'}(\chi)$. Hence $\underline{V}(A) = \underline{V'}(A)$, completing the case.

(iiia) A is of the form $of_1 \ldots f_k\chi$. By the argument for (i) or inductive hypothesis, $\underline{V}(\chi) = \underline{V}(\chi)$. Hence $\underline{V}(A) = \underline{V'}(A)$.

(iiib) A is of the form $o\delta_1 \ldots \delta_k\chi$. By the argument for (i) or inductive hypothesis, $\underline{V}(\chi) = \underline{V'}(\chi)$. By the argument for (ii) or (iiia) and the inductive hypothesis, $\underline{V}(\delta_h) = \underline{V'}(\delta_h)$, $1 \leqslant h \leqslant k$.

Hence $\underline{V}(A) = \underline{V'}(A)$.

Proof: *ad* (2). If $n = 0$, the case is immediate from (1). If $n > 0$, the argument for (1)(i) suffices.

Lemma 2. If $\langle \underline{S}, V \rangle$ is a regular model, then for any wff A, $V(A) \in D[1,0]$.

Proof: We proceed by induction on the length of A over all variants V' of V. Clearly if $A \in S[1,0]$, $V'(A) \in D[1,0]$. Let $A = \delta\phi$, $\delta \in \Gamma[m,n]$ and $\phi \in \Sigma[m,n]$. Suppose $\langle\langle A_1, \ldots, A_x\rangle, \langle v_1, \ldots, v_z\rangle\rangle$ is a part of a well-formed subpart of A of the form (1) $\delta_1 A_1 \ldots A_x v_1 \ldots v_z$, (2) $a A_1 \ldots A_x v_1 \ldots v_z \chi$ or (3) $a_1 \psi A_1 \ldots A_x$ ($z = 0$), where $\delta_1 \in \Gamma[x,z]$, $\chi \in \Sigma[x,0]$, $\psi \in \Sigma[k,x]$, $a_1 \in F[k,x]$.

(1) By inductive hypothesis, for any appropriate $X_1, \ldots, X_z$, $V'[v_1/X_1, \ldots, v_z/X_z](\langle A_1, \ldots, A_x\rangle) \in D[x,0]$. If $\langle x,z\rangle = \langle 1,1\rangle$, by regularity where F is such that for $X \in D[1,0]$, $F(X) = \text{card}(X)$ where $X = \{V'': V''$ differs from V at most at v_1 and $V''(A_1) = X\}$ if $\text{card}(X)$ is finite, and otherwise $F(X) = V'(\langle\langle A_1\rangle, \langle v_1\rangle\rangle)(X)$, $F \in D[1,1]$. But by clause (6) of the definition of valuations $V'(\langle\langle A_1\rangle, \langle v_1\rangle\rangle) = F$, for some such. F. If $\langle x,z\rangle \neq \langle 1,1\rangle$, by regularity where F is such that for $X \in D[x,0]$, $F(X) = V'(\langle\langle A_1, \ldots, A_x\rangle, \langle v_1, \ldots, v_z\rangle\rangle)(X)$, $F \in D[x,z]$. But by clause (7) of the definition of valuations $V'(\langle\langle A_1, \ldots, A_x\rangle, \langle v_1, \ldots, v_z\rangle\rangle) = F$ for some such F.

(2) The argument for (1) establishes that $V'(\langle\langle A_1, \ldots, A_x\rangle, \langle v_1, \ldots, v_z\rangle\rangle) \in D[x,z]$.

(3) on the inductive hypothesis $V'(\langle A_1, \ldots, A_x\rangle) \in D[x,0]$.

Hence for any well-formed subpart of A of the form δ_1, $\delta_1 \in \Gamma[x,z]$, $V'(\delta_1) \in M[x,z]$. Thus $V'(\delta) \in M[m,n]$. If ϕ is $\langle\langle A_1, \ldots, A_m\rangle, \langle v_1, \ldots, v_n\rangle\rangle$, $V'(\phi) \in D[m,n]$. If $\phi \in S[m,n]$, $V'(\phi) \in D[m,n]$. Hence $V'(A) \in D[m,n]$. Hence $V'(A) \in D[1,0]$.

Lemma 3. Where $S = \langle W,D,a\rangle$ and $\langle \underline{S},V\rangle$ is a model such that $V((\forall v)A) \in D[1,0]$, for all $w \in W$, $w \in V((\forall v)A)$ iff $w \in V'(A)$, for any variant V' differing from V at most at v.

Proof: Notice that $d_\forall(V(\langle\langle A\rangle, \langle v\rangle\rangle)) = \cap\{Y \in D[1,0]: Y = V'(A)$ for some V' differing from V at most at v$\}$. From this the proof is obvious.

Lemma 4. $\langle \underline{S},V\rangle \mid\vdash (A \wedge B)$ iff $(\langle \underline{S},V\rangle \mid\vdash A$ and $\langle \underline{S},V\rangle \mid\vdash B)$.

Lemma 5. $\langle \underline{S},V\rangle \mid\vdash (A \leftrightarrow B)$ iff $(\langle \underline{S},V\rangle \mid\vdash A$ iff $\langle \underline{S},V\rangle \mid\vdash B)$.

Lemma 6. If $\langle \underline{S},V\rangle$ is a normal model and the valuations below are all defined, $\underline{S} = \langle W,\underline{D},O\rangle$, and $w \in W$,

(1) for any $\phi,\psi \in \Sigma[m,O]$, $w \in V(\phi = \psi)$ iff $V(\phi) = V(\psi)$,
(2) for any $\delta,\gamma \in \Gamma[m,n]$, $w \in V(\delta = \gamma)$ iff $V(\delta) = V(\gamma)$,

(3) for any $a_1, a_2 \in F[m,n]$, $w \in V(a_1 = a_2)$ iff $V(a_1) = V(a_2)$,
(4) for any $o_1, o_2 \in O[m,n,k]$, $w \in V(o_1 = o_2)$ iff $V(o_1) = V(o_2)$.

Proof: ad (1). Assume hypothesis. $(\phi = \psi) =_{df} (\forall f)(f\phi \leftrightarrow f\psi)$, where $f \in U[m,n]$ and f is not free in either ϕ or ψ. If $\underline{S}_w = \langle W, \underline{D}, w \rangle$, $\langle \underline{S}_w, V \rangle$ is a normal model. Since $V(\phi = \psi)$ is defined, if $w \in V(\phi = \psi)$, $w \in V[\bar{f}/d](f\phi)$ iff $w \in V[\bar{f}/d](f\psi)$, i.e., $w \in d(V(\phi))$ iff $w \in d(V(\psi))$, for all $d \in M[m,n]$. By normality $V(\phi) = V(\psi)$. The converse is straightforward.

ad (2). If $w \in V(\delta = \gamma)$, then for any V' differing from V at most at P ($P \in S[m,n]$), $w \in V'(\delta P = \gamma P)$. By (1) $V'(\delta P) = V'(\gamma P)$, i.e., $V'(\delta)V'(P) = V'(\gamma)V'(P)$. But P is not free in either δ or γ, so $V(\delta)V'(P) = V(\gamma)V'(P)$. So $V(\delta) = V(\gamma)$. If, on the other hand, $V(\delta) = V(\gamma)$, then for any V' differing from V at most at f ($f \in U[1,0]$) and P, $V'(f\delta P) = V'(f\gamma P)$. By Lemma 3, $w \in V(\phi = \gamma)$.

ad (3) and (4). The strategy parallels that of (2).

Lemma 7. Where $\langle \underline{S}, V \rangle$ is a 2AGMS model. A is a wff and v is free for u in A, $V(A[v/u]) = V[v/\overline{V}(u)](A)$.
Proof: By induction on the length of A over all variants V' of V.

Lemma 8. If $\langle \underline{S}, V \rangle$ is a regular model, then for any $\phi \in \Sigma\{m,n\}$, $V(\phi) \in D[m,n]$.
Proof: Since $\langle \underline{S}, V' \rangle$ is a regular model for any variant V' of V, the result follows immediately from Lemma 2, regularity and the definition of a valuation.

Lemma 9. If $\langle \underline{S}, V \rangle$ is a regular model, then where A is a wff and $p_1, \ldots, p_n$ are distinct propositional variables $V((\lambda p_1) \ldots (\lambda p_m)A) \in M[m,0]$.
Proof: By Lemma 2, for any $\langle X_1, \ldots, X_m \rangle \in D[m,0]$, $V[p_1/X_1, \ldots, p_m/X_m](A) \in D[1,0]$. So $V((\lambda p_1) \ldots (\lambda p_m)A)$ is represented in $\langle \underline{S}, V \rangle$ by $\langle\langle A \rangle, \langle p_1, \ldots, p_m \rangle\rangle$. Hence by regularity, $V((\lambda p_1) \ldots (\lambda p_m)A) \in M[m,0]$.

Lemma 10. If $\langle \underline{S}, V \rangle$ is a regular model, then where A is a wff and $P \in S[m,n] - SC[m,n]$, $V((\lambda P)A) \in M[m,n]$.
Proof: By Lemma 2, where $X \in D[m,n]$, $V[P/X](A) \in D[1,0]$. Hence $V((\lambda P)A)$ is defined and by M-regularity is in $M[m,n]$.

Lemma 11. If $\langle \underline{S}, V \rangle$ is a regular model, then where A is a wff, $P, R \in S[m,n] - SC[m,n]$, $Q \in \overline{S}[m,0] - SC[m,0]$, $V((\lambda P)(\lambda Q))V((\lambda R)A) \in J[m,n]$.
Proof: $V((\lambda P)(\lambda Q)(\lambda R)A)$ is represented in $\langle \underline{S}, V \rangle$ by $\langle\langle A \rangle, \langle P,Q,R \rangle\rangle$. The conclusion follows immediately by J-regularity.

Lemma 12. If $\langle \underline{S}, V \rangle$ is a regular model, then where A is a wff, $f_1, \ldots, f_k$ are distinct members of $U[m,n] - UC[m,n]$ and $P \in S[m,n] - SC[m,n]$, then $V((\lambda f_1) \ldots (\lambda f_k)) V((\lambda P) A) \in L[m,n,k]$.

Proof: The strategy for Lemma 11 suffices.

Lemma 13. If $\langle \underline{S}, V \rangle$ is a regular model, $\langle \underline{S}, V \rangle$ is a general model.

Proof: See Cocchiarella [8].

ad AxC1. $V'(\phi) \in D[m,n]$, $m \geqslant 1$, $n \geqslant 0$, by Lemma 8. Since P is not free in ϕ, $V'[P/V'(\phi)](P) = V'[P/V'(\phi)](\phi)$. By Lemma 6 and the normality of regular models, $O \in V'[P/V'(\phi)](P = \phi)$, and so $O \in V'((\exists P)(P = \phi))$.

ad AxC2. $V'(\phi) = D[m,0]$ by Lemma 8. Thus $V'(\phi) = \langle X_1, \ldots, X_m \rangle$, for $1 \leqslant i \leqslant m$, $X_i = D[1,0]$. Since none of $p_1, \ldots, p_m$ are free in ϕ $V'[p_1/X_1, \ldots, p_m/X_m](\langle p_1, \ldots, p_m \rangle) = V'[p_1/X_1, \ldots, p_m/X_m](\phi)$. By Lemma 6 and normality, $O \in V'[p_1/X_1, \ldots, p_m/X_m](\langle p_1, \ldots, p_m \rangle = \phi)$ and so $O \in V((\exists p_1) \ldots (\exists p_m)(\langle p_1, \ldots, p_m \rangle = \phi))$.

ad AxC3. $V'((\lambda p_1) \ldots (\lambda p_m) A) \in M[m,0]$ by Lemma 9. Thus $V'[f/V'((\lambda p_1) \ldots (\lambda p_m) A)](f) = V'[f/V'((\lambda p_1) \ldots (\lambda p_m) A)]((\lambda p_1) \ldots (\lambda p_m) A)$, since f is not free in A and is distinct from $p_1, \ldots, p_m$. Consequently, for all $X_1, \ldots, X_m \in D[1,0]$, $V'[f/V'((\lambda p_1) \ldots (\lambda p_m) A), p_1/X_1, \ldots, p_m/X_m](fp_1 \ldots p_m) = V'[f/V'((\lambda p_1) \ldots (\lambda p_m) A), p_1/X_1, \ldots, p_m/X_m](A)$. By Lemma 3, $O \in V'[f/V'((\lambda p_1) \ldots (\lambda p_m) A)]((\forall p_1) \ldots (\forall p_m)(fp_1 \ldots p_m = A))$. Hence $O \in V'((\exists f)(\forall p_1) \ldots (\forall p_m)(fp_1 \ldots p_m = A))$.

ad AxC4. $V'((\lambda P) A) \in M[m,n]$, $m \geqslant 1$, $n \geqslant 0$, by Lemma 10. $V'[f/V'((\lambda P) A)](fP) = V'[f/V'((\lambda P) A)](A)$ since f is not free in A. Thus for all $X \in D[m,n]$, $V'[f/V'((\lambda P) A), P/X](fp) = V'[f/V'((\lambda P) A), P/X](A)$. Thus by Lemma 6 and normality, $O \in V'[f/V'((\lambda P) A), P/X](fP = A)$ for all $X \in D[m,n]$. By Lemma 3, $V'[f/V'((\lambda P) A)]((\forall P)(fP = A))$. Hence $O \in V'((\exists f)(\forall P)(fP = A))$.

The cases for AxC5 and AxC6 proceed as above, using Lemmas 11 and 12 respectively.

Lemma 14. If $\langle \underline{S}, V \rangle$ is a general model, $\langle \underline{S}, V \rangle$ is a regular model.

Proof: It is sufficient to show that $\underline{S}$ is hereditary and $\langle \underline{S}, V \rangle$ is $\underline{D}$-, $\underline{M}$-, $\underline{J}$- and $\underline{L}$-regular.

That condition (6) is satisfied in $\underline{S}$ follows from the validity of AxC6 and normality. We have that for some $\delta \in M[m,0]$, and any $X_1, \ldots, X_m \in D[1,0]$, $O \in V[f/\delta, p_1/X_1, \ldots, p_m/X_m](fp_1 \ldots p_m = p_i)$, $1 \leqslant i \leqslant m$. That is, $\delta X_1 \ldots X_m = X_i$, for any $X_1, \ldots, X_m \in D[1,0]$, δ is a projection function.

That condition (7) is satisfied is shown as follows: Where $q \in S[1,0] - SC[1,0]$ and q is distinct from P, $O \in V((\forall q)(\exists f)(\forall P)(fP = q))$. Hence for all $X \in D[1,0]$, there is a $d \in M[m,n]$ such that for all $Y \in D[m,n]$, $O \in V[q/X, f/d, P/Y](fP = q)$. So by normality, for all $Y \in D[m,n]$, $d(Y) =$

$V[q/X](q) = X$. Hence d is a constant function and for each $X \in D[1,0]$, $M[m,n]$ contains such a constant function mapping to X.

For clause (b) of D-regularity, assume that V' is a variant of V, v is a variable, A is a wff and for any variant V'' of V' differing from V' at most at v, $V''(A) \in D[1,0]$. Since $\langle \underline{S}, V \rangle$ is general, $O \in V'((\exists P)(P = \langle\langle A \rangle, \langle v \rangle\rangle))$. So by normality for some $F \in D[1,1]$, $F = V'(\langle\langle A \rangle, \langle v \rangle\rangle)$. By the definition of a valuation, F behaves as it should.

For clause (c) of D-regularity, assume that V' is a variant of V, $v_1, \ldots, v_n$ are variables, $A_1, \ldots, A_m$ are wffs and for any variant V'' of V' that differs at most at $v_1, \ldots, v_n$, $V''(\langle A_1, \ldots, A_m \rangle) \in D[m,0]$. Since $\langle \underline{S}, V \rangle$ is general, $O \in V'((\exists P)(P = \langle\langle A_1, \ldots, A_m \rangle, \langle v_1, \ldots, v_n \rangle\rangle))$. So by normality for some $F \in D[m,n]$, $F = V'(\langle\langle A_1, \ldots, A_m \rangle, \langle v_1, \ldots, v_n \rangle\rangle)$. By the definition of a valuation F behaves as it should.

For M-regularity, assume first that V' is a variant of V and d is represented in $\langle S, V' \rangle$ by $\langle\langle A \rangle, \langle P \rangle\rangle$, $P \in S[m,n]$. We must show that $d \in M[m,n]$. Since $\langle \underline{S}, V' \rangle$ is a general model, $O \in V'((\exists f)(\forall P)(fP = A))$. So for some $d' \in M[m,\overline{n}]$, $O \in V'[f/d']((\forall P)(fP = A))$, it remains to show that $d = d'$. By Lemma 3, for all $X \in D[m,n]$, $O \in V'[f/d',P/X](fP = A)$. By Lemma 6, $d'(X) = V'[f/d',P/A](A) = V'[P/A](A)$ (since f is not free in A) $= d(X)$. Assume secondly that V' is a variant of V and d is represented in $\langle \underline{S}, V' \rangle$ by $\langle\langle A \rangle, \langle p_1, \ldots, p_m \rangle\rangle$. We must show that $d \in M[m,0]$. By generality, $O \in V'((\exists f)(\forall p_1) \ldots (\forall p_m)(fp_1 \ldots p_m = A))$, $f \in U[m,0]$. So for some $d' \in M[m,0]$, $O \in V'[f/d']((\forall p_1) \ldots (\forall p_m)(fp_1 \ldots p_m = A))$. It remains to show that $d = d'$. For all $\langle X_1, \ldots, X_m \rangle \in D[m,0]$, $d'(\langle X_1, \ldots, X_m \rangle) = (V'[f/d'](f))(\langle X_1, \ldots, X_m \rangle) = V'[f/d',p_1/X_1, \ldots, p_m/X_m](fp_1 \ldots p_m) =$ (by Lemma 6) $V'[f/d',p_1/X_1, \ldots, p_m/X_m](A) =$ (since f is not free in A) $V'[p_1/X_1, \ldots, p_m/X_m](A) = V'((\lambda p_1) \ldots (\lambda p_m)A)(\langle X_1, \ldots, X_m \rangle) = d(\langle X_1, \ldots, X_m \rangle)$.

For J-regularity, assume that V' is a variant of V and d is represented in $\langle S, V' \rangle$ by $\langle\langle A \rangle, \langle P, Q, R \rangle\rangle$, where $P, R \in S[m,n]$ and $Q \in S[m,0]$. Since $\langle \overline{S}, V' \rangle$ is general, where $a \in F[m,n]$, for some $d' \in J[m,n]$, $O \in V'[a/d']((\forall P)(\forall Q)(\forall R)(aPQR = A))$. It remains to show that $d' = d$. For all $X, Z \in D[m,n]$ and $Y \in D[m,0]$, $(d'(X,Y))(Z) = V'[a,d'](a)(\langle V'[P/X](P), V'[Q/Y](Q) \rangle)(Z) = V'[a/d',P/X,Q/Y](aPQ)(Z) = V'[a/d',P/X,Q/Y,R/Z](aPQR) = V'[P/X,Q/Y,R/Z](A)$ (since a is not free in A) $= d(X,Y,Z)$.

The strategy for J-regularity may be used to show L-regularity, completing the proof.

This establishes that general and regular models coincide.

Lemma 15. If $\langle S, V \rangle$ is a regular model, $V(0) = d_0$.

Proof: By (D15), $V(0) = V(\alpha(\langle\langle \sim \exists pp \rangle, \langle p \rangle\rangle, \exists pp)) = j(V(\langle\langle \sim \exists pp \rangle, \langle p \rangle\rangle), V(\exists pp))$, $\alpha = \alpha[1,1]$, $j = j[1,1]$. Clearly $V(\langle\langle \sim \exists pp \rangle, \langle p \rangle\rangle)$

$(V(\exists pp)) = 0$. By condition (3)(j) for a 2AGMS, $j(V(\langle\langle\langle\sim\exists pp\rangle,\langle p\rangle\rangle\rangle)$, $V(\exists pp)) = d_0$.

Lemma 16. Where $\langle \underline{S},V\rangle$ is a regular model, for all $N \in \omega$, $V(N) = d_N$.

Proof: The claim has already been established for $N = 0$ by Lemma 15. Notice that for $N \in \omega$, by (D19), $V(N+1) = V(\alpha(\langle\langle\langle [\vee (f = M), \; 1 \leqslant M \leqslant n]\rangle,\langle f\rangle\rangle,\exists pp)) = j(V(\langle\langle\langle [\vee (f = M), \; 1 \leqslant M \leqslant n]\rangle,\langle f\rangle\rangle),V(\exists pp)) = N+1$. To show the latter, it is sufficient to show, by strong induction on the natural numbers that

(1)   for $0 \leqslant M_1 < M_2 \leqslant N$, $d_{M_1} \neq d_{M_2}$,
(2)   where $V^1 = V[f/d_I]$, $0 \leqslant I \leqslant N$, $V^1([\vee (f = M), \; 0 \leqslant M \leqslant N]) = V(\exists pp)$ and
(3)   where V^2 differs from V at most at f and $V^2(f) \neq d_I$, for any $1 \leqslant I \leqslant N$, then $V^2([\vee (f = M), 0 \leqslant M \leqslant N]) = V(\forall pp)$.

Assume that the claim holds for $M < N$ and show for N.

Case (1). $N = 0$. (1) is satisfied vacuously.

ad (2). If $V^1 = V[f/d_0]$ and $w \in W$, $w \in V^1(f = 0)$ iff $V^1(f) = V^1(0)$ by Lemma 6.2 iff $d_0 = d_0$ by definition of V^1 and Lemma 2.

ad (3). If $V^2 = V[f/d]$, where $d \neq d_0$, clearly by the above strategy, $V^2(f = 0) = \varnothing$.

Case (2). $N > 0$. *ad* (1). By inductive hypothesis, for $0 \leqslant M_1 < M_2 \leqslant N - 1$, $d_{M_1} \neq d_{M_2}$. Assume, *per reductio*, that for some M, $M < N$, $d_M = d_N$. $M \neq 0$, since if otherwise by the fact that $j(V(\langle\langle\langle\sim\exists pp\rangle,\langle p\rangle\rangle$, $V(\exists pp)) = d_0$, we have that $j(V(\langle\langle\langle\sim\exists pp\rangle,\langle p\rangle\rangle),V(\exists pp)) = d_N$ and $V(\langle\langle\langle\sim\exists pp\rangle,\langle p\rangle\rangle)(V(\exists pp)) = N$, which is impossible. So $M > 0$. We have by inductive hypothesis that $V(\langle\langle\langle [\vee (f = I), 0 \leqslant I \leqslant M-1]\rangle,\langle f\rangle\rangle)$ $(V(\exists pp)) = M = N$, by hypothesis and condition (3)(j.1) of a 2AGMS. But this is again impossible. (2) and (3) are obvious.

Corollary 17. For $M \neq N$, $d_M \neq d_N$.

Lemma 18. Where $\langle \underline{S},V\rangle$ is a regular model, $V(\langle\langle\langle [\vee (f = M), 0 \leqslant M \leqslant N]\rangle,\langle f\rangle\rangle)(V(\exists pp)) = N+1$.

Proof: We proceed by strong induction on the natural numbers. Assuming the lemma holds for all $m < n$, we show for n.

Base case $n = 0$. Notice where V' differs from V at most at f, either $V'(f = 0) = W$ and $V(f) = d_0$, or $V'(f = 0) = \varnothing$ and $V(f) \neq d_0$ by Lemma 6.2. But from this it is obvious that $V(\langle\langle\langle (f = 0)\rangle,\langle f\rangle\rangle)(V(\exists pp)) = 1$.

Inductive case. Assume, *per reductio,* that $V(\langle\langle[\vee(f = M), 0 \leqslant M \leqslant N]\rangle\langle f\rangle\rangle)(V(\exists pp)) \neq N+1$. Then $d_N = d_M$, for some $m < n$. By IH, $V(\langle\langle[\vee(f = I), 0 \leqslant I \leqslant M-1]\rangle,\langle f\rangle\rangle)(V(\exists pp)) = M$. By condition $(3)(j.1)$ of a 2AGMS, $j(V(\langle\langle[\vee(f = I), 0 \leqslant I \leqslant M-1]\rangle,\langle f\rangle\rangle),V(\exists pp)) = d_M$. So $V(\langle\langle[\vee(f = I), 0 \leqslant I \leqslant M-1]\rangle,\langle f\rangle\rangle)(V(\exists pp)) = N$, again by $(3)(j.1)$. But this is impossible.

Section 8
Soundness

This section is devoted to establishing one result: *Theorem 1.* If $\vdash A$, then $\Vdash A$.

The AxPC and AxQC schemas require no argument. Since all 2AGMS models are regular models, and since all regular models are general models, the AxC schemas are sound. The AxM schemas are sound by virtue of atomicity.

ad AxI1. Assume that $O \in V((\forall v_1) \ldots (\forall v_k)(\phi = \psi))$, $\phi,\psi \in \Sigma[m,n]$. We establish the following by inducting on the length of A over all variables u, sets of variables u, and valuations V'. Where V' differs from v at most at u, if $u \in u$ and u does not occur free in $(\forall v_1) \ldots (\forall v_k)(\phi = \psi)$, $V'(A) = V'(B)$.

(1) Assume that $A \in S[1,0]$. Then A is ϕ and B is ψ. By hypothesis $O \in V((\forall v_1) \ldots (\forall v_k) (A = B))$. By Lemma 7.1, $O \in V'((\forall v_1) \ldots (\forall v_k) (A = B))$. By construction and Lemma 7.6.1, $V'(A) = V'(B)$.

(2) Assume that A is of the form fP, $f \in U[x,z]$, $P \in S[x,z]$. Then $x = m$, $z = n$, A is $f\phi$ and B is $f\psi$. By IH, Lemma 7.1, construction and Lemma 7.6.1, $V'(\phi) = V'(\psi)$. Hence $V'(A) = V'(f)V'(\phi) = V'(B)$.

(3) A is of the form $fC_1 \ldots C_x w_1 \ldots w_z$, where $f \in U[x,z]$. By IH exactly one occurrence of ϕ is replaced by ψ in exactly one C_h, $1 \leqslant h \leqslant x$. Let C_h^* be either C_h or the result of making this replacement, as the case may be. By construction and IH, for any appropriate set of variables u and V' differing from V at most at u, $V'(\langle C_1,\ldots, C_x\rangle) = V(\langle C_1^*,\ldots, C_x^*\rangle)$. If $z = 0$, we are done.

   (a) $\langle x,z\rangle = \langle 1,1\rangle$. So A is $fC_1 w_1$ and B is $fC_1^* w_1$. Assume that $X \in D[1,0]$ and let $X = \{V''(C_1): V''$ differs from V' at most at w_1 and $V''(C_1) = X\}$. By construction u does not occur free in $(\forall v_1) \ldots (\forall v_k)(\phi = \psi)$. By IH, for each V'', $V''(C_1) = V''(C_1^*)$, and so if card (X) is finite, $V''(\langle\langle C_1\rangle,\langle w_1\rangle\rangle) = V'(\langle\langle C_1^*\rangle,\langle w_1\rangle\rangle)$. If card$(X)$ is not finite, the result is immediate by construction of V'.

   (b) $\langle x,z\rangle \neq \langle 1,1\rangle$. A is $fC_1 \ldots C_x w_1 \ldots w_z$ and B is $fC_1^* \ldots C_x^* w_1 \ldots w_z$.

By construction u does not occur free in $(\forall v_1) \ldots (\forall v_k)(\phi = \psi)$. By IH and construction of V', the case is immediate.

(4)   A is of the form $a\pi\rho\chi$, $\pi,\chi \in \Sigma[x,z]$, $\rho \in \Sigma[x,0]$. If $m = x$, $n = z$ and $\phi = \pi$ or χ, or if $m = x$, $z = 0$ and $\phi = \rho$, there is nothing to prove.

(a) ρ is $C_1 \ldots C_x$. Let $C_h{}^*$ be either C_h or the result of making the replacement of ϕ by ψ. By construction of V' and IH, $V'(\langle C_1, \ldots, C_x \rangle) = V'(\langle C_1{}^*, \ldots, C_x{}^* \rangle)$. The result follows immediately.

(b) π or χ is $\langle\langle C_1, \ldots, C_x \rangle, \langle w_1, \ldots, w_z \rangle\rangle$ and $C_h{}^*$ is as in (a), $i \leqslant h \leqslant x$. The argument proceeds as in (3)(a) and (3)(b).

(5)   A is of the form $o\delta_1 \ldots \delta_i\chi$, where $o \in O[x,z,i]$ and $\delta_1, \ldots, \delta_i \in \Gamma[x,z]$. Notice that either

(a) $m = x$, $n = z$ and

     (i) $\phi = \chi$ or

     (ii)   for some $0 \leqslant r \leqslant i$ there is a sequence $\gamma_1, \ldots, \gamma_v$ such that $\gamma_1 = \delta_r$, $\gamma_v = a\phi\pi$, $\pi \in \Sigma[x,0]$, $a \in F[x,z]$, and for $1 \leqslant s \leqslant v-1$ there is a μ such that $\gamma_s = o'\zeta_1 \ldots \gamma_{s+1} \ldots \zeta_\mu$, $\zeta_1, \ldots, \zeta_\mu \in \Gamma[x,z]$ and $o' \in O[x,z,\mu]$ or

(b) $m = x$, $n = 0$, $a\pi\phi$, and δ_r are as in (5)(a)(ii) for some $1 \leqslant r \leqslant i$ or

(c)   there is a $\langle\langle C_1, \ldots, C_x \rangle, \langle w_1, \ldots, w_z \rangle\rangle$ in A such that the occurrence of ϕ replaced by ψ in B occurs in C_h, $1 \leqslant h \leqslant i$, and we may assume that $\langle\langle C_1, \ldots, C_x \rangle, \langle w_1, \ldots, w_z \rangle\rangle = \chi \in \Sigma[x,z]$, or for some δ_r, $1 \leqslant r \leqslant i$, there are a and π such that δ_r and $a\langle\langle C_1, \ldots, C_x \rangle, \langle w_1, \ldots, w_z \rangle\rangle\pi$ are related as in (5)(a)(ii), or where δ_r and a are as above, there is a $\pi \in \Sigma[x,z]$ such that δ_r and $a\pi\langle C_1, \ldots, C_x \rangle$ are related as in (5)(a)(ii).

In cases (5)(a) and (5)(b) the result is immediate. The argument for (5)(c) proceeds as in (3)(a) and (3)(b).

ad AxI2. Assume that $O \in V((\forall u_1) \ldots (\forall u_k)(\delta_1 = \delta_2))$. It is sufficient to show that $V(A) = V(B)$. We prove the following by induction on the length of A. If u is any set of variables such that no member of u occurs free in $(\forall u_1) \ldots (\forall u_k)(\delta_1 = \delta_2)$ and V' differs from V at most at u, then $V'(A) = V'(B)$.

Since by hypothesis δ_1 actually occurs in A, the case where $A \in S[1,0]$ follows vacuously. We have then that A is of the form $\gamma\phi$, $\gamma \in \Gamma[x,z]$, $\phi \in \Sigma[x,z]$. Assume that u and V' are as described. By Lemmas 7.1 and 7.5, for any V'' differing from V' at most at $u_1, \ldots, u_k$, $V''(\delta_1) = V''(\delta_2)$. Assuming below that the occurrence of δ_1 mentioned is the occurrence in A replaced by δ_2 in B, if $\gamma = \delta_1$ or if there is a sequence of quantifiers $\gamma_1, \ldots, \gamma_i$ such that $\gamma_1 = \gamma$, $\gamma_i = ov_1 \ldots \delta_1 \ldots v_k$, $o \in O[m,n,k]$, $v_1, \ldots, v_k \in \Gamma[m,n]$ and for h, $1 \leqslant h \leqslant i-1$ $\gamma_h = o'\sigma_1 \ldots \gamma_{r+1} \ldots \sigma_r$, $o' \in O[m,n,r]$, $\sigma_1, \ldots, \sigma_r \in \Gamma[m,n,r]$ there is nothing to prove.

If not, then there is some sequence $\langle\langle C_1, \ldots, C_i \rangle, \langle v_1, \ldots, v_h \rangle\rangle$, $1 \leqslant i$,

$0 \leqslant h$, such that either for some $\delta \in \Gamma[i,h]$, $\delta C_1 \ldots C_i v_1 \ldots v_h$ is a well-formed subpart of A, or for some $a \in F[i,h]$ and $\pi \in \Sigma[i,0]$, $aC_1 \ldots C_i v_1 \ldots v_h \pi$ is a well-formed subpart of A, or $h = 0$ and there are $a \in F[i,r]$ and $\pi \in \Sigma[i,r]$ such that $a\pi C_1 \ldots C_i$ is a well-formed subpart of A, and for some $1 \leqslant s \leqslant i$, the occurrence of δ_1 in A replaced by δ_2 in B is a well-formed subpart of C_s. Let us designate the corresponding formula in B by D_s.

Let $w_1, \ldots, w_\sigma$ be all the variables occurring free in $(\langle\langle C_1, \ldots, C_s, \ldots, C_i\rangle, \langle v_1, \ldots, v_h\rangle\rangle = \langle\langle C_1, \ldots, D_s, \ldots, C_i\rangle, \langle v_1, \ldots, v_h\rangle\rangle)$ which are bound in A or B at the appropriate replacement occurrence. By hypothesis none of $w_1, \ldots, w_\sigma$ occur free in $(\forall v_1) \ldots (\forall v_k)(\delta_1 = \delta_2)$. By IH and the argument showing the validity of AxI1, for any V'' differing from V' at most at $w_1, \ldots, w_\sigma$, $V''(\langle\langle C_1, \ldots, C_s, \ldots, C_i\rangle, \langle v_1, \ldots, v_h\rangle\rangle) = V''(\langle\langle C_1, \ldots, D_s, \ldots, C_i\rangle, \langle v_1, \ldots, v_h\rangle\rangle)$. By Lemmas 7.3 and 7.6, $O \in V'((\forall w_1) \ldots (\forall w_\sigma)(\langle\langle C_1, \ldots, C_s, \ldots, C_i\rangle, \langle v_1, \ldots, v_h\rangle\rangle = \langle\langle C_1, \ldots, D_s, \ldots, C_i\rangle, \langle v_1, \ldots, v_h\rangle\rangle))$. By the validity of AxI1, $V'(A) = V'(B)$, completing the case.

Verification of Ax13 is easy and can be found in Daniels and Freeman [1].

ad AxN1. Assume that V' differs from V at most at P and $O \in V'(0P)$. Hence for all $Y \in D[1,0]$ such that $O \in Y$, $V'(P)(Y) = 0$. So where $X = \{Y \in D[1,0] : V'(P)(Y) \neq 0\}$, $O \notin \cup X = V'(\exists P)$. So $O \in V(\sim \exists p)$. The steps are clearly reversible.

ad AxN2. Assume that $O \in V((1v)A)$. By construction there is exactly one V' differing from V at most at v such that $O \in V'(A)$. Assume that V'' differs from V' at most at u and $O \in V''(A[v/u])$. By Lemma 7.7, $O \in V''[v/V''(u)](A)$. But since u is not free in A, $O \in V[v/V''(u)](A)$. By hypothesis $V''(v) = V''(u)$, and by Lemma 7.6, $O \in V''(v = u)$. For the converse direction, assume that $O \in V((\exists v)(A \wedge (\forall u)(A[v/u] \to (v = u))))$, where u does not occur free in A. So for some V_1 differing from V at most at v, $O \in V_1(A)$. Assume that V_2 differs from V at most at v and $O \in V_2(A)$. We must show that $V_1(v) = V_2(v)$. Let $V_3 = V_1[u/V_2(v)]$. $V_2(A) = V_3[v/V_3(u)](A) = V_3(A[v/u])$. Hence, $O \in V_3(u = v)$, $V_1(v) = V_2(v)$, and V_1 is unique. So card$\{V' : V'$ differs from V at most at v and $V'(A) = V_1(A)\} = 1$, $\Sigma\{V(\langle\langle A\rangle, \langle v\rangle\rangle)X : X \in D[1,0]$ and $O \in X\} = 1$, and $O \in V((1v)A)$.

ad AxN3. If $O \in V((Nv)A)$, then $\Sigma\{$card$\{V' : V'$ differs from V at most at v and $V'(A) = X\} : X \in D[1,0]$ and $O \in X\} = N$. Let $V_1, \ldots, V_n$ be these n distinct valuations. Let $V' = V[v_1/V_1(v), \ldots, v_n/V_n(v)]$. Clearly for $1 \leqslant i < h \leqslant n$, $V_i(v) \neq V_h(v)$. By Lemma 7.6, $O \in V'(\neq(v_1, \ldots, v_n))$. For $1 \leqslant i \leqslant n$, $O \in V_i(A)$. But $V_i(A) = V[v/V'(v_i)](A) = V'[v/V'(V_i)](A)$ (by Lemma 7.1) $= V'(A[v/v_i])$ (by Lemma 7.7). Let V'' differ from V' at most at u and assume that $O \in V''(A[v/u])$. So $O \in V''[v/V''(u)](A) = V[v/V''(u)](A)$. For some $1 \leqslant i \leqslant n$, $V''(u) = V_i(v) = V'(v_i) = V''(v_i)$. Hence by Lemma 7.6, $O \in V''(u = v_i)$.

For the converse, assume that the right-hand side holds. Hence there is a V' differing from V at most at $v_1, \ldots, v_n$ such that $O \in V'((\neq (v_1, \ldots, v_n) \wedge A[v/v_1] \wedge \ldots \wedge A[v/v_n] \wedge (\forall u)(A[v/u] \to ((u = v_1) \vee \ldots \vee (u = v_n)))))$. Let $V_1, \ldots, V_n$ be such that for $1 \leqslant i \leqslant n$, $V_i = V[v/V'(v_i)]$. By Lemma 7.6, for $1 \leqslant i < h \leqslant n$, V_i and V_h are distinct valuations. Notice that for $1 \leqslant i \leqslant n$, $V'(A[v/v_i]) = V'[v/V'(v_i)](A)$ (by Lemma 7.7) $= V[v/V'(v_i)](A)$ (by Lemma 7.1) $= V_i(A)$. So $O \in V_i(A)$. Let V'' differ from V at most at v and $O \in V''(A)$. $V''(A) = V'[v/V''(v)](A)$. So $O \in V'[v/V''(v)]((v = v_1) \vee \ldots \vee (v = v_n))$. Hence for some $1 \leqslant i \leqslant n$, $V''(v) = V'(v_i) = V_i(v)$. So $V'' = V_i$ for some $1 \leqslant i \leqslant n$. Consequently card $\{V' : V'$ differs from V at most at v and $O \in V'(A)\} = N$. Hence by (6) of the definition of a valuation, $\Sigma\{V(\langle\langle A\rangle,\langle v\rangle\rangle)X : X \in D[1,0]$ and $O \in X\} = N$. By Lemma 7.16, $O \in d_N V(\langle\langle A\rangle,\langle v\rangle\rangle) = V(N)V(\langle\langle A\rangle,\langle v\rangle\rangle) = V((Nv)A)$.

Verification of AxN4 is trivial.

ad AxN5. Notice that $O \in V((0p)(p \wedge \sim p))$. So $O \in V(((\exists P)0P)0P)$. By Lemma 7.18, for any $N \in \omega$, $V(\langle\langle [\vee (f = M), 0 \leqslant m \leqslant n]\rangle,\langle f\rangle\rangle)V(\exists pp) = N + 1$. Notice that if $O \in X$, for any $X \in D[1,0]$ and $X \neq V(\exists pp)$, $V(\langle\langle [\vee (f = M), 0 \leqslant m \leqslant n]\rangle,\langle f\rangle\rangle)X = 0$. So for all $N \in \omega$, $O \in V((N+1f)((f = 0) \vee \ldots \vee (f = N)))$, and hence $O \in V((\exists P)N + 1P)$, $P \in S[1,1]$.

ad AxN6. Assume that V^1 differs from V at most at P, f and g, $P \in S[m,n]$, $f,g \in U[m,n]$ and that $O \in V^1((\text{Num } f) \wedge (\text{Num } g) \wedge ((fP \wedge gP) \neq F))$. By (D14) and the definition of valuations, there are V^2 and V^3 differing from V^1 at most at Q and R, $Q \in S[m,n]$ and $R \in S[m,0]$, such that $V^1(f) = j(m,n)(V^2(Q),V^2(R))$ and $V^1(g) = j[m,n](V^3(Q),V^3(R))$. By construction and condition (3)(j), $V^1(f) = d_x$, $V^1(g) = d_z$, for some $x,z \in \chi[m,n]$. Assume that $x \neq z$ and that $\langle m,n\rangle = \langle 1,1\rangle$. Four cases arise.

(1) $x,z \in \omega$. Now for some $w \in W$, $w \in d_N(V'(P)) \cap d_M(V'(P))$. But this is clearly impossible by condition (3)(h).
(2) $x \in \omega$, $z \in \chi - \omega$, or
(3) $x \in \chi - \omega, z \in \omega$. (Cases (2) and (3) are symmetrical and are both ruled out by condition (3)(k).
(4) $x,y \in \chi - \omega$. The case is ruled out by (3)(l.1).

Now assume that $\langle m,n\rangle \neq \langle 1,1\rangle$. $x,z \in \chi[m,n]$. But this is ruled out by (3)(l.2).

Hence $x = z$ and by Lemma 7.6, $O \in V(f = g)$.

That the Ax*ns* axiom schemata are valid is practically immediate from conditions (3)(m), (n) and (o) for a 2AGMS.

ad Axα1. Let V^1 differ from V at most at $p_1, \ldots, p_k, P$, $P \in S[1,1]$, and assume that $O \in V^1((\neq (p_1, \ldots, p_k) \wedge [\wedge (\alpha(P,p_i) = M_i), 1 \leqslant i \leqslant k] \wedge [\wedge p_i, i \leqslant i \leqslant k] \wedge (\forall p_0)(((\alpha(P,p_0) \neq 0) \wedge p_0) \to [\vee (p_0 = p_i), 1 \leqslant i \leqslant k]))$.

Assume that $X \in D[1,0]$, $O \in X$, and $j(V^1(P),X) \neq d_0$. Where $V^2 = V^1[p_0/X]$, $V^2(p_0) = V^1(p_i)$ for some $1 \leqslant i \leqslant k$. So $\Sigma\{V^1(P)X : X \in D[1,0]$ and $O \in X\} \leqslant \Sigma\{M_i : 1 \leqslant i \leqslant k\}$. But furthermore, for $1 \leqslant i \leqslant k$ and $O \in V^1(p_i)$, $V^1(P)V^1(p_i) = M_i$, and for $1 \leqslant i < h \leqslant k$, $V^1(p_i) \neq V^1(p_h)$. So $\Sigma\{V^1(P)X : X \in D[1,0]$ and $O \in X\} = \Sigma\{M_i : 1 \leqslant i \leqslant k\} = N$ and $O \in V^1(NP)$.

ad Axα2. Let V^1 differ from V at most at P and assume that $O \in V^1(NP)$. Hence $\Sigma\{V^1(P)X : X \in D[1,0]$ and $O \in X\} = N$. Clearly there are at most n $X \in D[1,0]$ such that $O \in X$, $V^1(P)X \neq 0$, and $V^1(P)X = M$, for some $M \in \omega - \{0\}$. Let $X_1, \ldots, X_k$ $(k \leqslant n)$ be an enumeration of these elements. Let $V^2 = V^1[p_1/X_1, \ldots, p_k/X_k, p_{k+1}/X_k, \ldots, p_n/X_k]$. By Lemmas 7.6 and 7.4, $O \in V^2([\wedge (\alpha(P,p_i) \neq 0), 1 \leqslant i \leqslant n])$. Clearly again by Lemma 7.4, $O \in V^2([\wedge p_i, 1 \leqslant i \leqslant n])$. Assume that V^3 differs from V^2 at most at p_0 and $O \in V^3((\alpha(P,p_0) \neq 0) \wedge p_0)$. So $O \in V^3(p_0)$ and $V^1(P)V^3(p_0) \neq 0$. Hence $V^3(p_0) = X_i$, for some $1 \leqslant i \leqslant k$. By Lemma 7.6, $O \in V^3([\vee (p_0 = p_i), 1 \leqslant i \leqslant n])$.

ad Axα3. Assume that V^1 differs from V at most at P and $O \in V^1(\forall P)$. Assume that V^2 differs from V^1 at most at p and $O \in V^2(\alpha(P,p) \neq 0)$. By Lemma 7.6, $V^2(\alpha(P,p)) \neq d_0$, and so by construction $V^1(P)V^2(p) \neq 0$ and $O \in V^2(p)$. For the converse direction, assume that $O \in V^1((\forall p)((\alpha(P,p) \neq 0) \to p))$. Let $X \in \{Y \in D[1,0] : V^1(P)Y \neq 0\}$. If $X = \varnothing$, then immediately by construction, $O \in V^1(\forall P)$. We must show that $O \in \cap X$, where $X \neq \varnothing$. Let $V^3 = V^1[p/Y]$, where $Y \in X$. By Lemma 7.6, $O \in V^3(\alpha(P,p) \neq 0)$. So $O \in V^3(p) = Y$. Hence $O \in \cap X$.

ad Axα4. Assume that V^1 differs from V at most at P and $O \in V^1(\exists P)$. Hence $X = \{Y \in D[1,0] : V^1(P)Y \neq 0\} \neq \varnothing$. Furthermore, there is a $Y \in X$ such that $O \in Y$. Let $V^2 = V^1[p/Y]$. By Lemma 7.6, $O \in V^2((\alpha(P,p) \neq 0) \wedge p)$. For the converse direction, assume that $O \in V^1((\exists p)((\alpha(P,p) \neq 0) \wedge p))$. Hence where for some $Y \in D[1,0]$, $V^3 = V^1[p/Y]$, $O \in V^3((\alpha(P,p) \neq 0) \wedge p)$. Clearly $Y \in X$ and $O \in \cup X$. So $O \in V^1(\exists P)$.

ad Axα5. Assume that V' differs from V at most at P and Q $(\in S[m,n])$, and that $O \in V'((\forall R)(\alpha(P,R) = \alpha(Q,R)))$, $R \in S[m,0]$. Hence for any $Y \in D[m,0]$, $V'(P)Y = V'(Q)Y$. Hence $V'(P) = V'(Q)$. By Lemma 7.6, $O \in V'(P = Q)$.

ad Axα6. Assume that V' differs from V at most at P and p, $P \in S[1,1]$, and that $O \in V'(NP \wedge (\alpha(P,p) \neq 0) \wedge p)$. By construction, $\Sigma\{V'(P)X : X \in D[1,0]$ and $O \in X\} = N$. Hence for some i, $1 \leqslant i \leqslant N$, $V'(P)V'(p) = i$. By construction and Lemma 7.6, $O \in V'((\alpha(P,p) = 1) \vee \ldots \vee (\alpha(P,p) = N))$.

ad Axα7. Let $X = \{V' : V'$ differs from V at most at v and $V'(A) = V(A[v/u])\}$, where v is free for u in A. Let $V' = V[v/V(u)]$. By Lemma 7.7, $V'(A) = V(A[v/u])$. So X is not empty. By construction, $V(\langle\langle A \rangle, \langle v \rangle\rangle)V(A[v/u]) = \text{card}(X)$, if $\text{card}(X)$ is finite, and is some

$x \in \chi[1,1] - \omega$ otherwise. In either case, $V(\alpha(\langle\langle A\rangle,\langle v\rangle\rangle, A[v/u])) \neq V(0)$, from which the case follows by Lemma 7.6.

ad Axα8. Assume that no variable occurs free in $\langle\langle A\rangle,\langle v\rangle\rangle$, V' differs from V at most at p, and $O \in V'((\exists v_1) \ldots (\exists v_n)[\neq (v_1, \ldots, v_n) \wedge [\wedge (A[v/v_i] = p), 1 \leq i \leq n] \wedge (\forall u)((A[v/u] = p) \to [\vee (u = v_i), 1 \leq i \leq n])])$. It is sufficient to show that card(X) $(= \{V'' : V''$ differs from V' at most at v and $V''(A) = V'(p)\}) = N$. Assume that $V^* \in X$, where $V^*(v) = e$. By Lemma 7.3, there is a V'' differing from V' at exactly $v_1, \ldots, v_n$ such that $O \in V''(\neq (v_1, \ldots, v_n) \wedge [\wedge (A[v/v_i] = p), 1 \leq i \leq n] \wedge (\forall u)((A[v/u] = p) \to [\vee (u = v_i), 1 \leq i \leq n]))$. Let $V+ = V''[u/e]$. By Lemma 7.7, $V+(A[v/u]) = V+[v/e](A) = V^*(A)$, by Lemma 7.1. Now $O \in V+(A[v/u] = p)$. So $O \in V+([\vee (u = v_i), 1 \leq i \leq n])$. So for some $1 \leq i \leq n$, $V+(u) = V''(v_i)$. But $V^*(v) = V+(u)$. Hence card(X) is not greater than N. Assume that $V^* = V'[v/V''(v_i)]$, for some $1 \leq i \leq n$. By Lemma 7.7, $V^*(A) = V''(A[v/v_i])$. So $V^* \in X$. But there are n distinct such V^* by Lemma 7.6. Hence card$(X) = N$.

For the converse direction, assume that $O \in V'(\alpha(\langle\langle A\rangle,\langle v\rangle\rangle,p)) = N$. By construction we may infer that card$(X) = N$, where X is as above. Let $V^1, \ldots, V^n$ be an enumeration of X, and let $V'' = V'[v_1/V^1(v), \ldots, v_n/V^n(v)]$. By Lemma 7.6, $O \in V''(\neq(v_1, \ldots, v_n))$. By Lemmas 7.7 and 7.1, $V''(A[v/v_m]) = V^m(A) = V''(p)$, and so by Lemma 7.4, $O \in V''([\wedge (A[v/v_m] = p), 1 \leq m \leq n])$. Let V^* differ from V'' at most at u and assume that $O \in V^*(A[v/u] = p)$. By Lemma 7.7, $V^*(A[v/u]) = V^*[v/V^*(u)](A) = V'[v/V^*(u)](A)$ by Lemma 7.1. Hence $V'[v/V^*(u)] = V^m$ for some $1 \leq m \leq n$. By construction $V^*(v_m) = V^*(u)$, and by Lemma 7.6, $O \in V^*([\vee (u = v_m), 1 \leq m \leq n])$.

ad Axα9. Assume that V' differs from V at most at p and $O \in V'(\alpha(\langle\langle A\rangle,\langle v\rangle\rangle,p) \neq 0)$. By construction for some V'' differing from V' at most at v, $V''(A) = V^*(p)$. Hence $O \in V'((\exists v)(p = A))$.

Section 9
Completeness

The aim of this section is to show the following:

Theorem (completeness of LQ). If K is a consistent set of LQ sentences, then there is a LQ model in which every member of K is true.

A set of sentences K is *consistent* just in case K $\nvdash$ F. Where L$'$ is an extension of the language LQ, a set of L$'$ sentences K$'$ is *complete* with respect to L$'$ just in case K$'$ is consistent and for any L$'$ sentence A, if K$' \cup \{A\}$ is consistent, $A \in K'$. Where L$'$ is an extension of LQ, K$'$ is *universal in* L′ just in case for each sentence in L′ of the form $\sim(\forall v)A$ such that K′ ⊢ $\sim(\forall v)A$, K′ ⊢ $\sim A[v/c]$, where c is some constant of L′.

Lemma 1. If K is a consistent set of LQ sentences, there exists a complete, universal extension K′ of K.

The proof is as usual. We refer the reader to Hughes and Cresswell [1].

We now use a complete, universal set K′ of sentences in the usual way to construct a LQ model $\langle \underline{MK'},V \rangle$. Let X(p) be a set of L′ sentences such that $A \in X(p)$ iff K′ ⊢ (p ent A).

We have the following lemmas.

Lemma 2. For each propositional constant p such that K′ ⊢ (Max p) and any wff A, if X(p) ⊢ A, K′ ⊢ (p ent A).

Lemma 3. For each propositional constant p such that K′ ⊢ (Max p), X(p) is a consistent, complete, universal set of sequences.

Continuing to construct $\langle \underline{MK'},V \rangle$, we let $W \in \{X(p): p$ is a propositional constant in L′ and K′ ⊢ (Max p)$\}$. $O = X(p)$, where p is a propositional constant in L′ and K′ ⊢ (p ∧ (Max p)). We now construct a structure **D** on W. Where A is a sentence in L′, $V(A) = \{w \in W: O \in w\}$. $D[1,0] = \{V(\overline{A}): A$ is a sentence of L′$\}$. We now specify the values V assigns to other constants in L′.

(1) V(p), for $p \in SC[1,0]$, is already defined.
(2) For m > 1 by AxC2, ⊢ $(\exists p_1)\ldots(\exists p_m)(P = \langle p_1,\ldots, p_m \rangle)$, for $P \in SC[m,0]$. Since K′ is universal, K′ ⊢ $(P = \langle q_1, \ldots, q_m \rangle)$ for some m-tuple of propositional constants $q_1, \ldots, q_m$. Let $V(P) = \langle V(q_1), \ldots, V(q_m) \rangle$.
(3) For $P \in SC[1,1]$, V(P) = F, where for all $V(p) \in D[1,0]$, (a) if for some $N \in \omega$, K′ ⊢ $(\alpha(P,p) = N)$, then F(V(p)) = N, (b) if otherwise, then since by AxC4 and (D8) K′ ⊢ $(f = \alpha(P,p))$, for some constant $f \in UC[1,1]$, F(V(p)) = {f: f is a constant in UC[1,1] and K′ ⊢ $(f = \alpha(P,p))$}. We let $\chi[1,1]$ be ω together with the set of those sets of quantifiers included in the range of some F in D[1,1].
(4) For $P \in SC[m,n]$, m ⩾ 1, n ⩾ 1, and $\langle m,n \rangle \neq \langle 1,1 \rangle$, V(P) = F, where for all $V(Q) \in D[m,0]$, F(V(Q)) = {f: f is a constant in UC[m,n] and K′ ⊢ $(f = \alpha(P,Q))$ for $\alpha \in FC[m,n]$}, since by AxC4 and (D8), K′ ⊢ $(f = \alpha(P,Q))$, for some constant f.
     For m ⩾ 1, n ⩾ 0, D[m,n] = {V(P): $P \in SC[m,n]$}.
(5) For m ⩾ 1 and n ⩾ 0, $V(f) \in D[1,0]^{D[m,n]}$ such that for $V(P) \in D[m,n]$, V(f)(V(P)) = V(fP).
     For m ⩾ 1 and n ⩾ 0, M[m,n] = {V(f): $f \in UC[m,n]$}.

(6) For $m,n \geqslant 1$, $a \in FC[m,n]$, $P,R \in SC[m,n]$, and $Q \in SC[m,0]$, $V(aPQ) \in D[1,0]^{D[m,n]}$ such that for $V(R) \in D[m,n]$, $V(aPQ)(V(R)) = V(aPQR)$.

(7) For $m,n \geqslant 1$ and a,P,Q as above, $V(a) \in M[m,n]^{D[m,n] \times D[m,0]}$ such that for $V(P) \in D[m,n]$ and $V(Q) \in D[m,0]$, $V(a)(\langle V(P),V(Q) \rangle) = V(aPQ)$.
For $m,n \geqslant 1$, $J[m,n] = \{V(a): a \in FC[m,n]\}$.

(8) For $m,r \geqslant 1$, $n \geqslant 0$, $o \in OC[m,n,r]$, and $f_1, \ldots, f_r \in UC[m,n]$, $V(of_1 \ldots f_r) \in D[1,0]^{D[m,n]^r}$ such that for $V(P) \in D[m,n]$, $V(of_1 \ldots f_r)(V(P)) = V(of_1 \ldots f_r P)$.

(9) For $m,r \geqslant 1$, $n \geqslant 0$, and $o,f_1, \ldots, f_r$ as above, $o \in OC[m,n,r]$, $V(o) \in M[m,n]^{M[m,n]^r}$ such that for all $V(f_1), \ldots, V(f_r) \in M[m,n]$, $V(o)(\langle V(f_1), \ldots, V(f_r) \rangle) = V(of_1 \ldots f_r)$.

For $m,r \geqslant 1$ and $n \geqslant 0$, $L[m,n,r] = \{V(o): o \in OC[m,n,r]\}$.

We extend V to all variables, where for $m,r \geqslant 1$ and $n \geqslant 0$, if $v \in S[m,n] - SC[m,n]$, $v \in U[m,n] - UC[m,n]$, $v \in F[m,n] - FC[m,n]$, or $v \in O[m,n,r] - OC[m,n,r]$, $V(v) \in D[m,n]$, $V(v) \in M[m,n]$, $V(v) \in J[m,n]$, or $V(v) \in L[m,n,r]$ respectively. This extension satisfies the following conditions by stipulation:

(1) Where $\langle \langle A_1, \ldots, A_m \rangle, \langle v_1, \ldots, v_n \rangle \rangle$ contains no free variables, by AxC1 and the universality of K', $K' \vdash (Q = \langle \langle A_1, \ldots, A_m \rangle, \langle v_1, \ldots, v_n \rangle \rangle)$ for some constant $Q \in S[m,n]$, $V(\langle \langle A_1, \ldots, A_m \rangle, \langle v_1, \ldots, v_n \rangle \rangle) = V(Q)$.

(2) For any $\langle \langle A_1, \ldots, A_m \rangle, \langle v_1, \ldots, v_n \rangle \rangle$, where $u_1, \ldots, u_k$ are all the variables occurring free in $\langle \langle A_1, \ldots, A_m \rangle, \langle v_1, \ldots, v_n \rangle \rangle$, $c_1, \ldots, c_k$ are constants such that for $1 \leqslant i \leqslant k$, $V(u_i) = V(c_i)$, and for $1 \leqslant h \leqslant m$, $A_h^* = A_h[u_1/c_1, \ldots, u_k/c_k]$, $V(\langle \langle A_1, \ldots, A_m \rangle, \langle v_1, \ldots, v_n \rangle \rangle) = V(\langle \langle A_1^*, \ldots, A_m^* \rangle, \langle v_1, \ldots, v_n \rangle \rangle)$.

(3) For any $\phi \in \Sigma[m,n]$ and $f \in U[m,n]$, $V(f\phi) = V(f)(V(\phi))$.

(4) For any $\phi \in \Sigma[m,n]$, $\psi \in \Sigma[m,0]$, and $a \in F[m,n]$, $V(a\phi\psi) = V(a)(\langle V(\phi),V(\psi) \rangle)$.

(5) For any $\phi,\chi \in \Sigma[m,n]$, $\psi \in \Sigma[m,0]$, and $a \in F[m,n]$, $V(a\phi\psi\chi) = (V(a)(\langle V(\phi),V(\psi) \rangle))(V(\chi))$.

(6) For any $\delta_1, \ldots, \delta_k \in \Gamma[m,n]$ and $o \in O[m,n,k]$, $V(o\delta_1 \ldots \delta_k) = V(o)(\langle V(\delta_1), \ldots, V(\delta_k) \rangle)$.

(7) For any $\delta_1, \ldots, \delta_k \in \Gamma[m,n]$, $\phi \in \Sigma[m,n]$, and $o \in O[m,n,k]$, $V(o\delta_1 \ldots \delta_k\phi) = (V(o)(\langle V(\delta_1), \ldots, V(\delta_k) \rangle))(V(\phi))$.

Any variant V' of V satisfying conditions (1) through (7) above maps all wffs into $D[1,0]$. We shall show that where A and A^* are sentences, c and c^* are constants such that $V(c) = V(c^*)$, and A and A^* are alike save that A has an occurrence of c where A* has one of c*, then $V(A) = V(A^*)$. This will show that any mapping V' is uniquely defined on formulae beginning with a quantifier.

Lemma 4. $V(F) = \varnothing$.

Lemma 5. If $K' \vdash (A = B)$, $V(A) = V(B)$ for all sentences A and B.
The proof of the lemma makes use of AxI1.

Lemma 6. If $K' \vdash (A = T)$ for a sentence A and $K' \vdash (Max\,p)$ for a propositional constant p, then $K' \vdash (p\,ent\,A)$.
The proof of the lemma makes use of 5.1.9 and AxI1.

Lemma 7. If A is a sentence and $V(A) = \varnothing$, $K' \vdash (A = F)$.
The proof of the lemma makes use of 5.1.11.

Lemma 8. For any $\langle m,n \rangle \in \omega - \{0\}\,x\omega$, if $f \in UC[m,n]$, $c,c^* \in SC[m,n]$, and $V(f(c)) = V(f(c^*))$, then $K' \vdash (fc = fc^*)$.
Proof: Assume the hypothesis and, *per reductio*, that $K' \vdash (fc \neq fc^*)$. If $K' \vdash (fc = F)$, then by Lemma 5 $V(fc) = V(F) = \varnothing = V(fc^*)$. Hence by Lemma 7 and AxI1, $K' \vdash (fc = fc^*)$, contrary to hypothesis. So $K' \vdash (fc \neq F)$ and by similar reasoning $K' \vdash (fc^* \neq F)$. By 5.1.21, $K' \vdash (Max\,p)\ \wedge$ $([(p\,ent\,fc) \wedge \sim(p\,ent\,fc^*)] \vee [(p\,ent\,fc^*) \wedge \sim(p\,ent\,fc)])$. Either $X(p) \in V(fc)$ and $X(p) \notin V(fc^*)$, or $X(p) \in V(fc^*)$ and $X(p) \notin V(fc)$, by construction. Either way $V(fc) \neq V(fc^*)$, contrary to the hypothesis.

Lemma 9. For any $\langle m,n \rangle \in \omega - \{0\}\,x\,\omega$, if $P \in SC[m,n]$, $c,c^* \in UC[m,n]$, $g \in UC[1,0]$, and $V(g(c(P))) = V(g(c^*(P)))$, $K' \vdash (g(c(P)) = g(c^*(P)))$.

Lemma 10. For any $m,n \in \omega - \{0\}$, if $P,R \in SC[m,n]$, $Q \in SC[m,0]$, $c,c^* \in FC[m,n]$, $g \in UC[1,0]$, and $V(g(cPQR)) = V(g(c^*PQR))$, then $K' \vdash ((g(cPQR)) = (g(c^*PQR)))$.

Lemma 11. For any $n \in \omega$ and $m,k \in \omega - \{0\}$, if $f_1, \ldots, f_k \in UC[m,n]$, $P \in SC[m,n]$, $c,c^* \in OC[m,n,k]$, $g \in UC[1,0]$, and $V(g(cf_1 \ldots f_kP)) = V(g(c^*f_1 \ldots f_kP))$, then $K' \vdash ((g(cf_1 \ldots f_k)P) = (g(c^*f_1 \ldots f_k)P))$.
The strategy for proving Lemmas 9, 10 and 11 is similar to that for Lemma 8.

Lemma 12. Where c and c* are constants and $V(c) = V(c^*)$, $K' \vdash (c = c^*)$.
Proof: If $c,c^* \in SC[1,0]$, the argument parallels that for Lemma 8. If $c,c^* \in SC[m,n]$, $\langle m,n \rangle \neq \langle 1,0 \rangle$, and $f \in UC[m,n]$, $V(fc) = V(fc^*)$. So $K' \vdash$

(fc = fc*) for any $f \in UC[m,n]$ by Lemma 8. Since K' is universal, $K' \vdash (\forall f)(fc \leftrightarrow fc^*)$, i.e. $K' \vdash (c = c^*)$. If $c,c^* \in UC[m,n]$, $m \in \omega - \{0\}$, $n \in \omega$, $g \in UC[1,0]$, and $P \in SC[m,n]$, $V(g(c(P))) = V(g(c^*(P)))$. So $K' \vdash ((g(c(P))) = (g(c^*(P))))$ by Lemma 9. Since K' is universal, $K' \vdash (\forall g)(\forall P)((g(c(P))) = (g(c^*(P))))$, i.e., $K' \vdash (c = c^*)$. The cases where $c,c^* \in FC[m,n]$ and $c,c^* \in OC[m,n,k]$ proceed similarly.

Lemma 13. Where c and c* are constants, $V(c) = V(c^*)$, and A and A* are sentences that are alike save that A has an occurrence of c where A* has one of c*, then $V(A) = V(A^*)$.

Proof: $K' \vdash (c = c^*)$ by Lemma 12. The result follows by AxI1 or AxI2 and (R2).

We now turn to showing that $\langle \underline{MK'}, V \rangle$ is a GCMFC2A model. We show first that $\underline{MK'}$ is an atomic normal 2AGMS. Clearly W is a set and $O \in W$. By construction $O = \langle D, M, J, L \rangle$ where $D = \langle D[m,n] \rangle$, $m \in \omega - \{0\}$, $n \in \omega$, $M \in \langle M[m,n] \rangle$, $m \in \omega - \{0\}$, $n \in \omega$, $J \in \langle J[m,n] \rangle$, $m,n \in \omega - \{0\}$ and $L = \langle L[m,n,k] \rangle$, $m,k \in \omega - \{0\}$, $n \in \omega$. Clearly $D[1,0] \subseteq \mathscr{P}(W)$. For $m > 1$, $\vdash (\forall p_1) \ldots (\forall p_m)(\exists P)(P = \langle p_1, \ldots, p_m \rangle)$, $P \in S[m,0]$, by AxC1 and (R2). So for $\langle V(q_1), \ldots, V(q_m) \rangle \in D[1,0]^m$, $K' \vdash (Q = \langle q_1, \ldots, q_m \rangle)$ for some constant $Q \in S[m,0]$. By construction $V(Q) = \langle V(q_1), \ldots, V(q_m) \rangle$ and $V(Q) \in D[m,0]$. So $D[1,0]^m \subseteq D[m,0]$. The reverse inclusion follows immediately by construction. Hence $D[m,0] = D[1,0]^m$.

Also by construction $D[m,n] \subseteq \{F: D[m,0] \to \chi[m,n]\}$, $M[m,n] \subseteq D[1,0]^{D[m,n]}$, $J[m,n] \subseteq M[m,n]^{D[m,n] \times D[m,0]}$ and $L[m,n,r] \subseteq M[m,n]^{M[m,n]^r}$. Hence $\langle D, M, J, L \rangle$ is a structure on W, and $\underline{MK'}$ satisfies conditions (1) and (2) of a 2AGMS. Now to condition (3):

ad (a). By Lemma 4 and construction.

(b) and (c) need no argument.

ad (d). Assume that $F \in D[1,1]$ and $X = \{Y \in D[1,0]: F(Y) \neq 0\}$. By construction $F = V(P)$ for some constant $P \in SC[1,1]$. It suffices to show that $V(\exists P) = \cup X$. If $X(p) \in V(\exists P)$, by Axα4 and construction $X(p) \in V((\alpha(P,q) \neq 0) \wedge q)$ for some constant q. So $X(p) \in V(q)$. By construction $V(P)(V(q)) \neq 0$, so $V(q) \in X$. Assume, on the other hand, that $X(p) \in \cup X$. Hence $X(p) \in V(q)$, where $V(P)(V(q)) \neq 0$. By construction $K' \vdash (p \, \text{ent}((\alpha(P,q) \neq 0) \wedge q))$. By Ax$\alpha$4, $K' \vdash (p \, \text{ent} \, \exists P)$. Hence $\cup X \in D[1,0]$.

Now assume that $X \neq \emptyset$. It suffices to show that $\cap X = V(\forall P)$. If $X(p) \in V(\forall P)$, $K' \vdash (p \, \text{ent}(\forall q)((\alpha(P,q) \neq 0) \to q))$ by Axα3. It follows from construction that for each $V(q) \in X$, $X(p) \in V(q)$. Assume, on the other hand, that $X(p) \in \cap X$. Then for each $V(q)$ such that $V(P)(V(q)) \neq 0$, $K' \vdash (p \, \text{ent}((\alpha(P,q) \neq 0) \to q))$. By Ax$\alpha$3 and construction, $X(p) \in V(\forall P)$.

ad (e). By AxC3, $\vdash (\forall p_1)(\forall p_2)(fp_1p_2 = (p_1 \to p_2))$ for some constant $f \in UC[2,0]$. $V_\to = V(f) \in M[2,0]$.

ad (f). $V(\forall) \in M[1,1]$. If $F \in D[1,1]$, $F = V(P)$ for some constant $P \in SC[1,1]$. Where $X = \{Y \in D[1,0]: F(Y) \neq 0\}$, if $X \neq \emptyset$, there is nothing to prove. If $X = \emptyset$, then $K' \vdash \sim(\exists q)(\alpha(P,q) \neq 0)$. Hence $K' \vdash (p\,ent\,(\forall q)((\alpha(P,q) \neq 0) \to q))$. By Ax$\alpha$3, $X(p) \in V(\forall P)$.

ad (g). See the proof for (d).

Lemma 14. For any $P,Q \in SC[m,n]$, if $K' \vdash (P = Q)$, then $V(P) = V(Q)$, for $m \geqslant 1$ and $n \geqslant 0$.

Proof: Assume hypothesis. If $m = 1$ and $n = 0$, the case is immediate from Lemma 5. If $m > 1$ and $n = 0$, then by AxC2 and the universality of K', for some constants $p_1, \ldots, p_m, q_1, \ldots, q_m$, $P \in SC[m,0]$, and $Q \in SC[m,0]$, $K' \vdash (\langle p_1, \ldots, p_m \rangle = P)$ and $K' \vdash (\langle q_1, \ldots, q_m \rangle = Q)$. By AxI1, $K' \vdash (\langle p_1, \ldots, p_m \rangle = \langle q_1, \ldots, q_m \rangle)$. By 5.1.23, for $1 \leqslant i \leqslant m$, $K' \vdash (p_i = q_i)$. Again by Lemma 5 and construction, $V(P) = V(Q)$. Assume that $n > 0$. By AxI1, for each constant $R \in SC[m,0]$, $K' \vdash (\alpha(P,R) = \alpha(Q,R))$. Clearly by construction, $V(P) = V(Q)$.

ad (h). For each $N \in \omega$, by construction $V(N) \in M[1,1]$. Assume that $X(p) \in V(NP)$, for $P \in S[1,1]$. By Axα2, for n distinct propositional constants $q_1, \ldots, q_n$, $K' \vdash (p\,ent\,([\wedge (\alpha(P,q_i) \neq 0), 1 \leqslant i \leqslant n] \wedge [\wedge q_i, 1 \leqslant i \leqslant n] \wedge (\forall q_0)([(\alpha(P,q_0) \neq 0) \wedge q_0] \to [\vee (q_0 = q_i), 1 \leqslant i \leqslant n])))$. By Ax$\alpha$6, for each $q_i, 1 \leqslant i \leqslant n$, $K' \vdash (\alpha(P,q_i) = M)$, where $1 \leqslant M \leqslant N$. Clearly we may assume without loss of generality that if for some $1 \leqslant i < h \leqslant n$, $K' \vdash (q_i = q_h)$, there is a k such that $k < h$. Hence $K' \vdash \neq (q_1, \ldots, q_k)$. By Ax$\alpha$1, $K' \vdash (p\,ent\,MP)$, where $m = \Sigma\{\alpha(P,q_h): 1 \leqslant h \leqslant k\} = \Sigma\{V(P)(V(q_h)): V(q_h) \in D[1,0]$ and $X(p) \in V(q_h)\}$. By AxN4, $M = N$.

For the converse, assume that $\Sigma\{V(P)(V(q)): V(q) \in D[1,0]$ and $X(p) \in V(q)\} = N$. For some $k \leqslant n$, there are pairwise distinct $V(q_1), \ldots, V(q_k)$ such that for $1 \leqslant i \leqslant k$, $V(P)(V(q_i)) \neq 0$, $X(p) \in V(q_i)$, and for all $V(q_0) \neq V(q_1), \ldots, V(q_k)$, if $X(p) \in V(q_0)$, $V(P)(V(q_0)) = 0$. By Lemma 5, $K' \vdash (p\,ent\,(\neq (q_1, \ldots, q_k)))$. Also $K' \vdash (p\,ent\,[\wedge (\alpha(P,q_i) = M_i), 1 \leqslant i \leqslant k])$ and $K' \vdash (p\,ent\,[\wedge q_i, 1 \leqslant i \leqslant k])$. Assume that q_0 is a constant distinct from $q_1, \ldots, q_k$, and $K' \vdash (p\,ent\,((\alpha(P,q_0) \neq 0) \wedge q_0))$. So $K' \vdash (\alpha(P,q_0) \neq 0)$, $X(p) \in V(q_0)$, and $V(P)(V(q_0)) \neq 0$. For some $1 \leqslant i \leqslant k$, $V(q_0) = V(q_i)$. By Lemma 12, $K' \vdash (p\,ent\,[\vee (q_0 = q_i), 1 \leqslant i \leqslant k])$. By Ax$\alpha$1, $K' \vdash (p\,ent\,NP)$, completing the case.

Lemma 15. Where A and B are sentences if $V(A) = V(B)$, $K' \vdash (A = B)$.

Proof: Assume the hypothesis and, *per reductio*, that $K' \nvdash (A = B)$. Then, since K' is maximal, $K' \vdash (A \neq B)$, i.e., $K' \vdash \sim(\forall f)(fA \leftrightarrow fB)$, for $f \in U[1,0]$. Clearly for any $V(f) \in M[1,0]$, $V(fA) = V(fB)$. Since K' is universal, $K' \vdash \sim(f_0 A \leftrightarrow f_0 B)$ for some constant $f_0 \in U[1,0]$. Where p is such that $K' \vdash (p \wedge (Max\,p))$, $K' \vdash (p\,ent \sim(f_0 A \leftrightarrow f_0 B))$. But $K' \vdash (p\,ent\,f_0 A)$ or

$K' \vdash (\text{p ent} \sim f_0 A)$. If the former, $K' \vdash (\text{p ent } f_0 B)$, and so by 5.1.15 and 5.1.20, $K' \vdash (\text{p ent } (f_0 A \leftrightarrow f_0 B))$, which is impossible. If the latter, $K' \vdash (\text{p ent} \sim f_0 B)$, and so $K' \vdash (\text{p ent } (\sim f_0 A \leftrightarrow \sim f_0 B))$, which is again impossible. So $K' \vdash (A = B)$.

Lemma 16. For any constants c and c*, if $K' \vdash (c = c^*)$, then $V(c) = V(c^*)$.

Proof: By Lemma 5, we need argue only the cases where $c,c^* \in UC[m,n]$ $(m \geqslant 1,\ n \geqslant 0)$, $FC[m,n]$ $(m,n \geqslant 1)$, or $OC[m,n,k]$ $(m,k \geqslant 1,\ n \geqslant 0)$.

(a) $c,c^* \in UC[m,n]$. By 5.1.25, $K' \vdash ((c = c^*) = T)$. By 5.1.28, $K' \vdash (\forall g)(\forall P)((gcP \leftrightarrow gc^*P) = T)$, for $P \in S[m,n]$ and $g \in U[1,0]$. By AxC4 and universality, $K' \vdash (\forall p)(f_0 p = p)$, for some constant $f_0 \in UC[1,0]$. So $K' \vdash (\forall P)((cP \leftrightarrow c^*P) = T)$. For all $V(Q) \in D[m,n]$ and $X(p) \in W$, $X(p) \in V(c)(V(Q))$ iff $K' \vdash (\text{p ent } cQ)$ iff $K' \vdash (\text{p ent } c^*Q)$ iff $X(p) \in V(c^*)(V(Q))$. So $V(c) = V(c^*)$.

Cases (b) and (c) proceed similarly using 5.1.26 and 5.1.27 respectively, instead of 5.1.25.

Lemma 17. For any constants $P \in S[m,n]$, $Q \in S[m,0]$, quantifier $f \in U[m,n]$, and $\alpha \in F[m,n]$, if $K' \vdash (\alpha(P,Q) = F)$, then $V(\alpha(P,Q)) = V(f)$.

Proof: If $K' \vdash (\alpha(P,Q) = f)$, then for any constant $R \in SC[m,n]$, $K' \vdash (\alpha(P,Q)R = fR)$. By Lemma 5, $V(\alpha(P,Q)R) = V(fR)$. Hence by construction $V(\alpha(P,Q))$ is the same function as $V(f)$.

Lemma 18. Where V' and V'' are any extensions of V to variables differing at most at v, and if A contains no free occurrences of any variable in v, then $V'(A) = V''(A)$.

Proof: By induction on the length of A.

Lemma 19. Where V' differs from V at most at v and $V'(v) = V(c)$, then $V'(A) = V(A[v/c])$.

Proof: We may assume that v occurs free in A. The result follows by an induction on the length of formulas, recalling the conditions for the extension of a valuation.

ad (i.1). Assume that $V(P),V(Q) \in D[1,1]$, $V(p),V(q) \in D[1,0]$, $V(P)(V(p)) \neq V(Q)(V(q))$, and neither $V(P)(V(p)) = N$ nor $V(Q)(V(q)) = M$ for any $N,M \in \omega$. Then $V(P)(V(p)) = X = \{f:\ K' \vdash (\alpha(P,p) = f)$ for $f \in U[1,1]\}$ and $V(Q)(V(q)) = Y = \{f:\ K' \vdash (\alpha(Q,q) = f)$ for $f \in U[1,1]\}$. Clearly $X \cap Y = \varnothing$. So we may pick f from X and g from Y and have that $K' \vdash (f \neq g)$. By Lemma 12, $V(f) \neq V(g)$. But clearly $V(f),V(g) \in M[1,1]$, and $V(f),V(g) \neq V(N)$, for any $N \in \omega$.

ad (i.2). Assume that $V(P),V(Q) \in D[m,n]$, $V(R),V(S) \in D[m,0]$ and $V(P)(V(R)) \neq V(Q)(V(S))$. Then $V(P)(V(R)) = X = \{f: K' \vdash (\alpha(P,R) = f)$ for $\alpha \in F[m,n]$ and $f \in U[m,n]\}$, and $V(Q)(V(S)) = Y = \{f: K' \vdash (\alpha(Q,S) = f)$ for $\alpha \in F[m,n]$ and $f \in U[m,n]\}$. Again $X \cap Y = \varnothing$. The argument proceeds as above.

ad (j.1). $V(\alpha) \in J[1,1]$. Assume that $V(P) \in D[1,1]$, $V(p) \in D[1,0]$, and $V(P)(V(p)) = N$. We must show that $V(\alpha)(\langle V(P),V(p)\rangle) = V(N)$. By construction, $K' \vdash (\alpha(P,p) = N)$. By Lemma 17, $V(\alpha(P,p)) = V(N)$, from which the result follows immediately by construction. For the converse, assume that $V(\alpha)(\langle V(P),V(p)\rangle) = V(N)$. So $V(\alpha(P,p)) = V(N)$. If $K' \nvdash (\alpha(P,p) = N)$, then either for some $M \neq N$, $K' \vdash (\alpha(P,p) = M)$ or for some constant $f \in UC[1,1]$, $K' \vdash (\alpha(P,p) = f)$ and $V(P)(V(p)) = \{f: K' \vdash (\alpha(P,p) = f)\}$. In the former case, by Lemma 17 and construction, $V(\alpha)(\langle V(P),V(p)\rangle) = V(M)$, and so $V(M) = V(N)$. Now for any constants $g \in UC[1,0]$ and $P \in SC[1,1]$, $V(gMP) = V(gNP)$. Hence $K' \vdash (M = N)$, since if otherwise by universality for some constants $h \in UC[1,0]$ and $Q \in SC[1,1]$, $V(hMQ) \neq V(hNQ)$. But by 5.11, $K' \vdash (M \neq N)$, which is impossible. In the latter case, $V(f) = V(N)$. By Lemma 13, $V(\alpha(P,p) = f) = V(\alpha(P,p) = N)$. So by Lemma 15, $K' \vdash (\alpha(P,p) = N)$, contrary to hypothesis.

Now assume that $V(P)(V(p)) = \{f: K' \vdash (\alpha(P,p) = f)\}$. Let g be the representative member of this set. The left-to-right direction now follows straightforwardly by construction and Lemma 17. The converse is also straightforward.

ad (j.2). Proved as in the last part of the proof of (j.1).

ad (k). Assume that $d_x, d_N \in M[1,1]$ and $V(Q) \in D[1,1]$. By construction $d_x \in V(f)$, where $K' \vdash (\alpha(P,p) = f)$ and for no $M \in \omega$ does $K' \vdash (\alpha(P,p) = M)$. So $K' \vdash (f \neq N)$. By AxN6, $V(fQ) \cap V(NQ) = \varnothing$.

The proofs concerning (l.1) and (l.2) are easy adaptations from the argument for (i) above.

Notice that $V(n) \in L[1,1,1]$. That $V(n)$ behaves as v should follows easily from the maximal consistency of K' and Ax*ns*1 (for (m)) and Ax*ns*2 (for (n)), $V(s) \in L[1,1,1]$. That $V(s)$ is one–one follows by Ax*ns*5. The remainder of condition (o) follows by Ax*ns*3 and Ax*ns*4.

Lemma 20. If $K' \vdash (\text{Max } q)$, $V(q) = \{X(q)\}$, where $q \in SC[1,0]$.

Proof: Assume the hypothesis. Clearly $K' \vdash (q \text{ ent } q)$. So $X(q) \in V(q)$. Assume that $X(p) \in V(q)$. Hence $K' \vdash (p \text{ ent } q)$. But $K' \vdash (\forall p)((q \text{ ent } p) \vee (q \text{ ent } \sim p))$. If $K' \vdash (q \text{ ent } p)$, $K' \vdash (p = q)$, and so $X(p) = X(q)$. If $K' \vdash (q \text{ ent } \sim p)$, $K' \vdash (p = F)$, which is impossible.

Lemma 20 shows that $\underline{MK'}$ is atomic.

For normality, assume that $X(q) \in W$, $\langle m,n \rangle \in \omega - \{0\} \times \omega$, and $X,Y \in D[m,n]$. By construction $V(P) \in X$ and $V(Q) = Y$ for some constants

$P,Q \in SC[m,n]$. Assume that $V(P) \neq V(Q)$. Hence by Lemma 14, $K' \vdash (P \neq Q)$. By Ax13 and Lemma 6, $K' \vdash (q \operatorname{ent}(P \neq Q))$. By definition $K' \vdash (q \operatorname{ent} \sim (\forall f)(fP \leftrightarrow f(Q)))$ for $f \in U[m,n]$. We may infer that there is a constant $g \in UC[m,n]$ such that $K' \vdash (q \operatorname{ent}(gP \leftrightarrow \sim gQ))$. Clearly $X(q) \in V(gP)$ iff $X(q) \notin V(gQ)$. But $V(gP) = V(g)(V(P))$, and $V(g) \in M[m,n]$. This establishes that $\underline{MK'}$ is normal.

That $\underline{MK'}$ is hereditary is an easy consequence of AxC3 and AxC4.

Lemma 21. Where $A_1, \ldots, A_m, B_1, \ldots, B_m$ are sentences such that A_i and B_i are alike, $1 \leqslant i \leqslant m$, save that for some constants c and c*, some of $B_1, \ldots, B_m$ have occurrences of c* where $A_1, \ldots, A_m$ have occurrences of c, and $V(c) = V(c^*)$, then $V(\langle A_1, \ldots, A_m \rangle) = V(\langle B_1, \ldots, B_m \rangle)$.

Proof: Notice that by Lemma 13, for $1 \leqslant i \leqslant m$, $V(A_i) = V(B_i)$. By construction there are constants $p_1, \ldots, p_m, q_1, \ldots, q_m$ such that $V(\langle A_1, \ldots, A_m \rangle) = \langle V(p_1), \ldots, V(p_m) \rangle$, $V(\langle B_1, \ldots, B_m \rangle) = \langle V(q_1), \ldots, V(q_m) \rangle$, $K' \vdash (\langle A_1, \ldots, A_m \rangle = \langle p_1, \ldots, p_m \rangle)$, and $K' \vdash (\langle B_1, \ldots, B_m \rangle = \langle q_1, \ldots, q_m \rangle)$. By 5.1.23, for $1 \leqslant i \leqslant m$, $K' \vdash (A_i = p_i)$ and $K' \vdash (B_i = q_i)$. By Lemma 5, $V(A_i) = V(p_i)$ and $V(B_i) = V(q_i)$. Hence $V(\langle A_1, \ldots, A_m \rangle) = V(\langle B_1, \ldots, B_m \rangle)$.

Lemma 22. Where $\phi, \psi \in \Sigma[m,0]$, if $K' \vdash (\phi = \psi)$, $V(\phi) = V(\psi)$.

Proof: Let $v_1, \ldots, v_n$ be all the variables occurring free in $(\phi = \psi)$. If we assume the hypothesis, we have $K' \vdash (\forall v_1) \ldots (\forall v_n)(\phi = \psi)$. If ϕ is a variable, there is a constant P* such that $V(\phi) = V(P^*)$. If $\phi = \langle A_1, \ldots, A_m \rangle$, by construction there are sentences $A_1^*, \ldots, A_m^*$, where some, not necessarily all, of $v_1, \ldots, v_n$ are replaced by constants, and $V(\langle A_1, \ldots, A_m \rangle) = V(\langle A_1^*, \ldots, A_m^* \rangle)$. The case is similar for ψ. If a variable v occurs in both ϕ and ψ, by Lemma 21 we may assume that v is replaced by the same constant in the construction. Let ϕ^* and ψ^* be the expressions such that $V(\phi) = V(\phi^*)$ and $V(\psi) = V(\psi^*)$. $K' \vdash (\phi^* = \psi^*)$. If $\phi^* = \langle A_1^*, \ldots, A_m^* \rangle$, by construction there is a constant Q such that $V(Q) = V(\langle A_1^*, \ldots, A_m^* \rangle)$. Similarly there is a constant R such that $V(R) = V(\psi^*)$. By construction there are constants $q_1, \ldots, q_m, r_1, \ldots, r_m$ such that $K' \vdash (Q = \langle q_1, \ldots, q_m \rangle)$, $K' \vdash (R = \langle r_1, \ldots, r_m \rangle)$, $V(Q) = \langle V(q_1), \ldots, V(q_m) \rangle$, and $V(R) = \langle V(r_1), \ldots, V(r_m) \rangle$. $K' \vdash \langle q_1, \ldots, q_m \rangle = \langle r_1, \ldots, r_m \rangle$. Hence by 5.1.23, $K' \vdash (q_i = r_i)$, $1 \leqslant i \leqslant m$. Hence by Lemma 5, $V(q_i) = V(r_i)$, completing the proof.

Lemma 23. Where $A_1, \ldots, A_m$ are wffs and V' is any variant of V, $V'(\langle A_1, \ldots, A_m \rangle) = \langle V'(A_1), \ldots, V'(A_m) \rangle$.

Proof: By construction there are sentences $A_1^*, \ldots, A_m^*$ such that $V'(\langle A_1, \ldots, A_m \rangle) = V'(\langle A_1^*, \ldots, A_m^* \rangle)$. By repeated applications of Lemma 13, for $1 \leqslant i \leqslant m$, $V'(A_i) = V'(A_i^*)$. Furthermore there is an m-tuple of constants $q_1, \ldots, q_m$ such that $K' \vdash (\langle A_1^*, \ldots, A_m^* \rangle = \langle q_1, \ldots, q_m \rangle)$

and $V'(\langle A_1^*, \ldots, A_m^* \rangle) = \langle V'(q_1), \ldots, V'(q_m) \rangle$. But for $1 \leqslant i \leqslant m$, $K' \vdash (A_i^* = q_i)$. Hence $V'(A_i^*) = V'(q_i)$. So $V'(A_i) = V'(q_i)$, and $V'(\langle A_1, \ldots, A_m \rangle) = \langle V'(A_1), \ldots, V'(A_m) \rangle$.

Lemma 24. Where A and A* are wffs such that for some variables $v_1, \ldots, v_n$, $A^* = A[v_1/c_1] \cdots [v_n/c_n]$, there is a variant V' of V such that $V'(A) = V(A^*)$.

Proof: Let V' be that variant of V such that for $1 \leqslant i \leqslant n$, $V'(v_i) = V(c_i)$ and otherwise agrees with V. We assume that $v_1, \ldots, v_n$ actually occur free in A. Let $u_1, \ldots, u_k$ be all the variables other than $v_1, \ldots, v_n$ actually occurring free in A. Let $d_1, \ldots, d_k$ be constants appropriate for $u_1, \ldots, u_k$ such that for $1 \leqslant i \leqslant k$, $V'(u_i) = V'(d_i)$. By construction and Lemmas 13 and 18, $V'(A) = V'(A^*[u_1/d_1] \cdots [u_k/d_k]) = V(A^*[u_1/d_1] \cdots [u_k/d_k]) = V(A^*)$.

We now verify that the conditions for a valuation associated with <u>MK'</u> are satisfied by V.

Conditions (1)–(5) are satisfied. For (6), assume that v is a variable and A a wff. Let $u_1, \ldots, u_k$ be all the variables free in $\langle \langle A \rangle, \langle v \rangle \rangle$, and let A* be $A[u_1/c_1] \cdots [u_k/c_k]$, where for $1 \leqslant i \leqslant k$, $V(u_i) = V(c_i)$. By construction $V(\langle \langle A \rangle, \langle v \rangle \rangle) = V(\langle \langle A^* \rangle, \langle v \rangle \rangle) = V(Q)$, where $Q \in S[1,1]$ and $K' \vdash (Q = \langle \langle A^* \rangle, \langle v \rangle \rangle)$ by AxC1. It remains to show that for $V(p) \in D[1,0]$, where $X = \{V' : V'$ differs from V at most at v and $V'(A) = V(p)\}$, $V(Q)(V(p)) = \mathrm{card}(X)$ if the latter is finite, and otherwise is some element in $\chi - \omega$.

Assume first that $\mathrm{card}(X) = N$, for some $N \in \omega$. Let us index the members of X by $\{1, \ldots, n\}$. Now there are constants $c_1, \ldots, c_n$ such that $K' \vdash \neq (c_1, \ldots, c_n)$. By Lemma 19, $V_i(A^*) = V(A^*[v/c_i])$. By Lemma 15, $K' \vdash [\wedge (A^*[v/c_i] = p), 1 \leqslant i \leqslant n]$. Suppose that $K' \vdash (A^*[v/c_0] = p)$. Then where V' differs from V only in that $V'(v) = V(c_0)$, $V' \in X$ by Lemma 19. Hence $V' = V_i$ for some $1 \leqslant i \leqslant n$, and so by Lemma 12, $K' \vdash (c_0 = c_i)$. Hence $K' \vdash (\forall u)((A^*[v/u] = p) \rightarrow [\vee (u = v_i), 1 \leqslant i \leqslant n])$. By Ax$\alpha$8, $K' \vdash (\alpha(\langle \langle A^* \rangle, \langle v \rangle \rangle, p) = N)$. By construction, $V(Q)(V(p)) = N$.

Now assume that $\mathrm{card}(X)$ is not finite. It is sufficient to show that $K' \nvdash (\alpha(\langle \langle A \rangle, \langle v \rangle \rangle) = N)$ for any $N \in \omega$. Assume, *per reductio*, that it does. By Axα8 and the universality of K', there are constants $c_1, \ldots, c_n$ such that $K' \vdash (\neq (c_1, \ldots, c_n) \wedge [\wedge (A[v/c_i] = p), 1 \leqslant i \leqslant n] \wedge (\forall u)((A[v/u] = p) \rightarrow [\vee (u = c_i), 1 \leqslant i \leqslant n]))$. But from this it follows that $\mathrm{card}(X)$ is at most N, contrary to hypothesis. By construction, $V(Q)(V(p)) = \{f : K' \vdash (\alpha(Q,p) = f)\}$. But the latter is clearly in $\chi - \omega$, which was to be shown. That the remaining conditions are satisfied is immediate.

To verify that V is a standard valuation, notice that conditions (1), (2), (5) and (6) are straightforward. (3), (4), (7) and (8) are similar, so we shall address (3). By hypothesis and construction, where ϕ^* and ψ^* are such that all free variables have been replaced by constants (the same constant if the same variable occurs in both), then $O \in V'((\forall v_1) \ldots (\forall v_k((\phi^* = \psi^*))$ and $K' \vdash (\phi^* = \psi^*)$. By AxI1, where A^*, B^* are A, B with appropriate replacements of ϕ by ϕ^* and ψ by ψ^* respectively, $K' \vdash (\langle\langle A^*\rangle, \langle v\rangle\rangle = \langle\langle B^*\rangle, \langle v\rangle\rangle)$. Where A^{**} and B^{**} are sentences such that $V'(\langle\langle A^*\rangle, \langle v\rangle\rangle) = V'(\langle\langle A^{**}\rangle, \langle v\rangle\rangle)$ and $V'(\langle\langle B^*\rangle, \langle v\rangle\rangle) = V'(\langle\langle B^{**}\rangle, \langle v\rangle\rangle)$, clearly $K' \vdash (\langle\langle A^{**}\rangle, \langle v\rangle\rangle = \langle\langle B^{**}\rangle, \langle v\rangle\rangle)$. So by Lemma 14, $V'(\langle\langle A^*\rangle, \langle v\rangle\rangle) = V'(\langle\langle B^*\rangle, \langle v\rangle\rangle)$, from which it follows by construction that $V'(\langle\langle A\rangle, \langle v\rangle\rangle) = V'(\langle\langle B\rangle, \langle v\rangle\rangle)$.

V is a standard valuation. $\langle \underline{MK'}, V\rangle$ is general and so regular. This establishes that $\langle \underline{MK'}, V\rangle$ is a 2AGMS model.

Lemma 25. $K' = O$.

Proof: Recall that $O = X(p_0)$, where $K' \vdash (p_0 \wedge (\text{Max } p_0))$. It suffices to show that $A \in K'$ iff $K' \vdash (p_0 \text{ ent } A)$ for all wffs A in L. If $A \in K'$, then $K' \vdash A$. Hence $K' \vdash (p_0 \rightarrow A)$. If $K' \vdash (p_0 \text{ ent } \sim A)$, then $K' \vdash (p_0 \rightarrow (A \wedge \sim A))$, and so $K' \vdash \sim p_0$ and K' is not consistent. For the converse, if $K' \vdash (p_0 \text{ ent } A)$, then $K' \vdash A$. Then by the completeness of K', $A \in K'$.

Lemma 26. For all sentences $A \in K'$, $\langle \underline{MK'}, V\rangle | \vdash A$.

Proof: If $A \in K'$, then by Lemma 25, $A \in O$, and so $O \in \{w \in W : A \in w\}$, i.e., $O \in V(A)$.

The completeness of GCMFC2A is now established.

Appendix 2

Mind

Section 1
The language of mind

We now present a variant of second-order logic which includes constants
representing the mental attitudes of (suppositional) believing, wanting and
wondering and some axioms to characterise these constants. Underlying
this language is a system of categories, or as we shall call them, *kinds*, having
a (finite) type-like structure, and pigeonholing most of the elements of the
language.

The set of kinds is the smallest set X containing x, t and p, and such that
whenever $a_1, \ldots, a_n$ are in X so is $\langle a_1, \ldots, a_n \rangle$, $n \in N$. In general, things in any
kind of the form $\langle a_1, \ldots, a_n \rangle$ may be thought of as functions taking n
arguments, of kinds $a_1, \ldots, a_n$ respectively, into (objects of) kind p.

Then the language LPA may be described as follows:

In each kind there is a denumerably infinite number of variables, perhaps
some constants, and in two cases indexicals. Each variable, constant and
indexical is in at most one kind. Also, there are two disjoint denumerably
infinite sets Q and $\underline{E}$ of variables and perhaps some constants, each of Q and
$\underline{E}$ being disjoint as well from all the sets of variables, constants and
indexicals in kinds.

We shall use
—x and t, with or without subscripts, as metavariables for things in kind x
  and t, respectively;
—p, A, C and D, with or without subscripts, as metavariables for things in
  kind p;
—u and v, with or without subscripts, as metavariables for things in
  unspecified kinds (usually as metavariables for variables);
—f and g, with or without subscripts, as metavariables for things in kinds of
  the form $\langle \alpha_1, \ldots, \alpha_n \rangle$, $n \geqslant 1$; for precision we write $f[\alpha_1, \ldots, \alpha_n]$;
—e, with or without subscripts, as metavariables for variables and
  constants in $\underline{E}$;

—q, with or without subscripts, as metavariables for things in Q.

Constants in the language include $\rightarrow$ in kind $\langle p,p\rangle$; B, L and W in kind $\langle x,t,p,\langle x,t\rangle\rangle$; indexicals i_x in kind x and i_t in kind t (which may be read as 'I' and 'now', respectively); q in Q; and syncategorematic $\forall$.

Now we wish to describe meaningful combinations of the variables and constants. Normally this is just the definition of wffs. However, since we must define other sorts of complexes, and because our ontological commitments make us wish to avoid brackets, we proceed as follows.

By a *primitive symbol* we mean any variable, constant or indexical in LPA so far, as well as things of the form $\forall v$, where v is a variable in LPA. By an *expression* we mean a non-empty, finite sequence of primitive symbols. We wish to consider quadruples of the form $\langle c,a,F,Q^*\rangle$, where c is an expression, a is a kind, Q, or $\underline{E}$, F is a set (the variables free in c) and Q^* is a set (the unquoted variables in c). Then we have the following axiom and five formation rules:

(A1) $\langle v,a,\{v\},\{v\}\rangle$, where v is atomic in a, which is a kind, Q, or $\underline{E}$.

(R1) $\langle c,p,F,Q^*\rangle \Rightarrow \langle \forall vc,p,F-\{v\},Q^* \cup \{\forall vc\}\rangle$.

(R2) $\langle A,p,F,Q^*\rangle$, $\langle A,p,F,Q^*\rangle \Rightarrow \langle AA,\underline{E},\varnothing,\varnothing\rangle$, where F contains no variables.

(R3) $\langle A,p,F_1,Q^*_1\rangle$, $\langle C,p,F_2,Q^*_2\rangle \Rightarrow \langle AC,\underline{E},\varnothing,\varnothing\rangle$, where $(F_1 \cup F_2) -(F_1 \cap F_2)$ contains no variables and $F_1 \cap F_2$ contains some variables.

(R4) $\langle q,Q,\{q\},\{q\}\rangle$, $\langle c,\underline{E},F,Q^*\rangle \Rightarrow \langle qc,\langle x,t\rangle,F \cup \{q\},Q^* \cup \{q,qc\}\rangle$.

(R5) $\langle f,\langle a_1,\ldots, a_n\rangle,F_0,Q^*_0\rangle$, $\langle u_1,a_1,F_1,Q^*_1\rangle,\ldots, \langle u_n,a_n,F_n,Q^*_n\rangle \Rightarrow \langle fu_1 \ldots u_n,p,F_0 \cup F_1 \cup \ldots \cup F_n,Q^*_0 \cup Q^*_1 \cup \ldots \cup Q^*_n\rangle$, $n \geqslant 1$.

A *derivation* is (as usual) a finite, tree-style array of quadruples, such that every quadruple is either an axiom or follows by one of the rules from the quadruple(s) immediately above it. Where d is a derivation, the quadruple in d which is not a rule premise is called the *conclusion* of d. The first element of the conclusion of d is also called the conclusion of d, letting context disambiguate. d is a *wff derivation* just when the conclusion is $\langle A,p,F,Q^*\rangle$ for some A, F and Q^* such that there are no indexicals in the set Q^*; and we say that A is a *wff*. v is a *wlff by (R2)* [(R3)] just when v is the conclusion of a derivation d in which the last rule applied is (R2) [(R3)]. d is a *wlff derivation* just when the conclusion v is a wlff by (R2) or (R3), and we say that v is a *wlff*, v *occurs unquoted* in A just when there is a derivation d with the conclusion $\langle A,a,F,Q^*\rangle$ for some a, F and Q^* such that $v \in Q^*$. v *occurs free* in A just when there is a derivation d with the conclusion $\langle A,a,F,Q^*\rangle$ for some a, F and Q^* such that $v \in F$. Inspection of (R2) and (R3) will show that no variable occurs free in a wlff. However, knowing full well that no variables occur free in wlffs, we shall nonetheless say that v occurs free in wlff AC when v occurs free in A.

Section 2
Well-formedness

As with LQ, the language LPA just described contains no punctuation marks. We must now show that these notions are well defined.

Lemma: Each expression can be the conclusion of at most one derivation.

Where $c'_1 \ldots c'_n$ is an expression of length n (i.e., each c'_i is a primitive expression, $1 \leqslant i \leqslant n$) and $c_1 \ldots c_m$ is an expression of length m, $m < n$, the latter is *an initial part* of the former iff for all i, $1 \leqslant i \leqslant m$, c_i is c'_i.

Proof of Lemma: We argue inductively on the length of expressions to show that (1) each expression can be the conclusion of at most one derivation and (2) no two derivations put an expression and one of its initial parts in the same kind or in $\underline{E}$.

Basis: Expressions of length 1. The derivations concerned can only be axioms, establishing (1), and there are no initial parts of such expressions, establishing (2) vacuously.

Induction hypothesis (IH): Assume that claims (1) and (2) hold for all expressions of length less than or equal to n.

Let $c^* = c_1 \ldots c_{n+1}$ be an expression of length $n+1$. Suppose d_1 and d_2 are distinct derivations with conclusion c^*. We consider cases according to which rule was applied last in d_1 and d_2. Clearly neither d_1 nor d_2 can be just an axiom, since $n \geqslant 1$.

Case 1. (R1) is the final rule applied in d_1 and d_2. Then apply the induction hypothesis to the premise of (R1) in each derivation.

Case 2. d_1 ends with (R1), d_2 with (R2). In d_2, c^* divides into two copies of some A in kind p. c^* begins with $\forall v$, where v is some variable (d_1). Hence A is $\forall vC$, where C is in kind p. But $c^* = \forall vC'$ for some C' in p (d_1). Then C is an initial part of C', in the same kind, contrary to clause (2) of IH.

Case 3. d_1 ends by (R1), d_2 by (R3). Reason as above.

Case 4. If d_1 ends by (R1), d_2 cannot end by (R4) or (R5), since c^* begins with $\forall v$, for some variable v.

Case 5. d_1 ends by (R2), d_2 ends by (R3). Let the premise of (R2) in d_1 be $\langle c',p,F_1,Q^*_1 \rangle$. Let the premises of (R3) in d_2 be $\langle c'_1,p,F_2,Q^*_2 \rangle$ and $\langle c'_2,p,F_2,Q^*_3 \rangle$, with the former on the left. If $c' = c'_1$, then by IH, $F_1 = F_2$, which is absurd since $F_1 = \varnothing \neq F_2$. If $c' \neq c'_1$, then one is an initial part of the other, violating IH (2).

Case 6. d_1 ends by (R2), d_2 ends by (R4). Since (R4) is used, $c_1 \in Q$ and

$c_2 \ldots c_{n+1}$ is in $\underline{E}$. Since (R2) is used, $n+1$ is even. Say $2m = n+1$. Also, $c_1 \ldots c_m$ is in kind p. But since $c_1 \in Q$, $c_1 \ldots c_{m-2}$ is in kind $\langle x,t \rangle$, c_{m-1} is in kind x, c_m is in kind t. Then $c_2 \ldots c_{m-2}$ must be in $\underline{E}$. Since $c_2 \ldots c_{2m}$ is in E also, we have the desired contradiction IH (2).

Case 7. d_1 ends by (R2), d_2 ends by (R5). Then $c^* = AA$ for some A in kind p, since (R2) is used. Since (R5) is used, some initial part of c^* must be in a kind of the form $\langle a_1, \ldots, a_n \rangle$, for $n \geqslant 1$, where a_i are kinds, $1 \leqslant i \leqslant n$. Call the initial part of c^* which is the first entry in the left-most premise in the final application of (R5) in d_2, f_2. f_2 is either atomic, or begins with c_1 in Q. Hence A must also be the conclusion of an application of (R5) in d_1. Let f_1 be the first entry in the left-most premise of the application of (R5) in d_1 with conclusion A. If f_1 or f_2 is an initial part of the other, then at least one of them, say, f_1, is non-atomic. Hence $c_1 \in Q$, and so f_2 also is non-atomic. Then f_1 and f_2 are in kind $\langle x,t \rangle$ in violation of the IH (2).

So we may suppose $f_1 = f_2$. By IH (1), they must be in the same kind. Suppose it is $\langle a_1, \ldots, a_n \rangle$. Let the arguments (thinking of f_1, f_2 as m-ary functions) be $u_1, \ldots, u_m$ in d_1 and $u'_1, \ldots, u'_m$ in d_2. Then $u_1 = u'_1$ or IH (2) is violated. Assuming $u_i = u'_i$, $1 \leqslant i < k < m$, consider u_k and u'_k. If $u_k \neq u'_k$, then one is an initial part of the other, violating IH (2). So $u_k = u'_k$. Hence $u_i = u'_i$, $1 \leqslant i \leqslant m$. But $f_1 u_1 \ldots u_m = A$ and $f_2 u'_1 \ldots u'_m = AA$, which is absurd.

Case 8. d_1 ends by (R3), d_2 ends by (R4) or (R5). See case 7.

Case 9. d_1 ends by (R4), d_2 ends by (R5). Then since (R4) is applied, $c_1 \in Q$. Let f_2 be the initial part of c^* which acts as the function (first component of first premise) in the final application of (R5) in d_2. Since $c_1 \in Q$, f_2 is non-atomic, and hence in kind $\langle x,t \rangle$. So $f_2 = c_1 \ldots c_{n-1}, c_n$ is in kind x, c_{n+1} is in kind t, $c_2 \ldots c_{n-1}$ is in $\underline{E}$. But in d_1, $c_2 \ldots c_{n+1}$ is in $\underline{E}$. Hence IH (2) is violated.

Case 10. d_1 and d_2 end by (R2). Then $c^* = A\overline{A}$ for some A in kind p in both d_1 and d_2. By IH (1), d_1 and d_2 must be the same derivation.

Case 11. d_1 and d_2 end by (R3). If the two premises have the same first elements in d_1 and d_2, we invoke IH (1) to show that d_1 and d_2 are the same derivation. If the two premises have different first elements, we use IH (2) to get the desired absurdity.

Case 12. d_1 and d_2 end by (R4). Apply IH (1) to $c_2 \ldots c_{n+1}$.

Case 13. d_1 and d_2 end by (R5). Apply IH (1) and IH (2) to the acting function in d_1 and d_2, and then inductively to its arguments.

This establishes claim (1). To establish claim (2) consider cases according to whether c^* and an initial part c' are assumed to be in $\underline{E}$, p or $\langle x,t \rangle$. These are the only possibilities.

Case 14. Both are in $\underline{E}$. c^* is not atomic and so does not begin with some $e_i \in E$. Hence $c' \notin E$. So we may suppose that $c^* = AA'$ and $c' = CD$, for some A,A',C,D in kind p. If A and C do not together violate IH (2), and $A = C$. But then A' and D violate IH (2).

Case 15. Both are in $\langle x,t \rangle$. Then $c_1 \in Q$. Suppose that $c' = c_1 \ldots c_m$ for some $m < n+1$. Then $c_2 \ldots c_{n+1}$ and $c_2 \ldots c_{m-1}$ are both in $\underline{E}$, in violation of IH (2).

Case 16. Both are in p. Then the final rule applied in d_1 is (R1) or (R5) and in d_2 the same. If it is (R1) in either of them, it is (R1) in both and $c_1 = \forall v$ for some variable v in LPA. Then where $c^* = \forall vA$ and $c' = \forall vA'$ for some A and A' in kind p, A and A' violate IH (2). If it is (R5) in both, we reason as in case 7, *mutatis mutandis*.

This completes the proof of the lemma.

We can also readily decide whether a given occurrence of a primitive symbol in a given expression is quoted or unquoted, and whether a given occurrence of a variable is free or bound in a given expression. These notions (quoted/unquoted, free/bound) only make sense in the context of expressions which are the conclusions of derivations. Where o is an occurrence of some primitive symbol in some expression c which is the conclusion of derivation d, we may trace the path of o in d up to an instance of some axiom. Working down from this axiom instance we may mechanically check at each stage to see whether o is quoted/unquoted and, if it is a variable, free/bound. (This can easily be made rigorous, and we leave it as an exercise to the reader so inclined.)

Section 3
Definitions

We draw heavily on definitions that have already appeared in Appendix 1. For convenience some are repeated here. We write $\rightarrow$ as an infixed operator and use parentheses liberally to help those readers not comfortable in Polish. We introduce the following defined constants:

'F' $=_{df}$ '$(\forall p)p$'.
'$\sim A$' $=_{df}$ '$(A \rightarrow F)$'.
'T' $=_{df}$ '$\sim F$'.
'$(A \lor B)$' $=_{df}$ '$(\sim A \rightarrow B)$'.
'$(A \land B)$' $=_{df}$ '$\sim(\sim A \lor \sim B)$'.
'$(A \leftrightarrow B)$' $=_{df}$ '$((A \rightarrow B) \land (B \rightarrow A))$'.
'$(v = u)$' $=_{df}$ '$(\forall f[a])(f[a]v \leftrightarrow f[a]u)$', where u and v are in kind a and f[a] is not free in u or v.
'$(A \text{ ent } B)$' $=_{df}$ '$((A \rightarrow B) = T)$'.

Where u and v are both in the same kind, in $\underline{E}$, or in Q, u is a variable, and v^* is an expression. '$v^*[u/v]$' denotes the result of replacing all free occurrences of u in v^* by v.

'(Max A)' $=_{df}$ '((A $\neq$ F) $\wedge$ ($\forall$p)((A ent p) $\vee$ (A ent $\sim$p)))', where p is not free in A.
'$\square$A' $=_{df}$ '(A = T)'.
'$\Diamond$A' $=_{df}$ '$\sim\square\sim$A'.
'($e_1 = e_2$)' $=_{df}$ '($\forall$q)(qe_1 = qe_2)', where e_1 and e_2 are in $\underline{E}$, q $\in$ Q and q is not free in e_1 or e_2.
'($q_1 = q_2$)' $=_{df}$ '($\forall$e)(q_1e = q_2e)', where $q_1,q_2 \in$ Q and e $\in \underline{E}$.

We now turn to substitution.

The *scope of an occurrence* o *of* $\forall$u *in expression* c* is the shortest expression in c* beginning immediately to the right of o and being in kind p, as well as o itself. An occurrence o of variable v in expression c* is *free for variable* u iff o is unquoted, u and v are both in the same kind, in $\underline{E}$, or in Q and o is not within the scope of an occurrence of $\forall$u in c*. The *scope of an occurrence* o *of* f[$a_1, \ldots, a_n$] in expression c* depends on how o functions in c*. o may be used as an argument of some other function symbol, or it may be applied to n arguments in the appropriate kinds to produce an expression in kind p. In the former case, the scope of o is null; in the latter case the scope is the n arguments.

Where a variable f in kind $\langle a_1, \ldots, a_n \rangle$ occurs free in expression c*, an *innermost free occurrence of* f *in* c* is a free occurrence of f which has no free occurrences of f in its scope.

In the formation rules, a variable or constant f in kind $\langle a_1, \ldots, a_n \rangle$ can occur either in the left-most quadruple or in some other quadruple, when it occurs in a premise of an application of (R5). In the former case, we say that it occurs as an *operator*, in the latter case, as an *argument*.

Where $a_1, \ldots, a_n$ are such that for $1 \leqslant i \leqslant$ n, a_i is a kind, Q, or $\underline{E}$, $v_1, \ldots, v_n$ are distinct atoms in $a_1, \ldots, a_n$ respectively, $C_1, \ldots, C_n$ are expressions in $a_1, \ldots, a_n$ respectively and A is a wff, $\underline{S}$ [$v_1, \ldots, v_n/C_1, \ldots, C_n$] A | is the result of simultaneously replacing each free occurrence of v_i in A by C_i, $1 \leqslant i \leqslant$ n.

Where a is a kind, Q, or $\underline{E}$, v is an atom in a, C is an expression in a and A is a wff, $\check{S}$ [v/C] A | is A unless no part of A of the form ($\forall$u)D in kind p contains a free occurrence of v where u is free in C, in which case it is $\underline{S}$ [v/C] A |.

Recursive definition: If $v_1, \ldots, v_n$ are distinct variables such that f$v_1 \ldots v_n$ is a wff, and A and C are wffs as well, then the notation $\check{S}_1$ [f$v_1 \ldots v_n$/C] A | stands for A unless

(1)   f is atomic and does not occur free in C,
(2)   where u is a variable in C other than $v_1, \ldots, v_n$, no well-formed part of A of the form ($\forall$u)D in kind p contains a free occurrence of f,
(3)   for each n-tuple $C_1, \ldots, C_n$ of LPA expressions which is the scope of an

innermost free occurrence of f in A, there is no variable v that occurs free in any C_i, $1 \leqslant i \leqslant n$, such that v_i occurs free in a well-formed part of C of the form $(\forall v)D$ in kind p.

(4) f does not occur free as an argument in A.

When these conditions are satisfied the notation stands for the result of replacing $fC_1 \ldots C_n$ in A by $\underline{S}\,[v_1, \ldots, v_n/C_1, \ldots, C_n]\,C\,|$ whenever the shown occurrence of f is an innermost free one in A.

Where $\check{S}_k\,[fv_1 \ldots v_n/C]\,A\,|$ is defined, $\check{S}_{k+1}\,[fv_1 \ldots v_n/C]\,A\,|$ stands for A unless conditions (1), (2) and (4) are again satisfied, and also condition (3'), which is just (3) with $\check{S}_k\,[fv_1 \ldots v_n/C]\,A\,|$ replacing A. If these conditions are satisfied, the notation stands for the result of replacing $fC_1 \ldots C_n$ in $\check{S}_k$ $[fv_1 \ldots v_n/C]\,A\,|$ by $\underline{S}\,[v_1, \ldots, v_n/C_1, \ldots, C_n]\,C\,|$ wherever the shown occurrence of f is an innermost free occurrence of f in $\check{S}_k\,[fv_1 \ldots v_n/C]\,A\,|$.

Clearly for any given $fv_1 \ldots v_n$, C and A, there is a greatest k such that $\check{S}_k\,[fv_1 \ldots v_n/C]\,A\,| \neq \check{S}_{k+1}\,[fv_1 \ldots v_n/C]\,A\,|$; and we set $\check{S}\,[fv_1 \ldots v_n/C]\,A\,|$ to stand for $\check{S}_z\,[fv_1 \ldots v_n/C]\,A\,|$, where z is the least natural number i such that $\check{S}_i\,[fv_1 \ldots v_n/C]\,A\,| = \check{S}_{i+1}\,[fv_1 \ldots v_n/C]\,A\,|$.

Section 4
Sameness of meaning

We wish to characterise sameness of meaning of wlffs. We define a relation $\cong$ between wlffs and let $\simeq$ be the transitive closure of $\cong$. Then we will say that A and C are synonymous iff $A \simeq C$. Intuitively, and roughly, two wlffs are synonymous iff they differ at most in their bound variables, in the order of their adjacent quantifiers of the same sort or in the free variables in erotetic wlffs that are subparts of them.

Now to make this precise, we describe certain transformations of formation trees of wlffs which generate the relation $\cong$. The relation $\cong$ holds between two wlffs iff the formation tree of one can be transformed into that of the other in certain ways. There are three basic transformation rules, named, α, β and γ. Rule α allows us to rewrite bound variables.

(α) Let AC be a wlff in LPA with formation tree d. Let D' be an entry in d in kind p of the form $(\forall v)D$ for some D. Let d' be the part of d with conclusion D'. Suppose the shown occurrence of $(\forall v)$ binds occurrences $o_1, \ldots, o_n$ of v in D, $n \geqslant 0$. Let v' be some variable not occurring unquoted in D and of the same sort as v. Clearly we may trace each o_i back to some axiom. Let $s(o_i)$ be the series of occurrences of v in d', or in entries in d', which proceeds from the appropriate axiom to occurrence o_i of v in D'. Let D'' be the result of replacing each occurrence of v in $s(o_i)$ by one of v',

$1 \leqslant i \leqslant n$, and replacing the initial $(\forall v)$ in the conclusion of d' by $(\forall v')$. Let d* be the result of proliferating this change throughout d in the obvious minimal way to get a formation tree. Where A*C* is the conclusion of d*, we lay it down that $AC \cong A^*C^*$.

(β) Rule β allows us to reorder adjacent quantifiers of the same sort. We use the admissible formation rule:

$$\langle A,p,F,Q^* \rangle \Rightarrow \langle (\exists v)A,p,F - \{v\},Q^* \cup \{(\exists v)A\} \rangle$$

Call this rule (R1a).

Transformation rule β asserts that where d is a formation tree and d' is the result of switching the order of two adjacent applications of (R1) or of (R1a) and proliferating the change through d in the obvious way, then where the conclusions of d and d' are, respectively, the wlffs e and e', $e \cong e'$.

(γ) Rule γ allows us to rewrite free variables in the two parts of erotetic wlffs.

Let d be the formation tree of wlff DE and let AC be an entry in d in $\underline{E}$ by (R3). Let v be a variable free in A and in C and let $o_1, \ldots, o_n$ be the free occurrences of v in A and in C. Each o_i can be traced to one axiom in d, call it a_i, $1 \leqslant i \leqslant n$. Let d' be the result of replacing each v in each a_i by v', where v' is a variable of the same sort as v which does not occur unquoted in A or in C, and proliferating these changes through d. Where D'E' is the conclusion of d', we lay it down that $DE \cong D'E'$.

Theorem. Synonymy and non-synonymy of wlffs is effective.

Proof: Let AC and A*C* be two wlffs. Every variable in AC (A*C*) is either bound or free in A or C (A* or C*), or free in some well-formed part of A or C (A* or C*) which is a wlff by (R3). That is, whenever variable v occurs in AC and is not bound, v occurs freely in some well-formed part of AC which functions as a wlff. Let d and d' be the formation trees of AC and A*C* respectively.

If d and d' are not isomorphic, that is, if they are not structurally identical (if they do not apply the same rules in all the same places), then AC and A*C* are not synonymous. This holds since applications of α, β or γ cannot change the shape of formation trees.

If d and d' do not contain all the same constants in all the same places, then AC and A*C* are not synonymous, since applications of α, β and γ do not change constants in any way. So let us suppose that d and d' are isomorphic and do not differ in their constants. Then we say they differ at most in their variables. We try to apply α, β and γ to transform d into d', always assuming that d and d' differ at most in their variables.

Each variable occurring in AC can be bound any number of times, subject only to the complexity of AC and can occur free in any number of subwlffs of AC (a subwlff of AC being a well-formed part of AC that functions in AC as a wlff), again subject to the complexity of AC. The first step in trying to transform d into d' is to transform d and d' into d_2 and d_2', respectively, such that each variable occurring in d_2 (d_2') occurs either free in one entry in d_2 (d_2') which is a wlff, or is bound exactly once (by one application of (R1)) in d_2 (d_2'), and not both, and does not occur at all in d_2' (d_2).

Before getting d_2 and d_2', we produce d_1 and d_1' from d and d' by applying rule α successively to each application of (R1) in d and d', so that in d_1 (d_1') each application of (R1) binds a distinct variable, distinct from all other variables in d_1 (d_1') and distinct from all variables in d_1' (d_1).

Then we create d_2 and d_2' from d_1 and d_1', respectively, by applying rule α successively to each variable free in each entry in d_1 (d_1') which is a wlff, to produce d_2 and d_2' in which no variable free in any entry in d_2 (d_2') which is a wlff, is free in any other entry in d_2 (d_2') which is a wlff, or is bound anywhere in d_2 (d_2'), or occurs anywhere in d_2' (d_2).

Now we begin to try to transform d_2 into d_2'. List the applications of (R3) in d_2 in some order: $ap_1, \ldots, ap_n$. Let ap_z', $1 \leqslant z \leqslant n$, be the corresponding application of (R3) in d_2'. That is, ap_z and ap_z' occur at the same structural place in d_2 and d_2' for all $1 \leqslant z \leqslant n$. Let the variables free in the conclusion of ap_z of (R3) in d_2, reading from left to right, be $v_1^z, \ldots, v^z m_z$, $1 \leqslant z \leqslant n$, and let the variables free in the conclusion of ap_z' of (R3) in d_2' be $v_1'^z, \ldots, v'^z m_z'$, $1 \leqslant z \leqslant n$. If $m_z \neq m_z'$, for some $1 \leqslant z \leqslant n$, then no number of applications of α, β and γ will transform d_2 into d_2', and so $AC \neq A^*C^*$. So suppose that $m_z = m_z'$, $1 \leqslant z \leqslant n$. Then we produce d_3 from d_2 by working from left to right successively, through ap_1 to ap_n successively, replacing v_r^z by $v_r'^z$, for all $1 \leqslant r \leqslant m_z$ and for all $1 \leqslant z \leqslant n$.

Now apply rule β to d_3 in all possible combinations of ways. This process yields some finite number of formation trees $d_{4_1}, \ldots, d_{4_n}$, for some n, which differ at most in the order of adjacent identical quantifiers. Now work through d_{4_i}, $1 \leqslant i \leqslant n$, successively applying rule α to the conclusion of each application of (R1) in turn to replace the bound variable by the corresponding bound variable in d_2', i.e., by the variable bound in d_2' by the corresponding application of (R1) in d_2'. This yields $d_{5_1}, \ldots, d_{5_n}$, where for all $1 \leqslant i \leqslant n$, d_{5_i} comes from d_{4_i} by applications of rule α as described. It is then routine to check whether any of the d_{5_i}, $1 \leqslant i \leqslant n$ is d_2'. If one of them is, then $AC \cong A^*C^*$, and if not, not.

Section 5
Axiomatisation

The axiom schemata of LPA are as follows, f being a variable in kind $\langle x,t \rangle$ unless otherwise specified:

(A1) $A \to (C \to A)$.

(A2) $(A \to (C \to D)) \to ((A \to C) \to (A \to D))$.

(A3) $\sim \sim A \to A$.

(A4) $(\forall v)A \to A[v/u]$, where u is a variable or constant, u and v are both in the same kind, in Q, or in $\underline{E}$ and v is free for u in A.

(A5) $(\forall v)(A \to C) \to (A \to (\forall v)C)$, where v is not free in A.

(A6) $(\forall v_1) \ldots (\forall v_n)(u = v) \to (D \leftrightarrow D^*)$, where $n \geqslant 0$, u and v are both in the same kind, in Q, or in $\underline{E}$, D^* is D with one unquoted occurrence of u in D replaced by one of v and no free occurrences of variables other than $v_1, \ldots, v_n$ in v become bound in D^*.

(A7) $(\exists p)(p \wedge (\text{Max } p))$.

(A8) $(\forall p_1)((\forall p_2)(\text{Max } p_2) \to (p_2 \text{ ent } p_1)) \to (p_1 = T))$.

(A9) $((A \leftrightarrow C) = T) \to (A = C)$.

(A10) $(u \neq v) \to ((u \neq v) = T)$, where u and v are both in the same kind, in Q, or in $\underline{E}$.

(A11) $(\exists u)(u = v)$, where u and v are both in p, $\langle x,t \rangle$, or $\underline{E}$ and u is not free in v.

(A12) $(\exists f)(\forall v_1) \ldots (\forall v_n)(fv_1 \ldots v_n = A)$, where $v_1, \ldots, v_n$ are distinct variables in kinds $a_1, \ldots, a_n$ respectively, f is in kind $\langle a_1, \ldots, a_n \rangle$, A is a wff and f is not free in A.

(A13a) $(AC = A^*C^*)$, where $AC \simeq A^*C^*$.

(A13b) $(AC \neq A^*C^*)$, where $AC \not\simeq A^*C^*$.

(A14) $(qe_1 = qe_2) \to (e_1 = e_2)$, where e_1 and e_2 are in $\underline{E}$.

(A15) $(\forall f)(\forall x)(\forall t)(\forall p)(\Diamond Gxtpf \to (\Diamond(Gxtpf \wedge fxt) \wedge \Diamond(Gxtpf \wedge \sim fxt)))$, where G is B, L or W.

(A16) $(\forall x)(\forall t)(\forall p_1)(\forall p_2)(\forall f)((Wxtp_1f \wedge Wxtp_2f) \to (Wxtp_1f = Wxtp_2f))$.

(A17) $(\forall f)(\Diamond(\exists x)(\exists t)(\exists p)(Bxtpf \vee Lxtpf \vee Wxtpf) \to (\forall x)(\forall t)(\forall x_1)(\forall t_1)(((x \neq x_1) \vee (t \neq t_1)) \to (\Diamond(fxt \wedge fx_1t_1) \wedge \Diamond(fxt \wedge \sim fx_1t_1))))$.

(A18) $(\forall x)(\forall t)((\exists p)WxtpqAC \to \sim (\exists p)Wxtpq((p_1 = (\exists v_1) \ldots (\exists v_n)A) \vee (\sim p_1 = (\exists v_1 \ldots (\exists v_n)A),p_1))$, where $v_1, \ldots, v_n$ are the variables free in A and p_1 is a variable.

(A19) $(\forall x)(\forall t)(\forall p)(\forall f)(\Diamond Wxtpf \to \sim \Diamond(Bxtpf \vee Lxtpf))$.

(A20) $(\forall q)(\forall x)(\forall t)(\forall p)(\forall e)(Gxtpqe \to (q = q))$, where G is B, L or W.

(A21) $(\forall x)(\forall t)(\forall p)(GxtpqA^*A^* \to (p = A))$, where A^*A^* is in $\underline{E}$ by formation rule (R2), A differs from A^* only in that all unquoted occurrences of i_x and i_t in A* are replaced by occurrences of x and t respectively, and G is either B or L.

(A22) $(\forall x)(\forall t)(\forall p) \sim WxtpqAA$, where AA is in $\underline{E}$ be formation rule (R2).

(A23) $(\forall x)(\forall t)(\sim(\exists v_1)\ldots(\exists v_n)A \to (\forall p)(Wxtpq\bar{A}*C* \to (p = F)))$, where A*C* is in $\underline{E}$ by formation rule (R3), $v_1, \ldots, v_n$ are exactly the variables occurring free in A*C*, x and t are not among $v_1, \ldots, v_n$ and A* and C* differ from A and C respectively only in that all unquoted occurrences of i_x and i_t in A* and C* are replaced by occurrences of x and t respectively in A and C.

(A24) $(\forall x)(\forall t)((\exists v_1)\ldots(\exists v_n)A \to (\forall p)(WxtpqA*C* \to (\exists v_1)\ldots(\exists v_n)(A \wedge (p = C))))$, where A*C* is as above and p is not among $v_1, \ldots, v_n$.

(A25) $(\forall x)(\forall t)((\exists p)WxtpqA*C* \to (\exists p)Bxtpq((\exists v_1)\ldots(\exists v_n)A*, (\exists v_1)\ldots(\exists v_n)A*)$, where A*C*, $v_1, \ldots, v_n$ are as in (A23).

(A26) $(\forall x)(\forall t)(\forall p) \sim GxtpqAC$, where AC is in $\underline{E}$ by formation rule (R3) and G is either B or L.

(A27) $(\forall x)(\forall t)(\forall p_1)(\forall p_2)(\forall f)((Gxtp_1 f \wedge Gxtp_2 f) \to (p_1 = p_2))$, where G is either B or L.

We write $\vdash A$ with the usual meaning. The rule schemata of LPA are as follows:

(R1)   If $\vdash A$ and $\vdash A \to C$, then $\vdash C$.

(R2)   If $\vdash A$, then $\vdash (\forall v)A$, where v is a variable.

(R3)   If $\vdash A \leftrightarrow C$, then $\vdash fA \leftrightarrow fC$, where f is any variable in kind $\langle p \rangle$.

Change of bound variables, the deduction theorem, universal instantiation of the forms $\vdash (\forall v)A \to \check{S}[v/C]A|$ and $\vdash (\forall f)A \to \check{S}[fv_1 \ldots v_n/C]A|$ (where f is in kind $\langle a_1, \ldots, a_n \rangle$, $v_1, \ldots, v_n$ are distinct variables in kinds $a_1, \ldots, a_n$ respectively, and C is in kind p), and that indiscernibility implies co-extensionality can all be proved. The proofs are long and uninteresting. We omit them.

Section 6
Semantics

We now give an interpretation to the language LPA.

For all $AC \in \underline{E}$, let $[AC] = \{DD* \in \underline{E}: AC \simeq DD*)$. Let $E = \{[AC]: AC \in \underline{E}\} \cup \chi$, where χ is a set. Let I, W and $\bar{T}$ be non-empty sets such that E, I, W and T are pairwise disjoint. Let D_0 be a non-empty set of $\mathscr{P}(W)$.

Where x and y are sets, we write $y[x]$ instead of the more familiar y^x. We define $\underline{D}$ as a set X such that

(a) $I, T, D_0 \in X$,
(b) if $a_1, \ldots, a_n$ are in X, for $n \in N$, so is a non-empty subset of $D_0[a_1 x \ldots, x_n]$, where $D_0[a_1 x \ldots x a_n]$ is the set of unary functions that map n-tuples in $a_1 x \ldots x a_n$ and perhaps other things into D_0,
(c) nothing else is in X.

Let $\underline{D} \uparrow D_0[IxT]$ denote the subset of $D_0[IxT]$ in $\underline{D}$. Let $D = \underline{D} \cup \Sigma$, where $\Sigma \subseteq (\underline{D} \uparrow D_0[IxT])[E]$ such that Σ contains at least one function which is one–one on equivalence classes $[AC]$ and where $(\underline{D} \uparrow D_0[IxT])[E]$ is the set of functions mapping E and nothing else into $\underline{D} \uparrow D_0[IxT]$, D is called a *structure* on W, I, T, E.

A *model structure* (MS) is a sextuple $S = \langle W, I, T, E, D, O \rangle$, where W, I, T, E, D are as above and

(a) $O \in W$,
(b) $|D \uparrow D_0[IxT]| \geqslant \omega$, i.e., the subset of $D_0[IxT]$ in D is at least countably infinite,
(c) D_0 is a group (in particular, $\emptyset \in D_0$; if $X \in D_0$, so is $W - X \, (= \bar{X})$; and D_0 is closed under finite union),
(d) $D \uparrow D_0[a_1 x \ldots x a_n] \cap D \uparrow D_0[b_1 x \ldots x b_m] = \emptyset$ when $\langle a_1, \ldots, a_n \rangle \neq \langle b_1, \ldots, b_m \rangle$, $m, n \in N$,
(e) there exist $\underline{B}, \underline{L}$ and $\underline{W}$ in $D \uparrow D_0[IxTxD_0 x(D_0[IxT])]$ which satisfy
   (i) $(\forall x \in I)(\forall t \in T)(\forall p_1 \in D_0)(\forall p_2 \in D_0)(\forall f \in D \uparrow D_0[IxT])$ (if $\underline{W}\langle x,t, p_1,f \rangle \cap \underline{W}\langle x,t,p_2,f \rangle \neq \emptyset$, then $\underline{W}\langle x,t,p_1,f \rangle = \underline{W}\langle x,t,p_2,f \rangle$),
   (ii) $(\forall x \in I)(\forall t \in T)(\forall p \in D_0)(\forall f \in D \uparrow \bar{D}_0[IxT])$ (if $\underline{B}\langle x,t,p,f \rangle \neq \emptyset$, then $\underline{B}\langle x,t,p,f \rangle \cap f\langle x,t \rangle \neq \emptyset$ and $\underline{B}\langle x,t,p,f \rangle \cap \bar{f}\langle x,t \rangle \neq \emptyset$),
   (iii) like (ii) with $\underline{L}$ for $\underline{B}$.
   (iv) like (ii) with $\overline{W}$ for $\overline{B}$,
   (v)   if for some $x \in I$, $t \in T$, $p \in D_0$, and $f \in D \uparrow D_0[IxT]$, $\underline{B}\langle x,t,p,f \rangle \cup \underline{L}\langle x,t,p,f \rangle \cup \underline{W}\langle x,t,p,f \rangle \neq \emptyset$, then $(\forall x \in I)(\forall x_1 \in I)(\forall t \in T)(\forall t_1 \in \bar{T})$ (if $x \neq x_1$ or $t \neq t_1$, then $f\langle x,t \rangle \cap f\langle x_1,t_1 \rangle \neq \emptyset$ and $f\langle x,t \rangle \cap \bar{f}\langle x_1,t_1 \rangle \neq \emptyset$),
   (vi) $(\forall x \in I)(\forall t \in T)(\forall p \in D_0)(\forall f \in D \uparrow D_0[IxT])$ (if $\underline{W}\langle x,t,p,f \rangle \neq \emptyset$, then $\underline{B}\langle x,t,p,f \rangle \cup \underline{L}\langle x,t,p,f \rangle = \emptyset$) and
   (vii) $(\forall x \in I)(\forall t \in T)(\forall f \in D \uparrow D_0[IxT])(\forall p_1 \in D_0)(\forall p_2 \in D_0)$ (if $\underline{G}\langle x,t,p_1,f \rangle \cap \underline{G}\langle x,t,p_2,f \rangle \neq \emptyset$, then $p_1 = p_2$), for $\underline{G} = \underline{B}$ or $\underline{G} = \underline{L}$.

A model structure is *atomic* iff $(\forall w \in W)(\{w\} \in D_0)$. $\underline{S}$ is *WITE based* iff D is defined as above on W, I, T, E. $\underline{S}$ is *normal* iff

(a) $(\forall w \in W)(\forall X \in Z)(\forall Y \in Z)$ (if $(\forall d \in D \uparrow D_0[Z])$ $(w \in d(X)$ iff $w \in d(Y))$, then $X = Y$ for all $Z \in \underline{D}$),

(b) $(\forall x,y \in E)$ (if $(\forall d \in Q)(d(x) = d(y))$, then $x = y$), where Q is $D \uparrow ((D_0[IxT])[E])$,

(c) $(\forall x,y \in Q)$ (if $(\forall z \in E)(xz = yz)$, then $x = y$).

Let f be a function which maps (perhaps all) expressions into D. f *validates* wff A iff $O \in f(A)$.

Where $\underline{S}$ is a MS which is *WITE* based, a *q-valuation on* $\underline{S}$ is a function V from a (possibly null) term extension of LPA and its kinds, $\underline{Q}$, and $\underline{E}$ into $\underline{S}$ such that

(a) for kinds x,t,p, $V(x) = I$, $V(t) = T$, and $V(p) = D_0$,

(b) for kind $\langle a_1,\ldots, a_n\rangle$, $n \in N$, $V(\langle a_1,\ldots, a_n\rangle) = D \uparrow D_0[V(a_1)x \ldots xV(a_n)]$, $V(\underline{E}) = E$, and $V(Q) = Q$,

(c) $V(v) \in V(a)$, where v is atomic in kind a,

(d) $V(q) \in Q$ such that $V(q)$ is one–one on $\{[AC] : AC \in \underline{E}\}$, and $V(q) \in Q$ for all $q \in Q$,

(e) $V(AC) = [AC]$, for all $AC \in \underline{E}$, and $V(e) \in E$ for all $e \in \underline{E}$,

(f) $V(\rightarrow) \in D \uparrow D_0[D_0xD_0]$, such that $(\forall p_1,p_2 \in D_0)(V(\rightarrow)\langle p_1,p_2\rangle = \overline{p_1} \cup p_2)$,

(g) $V(B) = \underline{B}$, $V(L) = \underline{L}$, and $V(W) = \underline{W}$.

(h) $V(fv_1 \ldots v_n) = V(\overline{f})\langle V(v_1), \ldots, V(\overline{v_n})\rangle$.

By a *variant* of V we mean a function which agrees with V except perhaps on some specified part of LPA. By the notation $V'[v_1,\ldots, v_n]$ or $V[v_1,\ldots, v_n]$, we mean a function which agrees with V except perhaps at $v_1,\ldots, v_n$. By $V[\alpha_1/\beta_1, \ldots, \alpha_n/\beta_n]$ we mean a function which agrees with V in general, but assigns β_i to α_i, $1 \leqslant i \leqslant n$. That is, $V[\alpha_i/\beta_i](\alpha_i) = \beta_i$, $1 \leqslant i \leqslant n$ and otherwise $V[\alpha_i/\beta_i](\gamma) = V(\gamma)$ for all atomic expressions γ in LPA distinct from $\alpha_1, \ldots, \alpha_n$.

(i) $V((\forall v)A) = \cap V'[v](A) = \{w \in W : w \in V'[v](A)$ for all $V'[v]\}$.

A q-valuation V is a *valuation*, on the same MS, iff the following conditions are met:

(j) for all $V'[x,t,p]$, if AC is in $\underline{E}$ by (R3) of the formation rules, $V'[x,t,p](GxtpqAC) = \varnothing$, where G is B or L,

(k) for all $V'[x,t,p]$, if A*A* is as in (A21), $V'[x,t,p](GxtpqA*A*) \subseteq V'[x,t,p](p = A)$, where G is B or L,

(l)   for all $V'[x,t,p]$, if AC is in $\underline{E}$ by (R2) of the formation rules, $V'[x,t,p](WxtpqAC) = \varnothing$,

(m)   for all $V'[x,t]$, if $A*C*, v_1, \ldots, v_n$ are as in (A23), $V'[x,t](\sim(\exists v_1)) \ldots (\exists v_n)A) \subseteq \cap_p V'[x,t,p](WxtpqA*C* \rightarrow (p = F))$,

(n)   for all $V'[x,t]$, if $A*C*, v_1, \ldots, v_n, p$ are as in (A24), $V'[x,t]((\exists v_1) \ldots (\exists v_n)A) \subseteq \cap_p V'[x,t,p](WxtpqA*C* \rightarrow (\exists v_1) \ldots (\exists v_n)(A \wedge (p = C)))$,

(o)   for all $e_1, e_2 \in \underline{E}$, $V(qe_1 = qe_2) \subseteq V(e_1 = e_2)$,

(p)   for all $V'[x,t]$, if $A*C*, v_i, \ldots, v_n$ are as in (A25), $V'[x,t]((\exists p)WxtpqA*C*) \subseteq V'[x,t]((\exists p)BxtpqA*A*)$, where $A*$ is $(\exists v_1) \ldots (\exists v_n)A$,

(q)   for all $V'[x,t,p,q,e]$, if $V'[x,t,p,q,e](Gxtpqe) \neq \varnothing$, then $V'[x,t,p,q,e](q) = V'[x,t,p,q,e](q)$, where G is B, L or W,

(r)   for all $V'[x,t]$, if $v_1, \ldots, v_n, p_1$ are as in (A18), $V'[x,t]((\exists p)WxtpqAC) \cap V'[x,t]((\exists p)Wxtpq((p_1 = (\exists v_1) \ldots (\exists v_n)A) \vee (\sim p_1 = (\exists v_1) \ldots (\exists v_n)A), p_1)) = \varnothing$.

A *model* is a pair $\langle \underline{S}, V \rangle$, where $\underline{S}$ is a normal atomic MS and V is a valuation on $\underline{S}$ which validates the universal closure of all instances of (A11) and (A12). Where $\underline{S}$ is a MS, $\langle \underline{S}, V \rangle$ is a model and A is a wff, we say that A is *true on* $\langle \underline{S}, V \rangle$, written $\langle \underline{S}, V \rangle | \vdash A$, iff $O \in V(A)$, where $\underline{S} = \langle W, I, T, E, D, O \rangle$. A is *true on* $\underline{S}$, written $\underline{S} | \vdash A$, iff for all V such that $\langle \underline{S}, V \rangle$ is a model, $\langle \underline{S} \rangle | \vdash A$. A is *valid*, written $| \vdash A$, iff for all MS $\underline{S}$, $\underline{S} | \vdash A$.

Lemma 1. Where u is a well-formed expression (a wfe) in LPA and υ is a set of variables which do not occur free in u and V and V' are valuations which agree except perhaps on υ then $V(u) = V'(u)$.

Proof: By induction on the complexity of u. (If u is in $\underline{E}$, the result is immediate.)

Let $\langle \underline{S}, V \rangle$ be a model in which $\underline{S}$ is *WITE* based.

Lemma 2. $V(F) = \varnothing$.

Proof: $V(F) = V((\forall p)p) = \{w \in W: \text{for any } V[p], w \in V[p](p)\} = Y$. Let $V(p) = X$. D_0 is closed under complementation, and so $\bar{X} \in D_0$. Let $V'[p](p) = \bar{X}$. If $w \in Y$, then $w \in X$ and $w \in \bar{X}$, which is absurd. Hence $Y = \varnothing$.

Lemma 3. $V(\sim A) = \overline{V(A)}$.

Lemma 4. $\langle \underline{S}, V \rangle | \vdash \sim A$ iff $\langle \underline{S}, V \rangle | \nvdash A$.

Lemma 5. $\langle \underline{S}, V \rangle | \vdash A \leftrightarrow C$ iff ($\langle \underline{S}, V \rangle | \vdash A$ iff $\langle \underline{S}, V \rangle | \vdash C$).

Lemma 6. $\langle \underline{S}, V \rangle | \vdash A \wedge C$ iff ($\langle \underline{S}, V \rangle | \vdash A$ and $\langle \underline{S}, V \rangle | \vdash C$).

Lemma 7. $\langle \underline{S},V \rangle \,|\vdash (A \text{ ent } C)$ iff $V(A) \subseteq V(C)$.

Lemma 8. $\langle \underline{S},V \rangle \,|\vdash u = v$ iff $V(u) = V(v)$, for u and v in any kind, in $\underline{E}$, or in Q.

Proof: Let u and v be in kind b, and f be in $\langle b \rangle$ and free in neither u nor v. Assume that $O \in V((\forall f)(fu \leftrightarrow fv))$ (i.e., $V(u = v)$). Then for all $d \in V(\langle b \rangle)$, $O \in V[f/d](fu \leftrightarrow fv)$ and, by Lemma 5, $O \in V[f/d](fu)$ iff $O \in V[f/d](fv)$. Thus $O \in V[f/d](f)V(u)$ iff $O \in V[f/d](f)V(v)$, since f is not free in u or v. Hence for all $d \in V(\langle b \rangle)$, $O \in d(V(u))$ iff $O \in d(V(v))$. By normality, $V(u) = V(v)$. The converse is clear. The cases where u and v are in $\underline{E}$ and in Q have arguments that proceed similarly.

Lemma 9. Where e is any non-atomic expression in E, $V(e) = V'(e)$ for all valuations V and V' on all MS.

Section 7
Soundness

Soundness theorem. If $\vdash A$, then $|\vdash A$.

Proof: We adopt the usual inductive strategy and begin by showing the axiom schemata valid. Let $\langle \underline{S},V \rangle$ be a model. The soundness of (A1) through (A5) follows at once from the definition of models.

ad (A6): $(\forall v_1) \ldots (\forall v_n)(u = v) \rightarrow (D \leftrightarrow D^*)$, where no variables free in $(\forall v_1)$ $\ldots (\forall v_n)(u = v)$ are bound in v in D^* where it replaces u, and v is not in a well-formed part of D^* of the form qu_1 where it replaces u unless v is the initial q or u_1 and u and v are atomic, i.e., v is unquoted in D^* where it replaces u and it replaces an unquoted occurrence of u.

We suppose that, where V' is a variant of V, $O \in V'((\forall v_1) \ldots (\forall v_n)(u = v))$ and will show that $O \in V'(D \leftrightarrow D^*)$. We argue inductively on the complexity of D. Let d be the wff-derivation with the conclusion D. Let d^* be the result of deleting from d all entries above conclusions of applications of (R2) and (R3) of the formation rules and all entries above the entry o which becomes the entry of u to be replaced. We truncate the derivations in light of the fact that $V'[v_1, \ldots, v_n](u) = V'[v_1, \ldots, v_n](v)$ for all $V'[v_1, \ldots, v_n]$ and the condition that the replaced occurrence of u be unquoted. Note that the entry o in question is in d^* since v is not quoted where it replaces u, and so the occurrence of u is not in the non-atomic part of D in $\underline{E}$.

Let d' be the corresponding truncated wff-derivation with conclusion D^* and G be the obvious one–one map from d^* onto d'. We will show that for all entries c in d*, $V'(c) = V'(G(c))$. We argue inductively from the uppermost entries in d* down. We say that an entry c in d* (d') is of depth n iff the longest branch in the part of d* (d') with conclusion c is of length n.

Let V* be an arbitrary $V'[v_1, \ldots, v_n]$.

Basis step: If c in d* is of depth 0, then $V'(c) = V'(G(c))$, since $c = G(c)$ unless c is o. In the latter case, from the supposition that $O \in V'((\forall v_1) \ldots (\forall v_n)(u = v))$, it follows that $O \in V*(u = v)$ for all V*, and hence, by Lemma 2.6.8, that $V*(u) = V*(v)$. This completes the basis step.

Inductive hypothesis: For all entries c in d* of depth $<n$ and all V*, suppose that $V*(c) = V*(G(c))$.

Inductive step: Suppose that c is of depth n. Consider cases according to whether (c) is the conclusion of formation rule (R1), (R4) or (R5).

Case (R1). The conclusion is $(\forall u_1)A$. The case in which $A = G(A)$ is trivial, so we turn to the other case. Here we must have u as a well-formed part of A and v as the corresponding well-formed part of G(A). By IH, $V*(A) = V*(G(A))$, for all V*. Hence $V*((\forall u_1)A) = V*(G((\forall u_1)A))$.

Case (R4). c is qe for some $q \in Q$ and $e \in \underline{E}$. *Ex hypothesi*, $V*(e) = V*(G(c))$ and $V*(q) = V*(G(q))$. Hence $V*(qe) = V*(q)V*(e) = V*(G(q))V*(G(e)) = V*(G(q)G(e)) = V*(G(qe))$ for all V*.

Case (R5). Like the preceding, using IH. $V*(gu_1 \ldots u_n) = V*(g)\langle V*(u_1), \ldots, V*(u_n)\rangle = V*(G(g))\langle V*(G(u_1)), \ldots, V*(G(u_n))\rangle = V*(G(g)(G(u_1), \ldots, G(u_n))) = V*(G(gu_1 \ldots u_n))$ as required.

This completes the inductive step.

Hence $V'(D) = V'(G(D)) = V'(D*)$, so $O \in V'(D)$ iff $O \in V'(D*)$ and finally $O \in V'(D \leftrightarrow D*)$ as required.

ad (A7): By atomicity, $\{O\} \in D_0$. Let $V' = V[p/\{O\}]$. It suffices to show that $O \in V'(p \wedge (\text{Max } p))$. By Lemma 2.6.6 and the definition of Max p, we must show that (1) $O \in V'(p)$, (2) $O \in V'(p \neq F)$ and (3) $O \in V'((\forall p_1)((p \text{ ent } p_1) \vee (p \text{ ent } \sim p_1)))$. (1) and (2) are immediate. For (3), assume that $X \in D_0$. Then either $\{O\} \subseteq X$ or $\{O\} \subseteq \bar{X}$. In the first case $V'[p_1/X](p) \subseteq V'[p_1/X](p_1)$. In the latter case, by Lemma 2.6.3, $V'[p_1/X](p) \subseteq V'[p_1/X](\sim p_1)$. In either case, $O \in V'[p_1/X]((p \text{ ent } p_1) \vee (p \text{ ent } \sim p_1))$ by Lemma 2.6.7.

ad (A8): Assume that $X \in D_0$ and $O \in V[p_1/X]((\forall p_2)((\text{Max } p_2) \rightarrow (p_2 \text{ ent } p_1)))$. Then from atomicity it follows that $O \in V[p_1/X, p_2/Y](\text{Max } p_2)$ iff $Y = \{y\}$, for some $y \in W$. Since, by atomicity again, $\{y\} \in D_0$ for all $y \in W$, by Lemma 2.6.7, for any such $y \in W$, $y \in X$. Hence $V[p_1/X](p_1) = V[p_1/X](T)$, and so $O \in V[p_1/X](p_1 = T)$.

ad (A9): If $O \in V((A \leftrightarrow C) = T)$, then by Lemma 2.6.8 $V(A \leftrightarrow C) = V(T)$. Then for all $w \in W$, $w \in V(A \leftrightarrow C)$, since $V(T) = W$ by Lemmas 2.6.2 and 2.6.3. Applying Lemma 2.6.8 again, we have $V(A) = V(C)$, i.e., $O \in V(A = C)$.

ad (A10): Suppose that $O \in V(u \neq v)$. Then by Lemmas 2.6.3 and 2.6.8, $V(u) \neq V(v)$. It suffices to show that for all $w \in W$, $w \in V(u \neq v)$. There are three cases, depending upon whether u and v are in some kind a, in $\underline{E}$ or in Q.

Case 1. u and v are in kind a. Assume that $w \in W$. By normality, there is a $g \in D\!\uparrow D_0[a]$ such that $w \in g(V(u))$ iff $w \notin g(V(v))$. Suppose, *per absurdum*, that $w \in V(u = v)$. Then $w \in V((\forall f)(fu \leftrightarrow fv))$ for some f in kind $\langle a \rangle$ that is not free in u or v. Then $w \in V[f](fu \leftrightarrow fv)$ for all $V[f]$. Then $w \in V[f](fu)$ iff $w \in V[f](fv)$, i.e., $w \in V[f](f)V(u)$ iff $w \in V[f](f)V(v)$, since f is not free in u or v. So $w \in g(V(u))$ iff $w \in g(V(v))$, since for some $V[f]$, $V[f](f) = g$.

Case 2. u and v are in $\underline{E}$. Let $w \in W$. By normality there is a $g \in D\!\uparrow((D_0[I\!xT])[E])$ such that $g(V(u)) \neq g(V(v))$. By normality again there is an $h \in D\!\uparrow D_0[D_0[I\!xT]]$ such that $w \in h(g(V(u)))$ iff $w \notin h(g(V(v)))$. Suppose, *per absurdum*, that $w \in V(u = v)$. Then $w \in V((\forall q)(qu = qv))$ and so $w \in V((\forall f)(\forall q)(fqu \leftrightarrow fqv))$, where f is in kind $\langle\langle x,t \rangle\rangle$. So $w \in V[f]((\forall q)(fqu \leftrightarrow fqv))$ for all $V[f]$ and then $w \in V[f,q](fqu \leftrightarrow fqv)$ for all $V[f,q]$. Hence $w \in V[f,q](fqu)$ iff $w \in V[f,q](fqv)$. But for some $V[f,q]$, $V[f,q](f) = h$ and $V[f,q](q) = g$, and we have the desired contradiction.

Case 3. u and v are in Q. Let $w \in W$. By normality there is an o in E such that $V(u)o \neq V(v)o$. By normality again there is an $h \in D\!\uparrow D_0[D_0[I\!xT]]$ such that $w \in h(V(u)o)$ iff $w \notin h(V(v)o)$. Suppose, *per absurdum*, that $w \in V(u = v)$. This case proceeds to a contradiction as in the preceding.

This completes the argument for the soundness of (A10).

(A11) and (A12) are sound by the definition of a model.

ad (A13): Both (A13a) and (A13b) are sound by construction and the definition of a valuation.

(A14) is sound by condition (o) of the definition of a valuation. (A15), (A16), (A17), (A19) and (A27) are all sound by condition (e) of the definition of a model structure. (A18), (A20), (A21), (A22), (A23), (A24), (A25) and (A26) are sound by, respectively, conditions (r), (q), (k), (l), (m), (n), (p) and (j) of the definition of a valuation.

This completes the base case of the soundness theorem.

For the inductive step we must show that the rules are valid. We do so with the aid of the following easily verified

Lemma: Where S is $\langle W,I,T,E,D,O \rangle$, $w \in W$, and $\underline{S}_w$ is $\langle W,I,T,E,D,w \rangle$, $\langle \underline{S},V \rangle$ is a model iff $\langle \underline{S}_w,V \rangle$ is a model.

Of the transformation rules only (R3) requires argument. Assume that $|\vdash (A \leftrightarrow C)$ and, *per impossibile*, that $|\nvdash (fA \leftrightarrow fC)$. Then there is some model $\langle \underline{S},V \rangle$ such that $\langle \underline{S},V \rangle |\nvdash (fA \leftrightarrow fC)$, i.e., $O \notin V(fA \leftrightarrow fC)$. So $O \in V(fA)$ and $O \notin V(fC)$, or $O \notin V(fA)$ and $O \in V(fC)$. In either case $V(A) \neq V(C)$. Thus for some $w \in W$, $w \in V(A)$ and $w \notin V(C)$, or $w \notin V(A)$ and $w \in V(C)$. By the lemma above, $\langle \underline{S}_w, V \rangle$ is a model and $\langle \underline{S}_w, V \rangle \not\Vdash (A \leftrightarrow C)$, contrary to the assumption that $\Vdash (A \leftrightarrow C)$.

This completes the proof of the soundness theorem.

Section 8
Completeness

We now establish the *completeness theorem*: if K is a consistent set of LPA wffs, then there is a model as described above in which every member of K is true.

A set K of wffs is *inconsistent* iff $K \vdash F$ and *consistent* iff it is not inconsistent. Where L is any (term) extension of LPA, a set of L-wffs K′ is *complete* with respect to L just in case for any L-wff A either $A \in K'$ or $\sim A \in K'$. Where L is an extension of LPA, K′ is *universal* (in L) iff for each L-wff of the form $\sim (\forall v)A$ such that $K' \vdash \sim (\forall v)A$, $K' \vdash \sim A[v/c]$, where c is some constant in L appropriate for v.

Lemma 10. If K is a consistent set of LPA wffs, there is a consistent, complete, universal extension K′ of K in some language L which extends LPA.

Proof: We adopt the strategy of Hughes and Cresswell [1], pp. 159–60. Let C′ be a denumerably infinite set of disjoint denumerably infinite sequences of constants foreign to LPA. Let $S = \{X: X \text{ is a kind in LPA}\} \cup \{Q, \underline{E}\}$, and let f be a one–one function from S into C′. Then we define $C\alpha$ as $f(\alpha)$ for all $\alpha \in S$.

Assume that K is a consistent set of LPA wffs. We construct a suitable K′ in L which is the language resulting from adding the elements of $C\alpha$ to α in LPA for all $\alpha \in S$ and forming all possible expressions according to the formation axiom schemata and rules given earlier.

By a U-wff with respect to c, we mean any wff of the form $\sim (\forall v)A \to \sim A[v/c]$, where c is some constant appropriate for v and A some wff in L. If two U-wffs differ only concerning the constants with respect to which they are U-wffs, we say that they are of the same U-form. A set of wffs J has the U-property just in case J contains a U-wff for every U-form.

Assume that all the U-forms can be put in some standard order indexed by ω. We expand K to a set J with the U-property by constructing the following sets of sentences:

$$J_0 = K$$
$$J_{n+1} = J_n \cup \{\sim (\forall v)A_{n+1} \to \sim A_{n+1}[v/c]\}, \text{ where the form of } \sim (\forall v)A_{n+1} \to$$

$\sim A_{n+1}[v/c]$ is the $n+1$st U-form, v and c are in α in S, and c is the first constant in $C\alpha$ which does not occur in any wff J_n or in A_{n+1}.

$J =$ the union of the J_n, $n \in \omega$.

J is consistent. If not, there is some finite subset J' of J and so of some J_i, $i \in \omega$, such that $J' \vdash F$. $J' \nsubseteq J_0$ since $J_0 = K$ and $K \nvdash F$. Let J_n be the first J_i which contains J'. $J_n = J_{n-1} \cup \{ \sim (\forall v)A_n \to \sim A_n[v/c]\}$. Clearly $\sim (\forall v)A_n \to \sim A_n[v/c] \in J'$. Since $J' \vdash F$, there is a sequence of wffs, $C_1, \ldots, C_m$, $C_m = F$ where for all C_i, $1 \leqslant i \leqslant m$, either C_i is J', C_i is an instance of an axiom scheme or C_i follows by (R1) or (R2) from an earlier C_k. Let u be a variable in α which does not occur in any C_i, or in any member of J'. Let $C'_1, \ldots, C'_m$ be the sequence of wffs which results from replacing each occurrence of c by u in all C_i, $1 \leqslant i \leqslant m$, i.e., $C'_i = C_i[c/u]$. Let $J'' = \{C : C \in J' \cap J_{n-1}\}$ $\cup \{ \sim (\forall v)A_n \to \sim A_n[v/c][c/u]\}$. Clearly, for each C'_i, $1 \leqslant i \leqslant m$, $J'' \vdash C'_i$ and $C'_m = C_m$. Hence J'' is inconsistent while $C(= \{C : C \in J' \cap J_{n-1}\})$ is consistent. Therefore $C \vdash \sim (\sim (\forall v)A_n \to \sim A_n[v/c][c/u])$, i.e., $C \vdash \sim (\forall v)A_n \wedge A_n[v/c][c/u]$. Then $C \vdash \sim (\forall v)A_n$ and $C \vdash A_n[v/c][c/u]$. But since c and u are not in any member of C or in A_n, we can easily derive $C \vdash (\forall u)A_n[v/c][c/u]$. But since $C \vdash (\forall u)A_n[v/c][c/u] \leftrightarrow (\forall v)A_n[v/c][c/u]$ $[u/v]$ (and the right-hand side is $(\forall v)A_n$), we have $C \vdash (\forall v)A_n$, which is absurd since C is consistent and $C \vdash \sim (\forall v)A_n$. Hence J is consistent.

We may expand J to a consistent, complete, universal set K' by the usual Lindenbaum construction. Since K' is closed under (R1) and has the U-property, K' is universal.

Since $K' \vdash (\exists p)(p \wedge (\text{Max } p))$ and K' is universal, $K' \vdash p_0 \wedge (\text{Max } p_0)$ for some constant p_0 in kind p. By universal instantiation and the completeness of K', for each wff A in L, $K' \vdash (p_0 \text{ ent } A)$ or $K' \vdash (p_0 \text{ ent } \sim A)$.

For each constant p_0 in kind p in L such that $K' \vdash \text{Max } p_0$, let $X(p_0)$ be the set $\{A : A$ is a wff in L and $K' \vdash (p_0 \text{ ent } A)\}$. We may now begin to construct model $\underline{SK'}$ as follows:

Let $\overline{W^*} = \{X(p) : p$ is a constant in L and $K' \vdash \text{Max } p\}$. Let $O = X(p_0)$, where $K' \vdash p_0 \wedge (\text{Max } p_0)$. There is such a unique p_0, as noted above, since if $K' \vdash p_0 \wedge (\text{Max } p_0)$ and $K' \vdash p_c \wedge (\text{Max } p_c)$, it is easy to show that $K' \vdash (p_0 \leftrightarrow p_c) = T$, and so $K' \vdash (p_0 = p_c)$, using (A9). Hence $X(p_0) = X(p_c)$.

We next define I^*, T^* and E^*. We begin by partitioning some expressions into equivalence classes. Where c is any expression in L, in Q, $\underline{E}$, or any kind save p, which contains no free variables, let $[c] = \{c' : c' \in L$ and $K' \vdash (c = c')$ and c' contains no free variables$\}$. Then form

$I^* = \{[c] : c$ is a constant in L in kind x$\}$

$T^* = \{[c] : c$ is a constant in L in kind t$\}$

$E^* = \{[e] : e$ is in $\underline{E}$ in L and not a variable$\}$.

Where A is any wff in L containing no free variables, let $V^*(A) = \{w : w \in W$ and $A \in w\}$ and let $D_0 = \{V^*(A) : A$ is a closed wff in L$\}$.

For any kind $\langle a_1, \ldots, a_n \rangle$, the notation $D_0[a_1 x \ldots x a_n]$ is defined inductively as before. The notation $(D_0[I^* x T^*])[E^*]$ is also defined as before.

(1) Where c is any expression in L in kind $\langle a_1, \ldots, a_n \rangle$ containing no free variables, and $c_1, \ldots, c_n$ are expressions in the appropriate kinds for $v_1, \ldots, v_n$ respectively also containing no free variables, $V^*(c)$ is defined to be a function in $D_0[a_1 x \ldots x a_n]$ such that $V^*(c)([c]) = V^*(T)$, for all c' in L for which $[c']$ exists if $K' \vdash (c \neq c')$, then $V^*(c)([c']) = V^*(F)$, and finally $V^*(c)\langle V^*(c_1), \ldots, V^*(c_n)\rangle = V^*(cc_1 \ldots c_n)$. (This defines $V^*(qe)$ where qe contains no free variables.)
(2) Where q is any constant in Q in L, $V^*(q)$ is a function in $(D_0[I^* x T^*])[E^*]$ such that all non-variables e in $\underline{E}$ in L, $V^*(q)(V^*(e)) = V(qe)$.
(3) We may now extend V^* to kinds and to Q and $\underline{E}$:
   (a) $V^*(x) = I^*$,
   (b) $V^*(t) = T^*$,
   (c) $V^*(p) = D_0$,
   (d) $V^*(\langle a_1, \ldots, a_n \rangle) = \{V^*(c) : c$ is in kind $\langle a_1, \ldots, a_n \rangle$ in L and contains no free variables$\}$,
   (e) $V^*(\underline{E}) = E^*$,
   (f) $V^*(\underline{q}) = \{V^*(q) : q$ is a constant in Q in L$\}$.
(4) We extend V^*, as defined above, to variables in L in such a way that
   (a) $V^*(v) \in V^*(\alpha)$ for all variables v in L in α in S,
   (b) If v is a variable in kind $\langle a_1, \ldots, a_n \rangle$, $c_1, \ldots, c_n$ are in $a_1, \ldots,$ a_n respectively and $V^*(c_i)$ is defined for all $1 \leqslant i \leqslant n$, then $V^*(v)\langle V^*(c_1), \ldots, V^*(c_n)\rangle = V^*(vc_1 \ldots c_n)$,
   (c) If either q in Q or e in $\underline{E}$ is a variable, c_1 is in x and c_2 in t, and $V^*(c_1)$ and $V^*(c_2)$ are defined, then $V^*(qe)\langle V^*(c_1), V^*(c_2)\rangle = V^*(qec_1c_2)$,
   (d) If q is in Q and e in $\underline{E}$, then $V^*(q)(V^*(e)) = V^*(qe)$,
   (e) If A is a wff in L, v is a variable, $v_1, \ldots, v_n$ are all the variables other than v that are free in A, $c_1, \ldots, c_n$ are constants such that for all $1 \leqslant i \leqslant n$, $V^*(v_i) = V^*(c_i)$, then $V^*((\forall v)A) = V^*((\forall v)A[v_1/c_1] \ldots [v_n/c_n])$.

Let $D^* = \cup\{V^*(\alpha) : \alpha$ is a kind or Q$\}$. Finally we set $\underline{S}^* = \langle W^*, I^*, T^*,$ $E^*, D^*, O \rangle$. Now we wish to show that $\langle S, V \rangle$ as defined is a model. We check the necessary properties in the order they were presented.

It is immediate from the construction that W^*, I^* and T^* are non-empty sets such that E^*, I^*, W^* and T^* are pairwise disjoint. Therefore, I^* suffices as I and T^* as T. It is also immediate that E^* suffices as E. We now show that S^* is a model structure by checking the necessary conditions in turn.

D^* is constructed from $\underline{D^*} = \cup\{V^*(\alpha): \alpha \text{ is a kind}\}$. Concerning $\underline{D^*}$, we must show

(a) $I^*, D_0, T^* \in \underline{D^*}$ where $D_0 = V^*(\text{kind p})$. This is immediate.
(b) If $a_1, \ldots, a_n$ are in $\underline{D^*}$ for $n \in N$, so are a non-empty subset of $D_0[a_1 x \ldots x a_n]$, where $D_0[a_1 x \ldots x a_n]$ is the set of unary functions mapping n-tuples in $a_1 x \ldots x a_n$ and perhaps other things into D_0. Observe that if $a_1, \ldots, a_n$ are in $\underline{D^*}$, then for some not necessarily distinct kinds $\beta_1, \ldots, \beta_n$, $V^*(\beta_i) = a_i$, $1 \leq i \leq n$. But then $V^*(\langle \beta_1, \ldots, \beta_n \rangle)$ will be the required non-empty subset of $D_0[a_1 x \ldots x a_n]$, since there are constants in L in kind $\langle \beta_1, \ldots, \beta_n \rangle$, and where c is such a constant $V^*(c)$ has the required properties, as inspection of the definition of V^* will verify (in particular clauses (1) and (4)). This completes the argument for (b).

Note that $D^* = \underline{D^*} \cup V^*(Q)$. We will now show that there is at least one function which is one–one on equivalence classes of non-atomic wlffs and that all functions in $V^*(Q)$ map E^* and nothing else into $D^* \uparrow D_0[I^* x T^*]$. The latter is immediate from clauses (2) and (4) in the definition of V^*. The former is satisfied by $V^*(q)$: $V^*(q)$ is one–one on equivalence classes in $\underline{E}$, for otherwise for some distinct classes $[e]$ and $[e']$ we would have $V^*(q)[e] = V^*(q)[e']$. But then $V^*(qe) = V^*(qe')$, and so $K' \vdash (qe = qe')$ by clause (1) in the definition of V^*. Then by (A14), $K' \vdash (e = e')$, which makes $[e] = [e']$ contrary to hypothesis.

Turning now from the definition of D^* to the definition of model structures, we check the clauses in turn.

ad (a): $(O \in W^*)$. By construction $O = V^*(p_0)$, where $K' \vdash p_0 \wedge (\text{Max } p_0)$.

ad (b): Given the above comments on $V^*(q)$, it suffices to show that there are infinitely many distinct equivalence classes of wlffs in order to show that $D^* \uparrow D_0[I^* x T^*]$ is infinite. Since there are infinitely many constants in L and two wlffs differ in meaning if they contain different constants, the result follows, inasmuch as wlffs with different meanings are in distinct equivalence classes.

ad (c): D_0 is a group, since L contains classical propositional logic and $V^*(F) = \emptyset \in D_0$. In particular, if $X \in D_0$, X is $V^*(A)$ for some wff A, and then $V^*(\sim A) = W^* - X$ by construction, and so $\bar{X} \in D_0$. D_0 is closed under finite union, since if $X, Y \in D_0$, then for some wffs A and C, $V^*(A) = X$ and $V^*(C) = Y$, and so using the properties of maximal propositions, $V^*(A \vee C) = X \cup Y$.

ad (d): If $\langle a_1, \ldots, a_n \rangle$ and $\langle b_1, \ldots, b_m \rangle$ are distinct kinds, then $D^* \uparrow D_0[a_1 x$

$\ldots xa_n] \cup D^* \uparrow D_0[b_1 x \ldots xb_m] = \varnothing$, since the domains of in the two classes are disjoint, as an easy inductive argument verifies.

ad (e): This condition is satisfied, since $V^*(B)$, $V^*(L)$ and $V^*(W)$ will suffice as the elements of $V^*(\langle x,t,p,\langle x,t\rangle\rangle)$ with the required properties, as a review of (A15), (A16), (A17), (A19) and (A27) will verify.

Clearly $\underline{S^*}$ is $W^*I^*T^*E^*$ based. We now show that $\underline{S^*}$ is atomic and normal.

For the former, it suffices to show that for all constants p in L such that $K' \vdash \mathrm{Max}\,p$, $V^*(p) = \{X(p)\}$. By definition $V^*(p) = \{w \in W^*: p \in w\}$. Clearly, $K' \vdash (p\,\mathrm{ent}\,p)$. Hence $p \in X(p)$, and so $X(p) \in V^*(p)$. Conversely, suppose that $X(p') \in V^*(p)$. Then $K' \vdash (p'\,\mathrm{ent}\,p)$. Since $K' \vdash \mathrm{Max}\,p$, $K' \vdash (p\,\mathrm{ent}\,p') \vee (p\,\mathrm{ent}\,{\sim}p')$. By the previous uniqueness argument, $K' \nvdash (p\,\mathrm{ent}\,{\sim}p')$. Since K' is complete, it follows that $K' \vdash (p\,\mathrm{ent}\,p')$. Hence $K' \vdash (p = p')$. Then $X(p) = X(p')$ and $V^*(p) = \{X(p)\}$.

Before turning to normality, we establish some lemmas.

Lemma 1. If $K' \vdash (A = C)$, then $V^*(A) = V^*(C)$ for all wffs A and C in L.
Proof: Assume that $K' \vdash (A = C)$. Then for any $X(p)$ in W^*, $X(p) \in V^*(A)$ iff $K' \vdash (p\,\mathrm{ent}\,A)$ iff, by (A6), $K' \vdash (p\,\mathrm{ent}\,C)$ iff $X(p) \in V^*(C)$.

Lemma 2. If $K' \vdash (A = T)$ and $K' \vdash \mathrm{Max}\,p$, then $K' \vdash (p\,\mathrm{ent}\,A)$, for any sentence A and constant p in L.

To establish that $\underline{S^*}$ is normal, we deal in turn with the clauses in the definition of normality.

ad (a): Suppose that α and β are in $V^*(a)$ for some kind a, for all $\gamma \in V^*(\langle a\rangle)$ $\gamma(\alpha) = \gamma(\beta)$, and, *per impossibile*, that $\alpha \neq \beta$. Then, by the definition of V^* and the construction of $\underline{S^*}$, there are constants c and c' in kind a in L such that $\alpha = V^*(c)$ and $\beta = \overline{V^*(c')}$ and $K' \vdash (c \neq c')$. Since K' is universal and complete, $K' \vdash g(c) \leftrightarrow {\sim}g(c')$ for some constant g in kind $\langle a\rangle$. Then $V^*(g) \in V^*(\langle a\rangle)$, and so for some γ in $V^*(\langle a\rangle)$, we have $\gamma(\alpha) = V^*(g)\langle V^*(c)\rangle = V^*(gc) \neq V^*(gc') = V^*(g)\langle V^*(c')\rangle = \gamma(\beta)$, contrary to the assumption that for all γ, $\gamma(\alpha) = \gamma(\beta)$.

ad (b): Reason as above, assuming now that α and β are in $V^*(\underline{E})$ and instead of considering $V^*(\langle a\rangle)$, consider $V^*(Q)$.

ad (c): (c) is analogous. Assume that α and β are in $V^*(Q)$ and, instead of $V(\langle a\rangle)$ and indiscernibility, consider $V^*(\underline{E})$ and co-extensionality.

This establishes that $\underline{S^*}$ is in fact a normal, atomic model structure. Turning to V^*, we begin by showing that it is a function. To demonstrate this, it chiefly suffices to show that V^* is uniquely defined on wffs beginning with a quantifier. So suppose that A and A' are wffs that are alike except that A has an occurrence of a constant c where A' has an occurrence of a constant c', where $V^*(c) = V^*(c')$. Then $V^*(A) = V^*(A')$.

Next we establish that V* is a q-valuation on $\underline{S^*}$. (a) through (h) are immediate. Turning to (i), we establish

Lemma 3. For all constants p in kind p in L, if $K' \vdash \text{Max p}$, then $X(p)$ is universal, consistent and complete.

Proof: The only non-trivial claim is that of universality. To prove universality, we suppose that $K' \vdash (p \text{ ent } A[v/c])$ for all constants c of the appropriate sort and $K' \vdash \text{Max p}$, where p is a constant in kind p in L. Then using quantifier logic, the theorem $\vdash (\forall v)(\forall f)(fv_1 \ldots v_n \leftrightarrow fu_1 \ldots u_n) \rightarrow (\forall f)(fv_1^* \ldots v_n^* \leftrightarrow fu_1^* \ldots u_n^*)$ [where both $v_1, \ldots, v_n$ and $u_1, \ldots, u_n$ are in kinds $a_1, \ldots, a_n$ respectively, f is in kind $\langle a_1, \ldots, a_n \rangle$, f does not occur free in any v_i or u_i, f is not v, and for $1 \leqslant i \leqslant n$, v_i and u_i are in kind a_i, $v_i^* (u_i^*)$ is v_i $(u_i$, respectively) if a_i is not p and is $(\forall v)v_i$ $((\forall v)u_i)$ otherwise, and v is free in v_i or u_i only if a_i is p], and the universality of K', we may derive $K' \vdash (\forall v)(p \text{ ent } A)$ and then $K' \vdash (p \text{ ent } (\forall v)A)$. The details are routine and left to the reader.

Lemma 4. If v is a variable in L, then for any wff $(\forall v)A$ in L and any $X(p)$ in W^*, $X(p) \in V^*((\forall v)A)$ iff $X(p) \in V^*(A[v/c])$ for all c appropriate for v containing no free variables.

The proof is straightforward using Lemma 3 and the definitions of $X(p)$ and (Max p). Then, arguing by induction on the complexity of wffs and using Lemma 4 for the quantifier case, we establish

Lemma 5. For any variable v in L, any closed expression c in L of the same sort as v and any wff A, if $V^*(c) = \alpha$, then $V^*(A[v/c]) = V^*[v/\alpha](A)$.

Using these last two lemmas, we finally derive

Lemma 6. Where v is any variable in L, A any L-wff, and $X(p)$ any element of W^*, $X(p) \in V^*((\forall v)A)$ iff $X(p) \in V[v/\alpha](A)$ for all α in $V^*(a)$, where a is a kind, q, or $\underline{E}$, and v is in a.

So V* does satisfy condition (i) and is hence a q-valuation.

We now proceed to verify that V* is a valuation on $\underline{S^*}$.

Conditions (j) through (r) on valuations are satisfied since all $w \in W^*$ contain all instances of (A26), (A21), (A22), (A23), (A24), (A14), (A25), (A20) and (A18) respectively. It remains to show that V* satisfies the universal closure of all instances of (A11) and (A12). This follows from the fact that K' contains a wffs and

Lemma 7. $K' = O$.

Proof: Recall that $O = X(p)$, where $K' \vdash (p \wedge (\text{Max p}))$. It suffices to show that $A \in K'$ iff $K' \vdash (p \text{ ent } A)$ for all wffs A in L. If $A \in K'$, then $K' \vdash A$. Hence

$K' \vdash (p \to A)$. If $K' \vdash (p \text{ ent } \sim A)$, then $K' \vdash (p \to (A \land \sim A))$, and so $K' \vdash \sim p$ and K' is not consistent. For the converse, if $K' \vdash (p \text{ ent } A)$, then $K' \vdash A$. Then by the completeness of K', $A \in K'$.

Completing the whole argument, we have

Lemma 8. For all wffs $A \in K'$, $\langle \underline{S^*}, V \rangle \, | \vdash A$.

Proof: We show that if $A \in K'$, then $O \in V^*(A)$. But by Lemma 7, if $A \in K'$, then $A \in O$ and so $O \in \{w \in W^* : A \in w\} = V^*(A)$.

Hence LPA is complete.

Appendix 3

Sign

Section 1
Formation of the language LS

The set of *kinds* of the language of word-strings LS is the smallest set X containing s and p and such that whenever $a_1, \ldots, a_n$ are in X, so is $\langle a_1, \ldots, a_n \rangle$, $n \in N$. There are also *categories* E_s and Q_s (dropping the subscript when convenient). Each kind and category is also called a *qkind*. In each kind is a denumerably infinite number of variables and scattered constants. In E_s and Q_s there is a denumerably infinite number of variables and constants of every finite type ≥ 2. $\forall$ and variables and constants in every kind are of type 1. All qkinds are pairwise disjoint, as are types within each category.

We have the following axioms and formation rules:

(A1) $\langle c, a, i, \{c\}, \{c\} \rangle$, where c is atomic in qkind a of type i,

(A2) $\langle \forall, \forall, 1, \{\forall\}, \{\forall\} \rangle$,

(R1) $\langle A, p, i, F, Q \rangle, \langle v, a, j, \{v\}, \{v\} \rangle \Rightarrow \langle \forall v A, p, \text{Max}(i,j), F - \{v\}, Q \cup \{\forall v A\} \rangle$, where v is a variable,

(R2) $\langle q, Q_s, i, \{q\}, \{q\} \rangle, \langle c, E_s, j, \emptyset, \emptyset \rangle \Rightarrow \langle qcq, s, i, \{q\}, \{qcq, q\} \rangle$, provided $i > j$,

(R3) $\langle q, Q_s, i, \{q\}, \{q\} \rangle, \langle e, E_s, i, \{e\}, \{e\} \rangle \Rightarrow \langle qeq, s, i, \{q,e\}, \{q,e,qeq\} \rangle$,

(R4) $\langle c, a, i, \{c\}, \{c\} \rangle \Rightarrow \langle c, E_s, i, \emptyset, \emptyset \rangle$, provided the premise is an axiom.

(R5) $\langle f, \langle a_1, \ldots, a_n \rangle, 1, F_0, Q_0 \rangle, \langle c_1, a_1, i_1, F_1, Q_1 \rangle, \ldots, \langle c_n, a_n, i_n, F_n, Q_n \rangle \Rightarrow \langle fc_1 \ldots c_n, p, \text{Max}(i_1, \ldots, i_n).[\cup F_i, 0 \leq i \leq n], [\cup Q_i, 0 \leq i \leq n] \cup \{fc_1 \ldots c_n\} \rangle$,

(R6) $\langle c_1, E_s, i, \emptyset, \emptyset \rangle, \langle c_2, E_s, j, \emptyset, \emptyset \rangle \Rightarrow \langle c_1 c_2, E_s, \text{Max}(i,j), \emptyset, \emptyset \rangle$.

Then we have formation trees in the obvious way. There are complex well-formed expressions in kinds p and s. Things in p are *wffs*, in s are *strings*. There are also complex expressions in E_s; we call them *ekspressions*. A *kwind* is any qkind other than E_s. We wish to show that anything in any kwind is unambiguous: it is in at most one kwind, and that in at most one way. As a preliminary, we need a criterion of identity for formation trees. The criterion is given recursively:

Formation trees t and t_1 are identical (write '$t = t_1$') if

(1) they have as conclusion the same sequence of syntactic atoms and they both put it in E_s, or
(2) if $t_2 = t_1$ and t^* is t with some part of t which is t_1 replaced by t_2, then $t^* = t$, or
(3) if $t = t_1$ and $t_1 = t_2$, then $t = t_2$.

A *grove* $[t]$ is such that $[t] = \{t_1 : t_1 = t\}$. All trees in a grove have as conclusion the same sequence of syntactic atoms which they put in the same qkind and type.

Lemma: Each expression is the conclusion of at most one grove which puts it in a kwind and type.

Proof: We argue inductively on the length of expressions (i.e., number of syntactic atoms) to show (i) each expression is put in a kwind and type by at most one grove and (ii) no expression is in the same kwind as one of its initial parts.

The basis step is immediate since kwinds are disjoint and there are no initial parts. The inductive hypothesis (IH) is as expected for all expressions of length $\leqslant n$. For the inductive step we pick an expression c of length $n + 1$ and pursue a reductio argument for claim (i). We proceed to consider cases depending on the last rule applied in trees representing two groves putting c in some kwind(s). For claim (ii) the possibilities are that c and an initial part of it are in p or s. We consider cases again depending on the last rule applied in a formation tree to get a reductio argument. We leave the details to the reader.

Our use of metavariables is as earlier for LPA with the addition of q^m and e^m being metavariables for things in Q_s or E_s, respectively of type m. Constants of the language include $\rightarrow[p,p]$, $S[s,s]$, q^m for all $m \geqslant 2$, $C[s,s,s]$, and syncategorematic $\forall$. v *occurs unquoted* in u just when there is a formation tree t with conclusion $\langle u,a,i,F,Q \rangle$ for some kwind a, with $v \in Q$. v *occurs quoted* in u just when there is a formation three t with conclusion $\langle u,a,i,F,q \rangle$ for some kwind a, $v \notin Q$, and v occurs in u. v *occurs free* in u just when there is a t as above with conclusion $\langle u,a,i,F,Q \rangle$ with $v \in F$. v *occurs bound* in u just when there is a t as above with v occurring in u, v is unquoted, and $v \notin F$.

We leave it to the reader to convince himself that these notions of 'free' and 'unquoted' and 'bound' and 'quoted' are effective, and that we can effectively decide whether a given occurrence of v in u is free and unquoted, or what. We have several defined constants as earlier in the description of LPA. In particular 'v*[u/v]' denotes the result of replacing all free occurrences of u in v* by v whenever u and v are of the same qkind and type. As earlier, we write $\rightarrow$ infixed and use frequent parentheses. The definitions of 'F', '$\sim$', etc., we take over from LPA. Identity is defined as indiscernibility for kinds. '(A = B)' $=_{df}$ '($\forall$v)(fA $\leftrightarrow$ fB)'; where u and v are in kind a other than p and f is in kind $\langle a \rangle$, '(u = v)' $=_{df}$ '($\forall$f)(fu = fv)'. Where q and q' are in Q_s of type m, '(q = q')' $=_{df}$ '($\forall e^m$)(qe^{m}q = q'e^{m}q')'; and where e and e' are in E_s of type $\leqslant$m, '(e $=_m$ e')' $=_{df}$ '($\forall q^m$)(q^{m}eq^m = q^{m}e'q^m)'. When u and v are in some unspecified qkind, we may write u $=_i$ v to encompass the three cases above. When $=_i$ is undefined, the notation stands for u = v.

We also have the following definitions:

'n' = '$q^3 e_n^2 q^3$', where 'e_n' is the nth variable in E_s of type 2, n $\in$ N.

'(Func f)' $=_{df}$ '($\forall$u)($\forall$v)(fuv $\rightarrow$ ($\forall v_1$)(fuv$_1$ $\rightarrow$ (v = v$_1$)))', where f is in kind $\langle a,b \rangle$, u is in a, and v and v$_1$ are in b.

'(1–1 f)' $=_{df}$ '(Func f) $\wedge$ ($\forall$u)($\forall$v)(fuv $\rightarrow$ ($\forall u_1$)(fu$_1$v $\rightarrow$ (u = u$_1$)))', where u and u$_1$ are in the same kind.

'(finite s)' $=_{df}$ '[($\exists s_1$)Sss$_1$ $\wedge$ $\sim$($\exists$f)((1–1 f) $\wedge$ ($\forall s_2$)($\forall s_1$)(fs$_2$s$_1$ $\rightarrow$ ((Ss$_1$s $\vee$ (s$_1$ = s)) $\wedge$ Ss$_2$s)) $\wedge$ ($\forall s_1$)((Ss$_1$s $\vee$ (s$_1$ = s)) $\rightarrow$ ($\exists s_2$)fs$_2$s$_1$) $\wedge$ ($\forall s_1$)(Ss$_1$s $\rightarrow$ ($\exists s_2$)fs$_1$s$_2$))]', where f is in kind $\langle s,s \rangle$.

We now turn to the matter of substitution.

The *scope of an occurrence* o *of ($\forall$v) in expression* c* is the shortest expression in c* beginning immediately to the right of o and being in kind p, as well as o itself. An occurrence o of variable v in expression c* is *free for variable* u iff o is unquoted, u and v are in the same qkind and type and o is not within the scope of an occurrence of $\forall$u in c*. *The scope of an occurrence* o *of* f[a_1,..., a_n] in expression c* depends on how o functions in c*. o may be applied to n arguments in the appropriate kinds to produce an expression in kind p, or not. In the former case, the scope of o is the n arguments; in the latter case, the scope of o is null. Where a variable f in kind $\langle a_1, \ldots, a_n \rangle$ occurs free in expression c*, an *innermost free occurrence of* f *in* c* is a free occurrence of f which has no free occurrences of f in its scope. In the formation rules, a variable or constant f in kind $\langle a_1, \ldots, a_n \rangle$ can occur as a premise of a formation rule either as the left-most premise of an application of (R5) or not. In the former case, we say that it occurs as an *operator*; in the latter case, as an *argument*.

Where $a_1, \ldots, a_n$ are such that for 1 $\leqslant$ i $\leqslant$ n, a_i is a qkind, $v_1, \ldots, v_n$ are distinct atoms in $a_1, \ldots, a_n$ respectively, $C_1, \ldots, C_n$ are expressions in $a_1, \ldots,$

a_n respectively such that for all $1 \leqslant i \leqslant n$, if a_i is Q or E, then C_i is of the same type as v_i, and atomic, or C_i is of a lower type than v_i, and A is a wff, $\underline{S}[v_1 \ldots v_n/C_1 \ldots C_n] A\,|$ is the result of simultaneously replacing each free occurrence of v_i in A by C_i, $1 \leqslant i \leqslant n$.

Where a is a kind, or Q or E, v is an atomic in a, C is an expression in a and A is a wff, $\check{S}[v/c] A\,|$ is A unless no part of A of the form $(\forall v)D$ in kind p contains a free occurrence of v where u is free in C, in which case it is $\underline{S}[v/C] A\,|$.

$\check{S}[fv_1 \ldots v_n/C] A\,|$ is defined as in Appendix 2, section 3.

Section 2
Axiomatisation

We carry over from LPA in Appendix 2 axiom schemata (A1) through (A12) and the three inference rules, *mutatis mutandis*. For reference we repeat these here:

(A1) $A \to (C \to A)$.

(A2) $(A \to (C \to D)) \to ((A \to C) \to (A \to D))$.

(A3) $\sim \sim A \to A$.

(A4) $(\forall v A \to A[v/u])$, where u is a variable or constant, v and u are both in the same qkind and type, and v is free for u in A.

(A5) $(\forall v)(A \to C) \to (A \to (\forall v)C)$, where v is not free in A.

(A6) $(\forall v_1) \ldots (\forall v_n)(u =_i v) \to (D \leftrightarrow D^*)$, where $n \geqslant 0$, u and v are in the same qkind, and D^* is D with one unquoted occurrence of u replaced by an occurrence of v, provided no free occurrences of variables other than $v_1, \ldots, v_n$ in v becomes bound in D^* and provided, of course, that D^* is well-formed.

(A7) $(\exists p)(p \wedge (\text{Max } p))$.

(A8) $(\forall p_1)((\forall p_1)((\text{Max } p_2) \to (p_2 \text{ ent } p_1)) \to (p_1 = T))$.

(A9) $((A \leftrightarrow C) = T) \to (A = C)$.

(A10) $(u \neq_i v) \to ((u \neq_i v) = T)$, where u and v are in the same qkind.

(A11a) $(\exists u)(u = v)$, where u and v are in p or s and u is not free in v.

(A11b) $(\exists e)(e =_i e')$, where e is in type i, e' is in type k, $i \geqslant k$, and e does not occur in e'.

(A12) $(\exists f)(\forall v_1) \ldots (\forall v_n)(fv_1 \ldots v_n = A)$, where $n \in N$, $v_1, \ldots, v_n$ are distinct variables in kinds $a_1, \ldots, a_n$ respectively, f is in kind $\langle a_1, \ldots, a_n \rangle$, A is in kind p, and f is not free in A.

(A13) $(\forall f)(fq^m a_1 \ldots a_n q^m \leftrightarrow fq^r a_1 \ldots a_n q^r)$, where f is in kind $\langle s \rangle$, $2 \leqslant m,r$, $n \in N$ and the type of all $a_1, \ldots, a_n < m,r$.

(A14) $Sn(n+1)$, for all $n \in N$.

(A15)　　$\sim(\exists s)Ss1$.

(A16)　　$(\forall s)(\forall s_1)(\forall s_2)((Sss_1 \wedge Ss_1s_2) \to Sss_2)$.

(A17)　　$\sim(\exists s)(\exists s_1)(Ss_1s \wedge Sss_1)$.

(A18)　　$\sim(\exists s)(Sis \wedge Ss(i+1))$, for all $i \in N$.

(A19)　　$(\forall s)((\exists s_3)Sss_3 \to (\exists s_1)(Sss_1 \wedge \sim(\exists s_2)(Sss_2 \wedge Ss_2s_1)))$.

(A20)　　$(\forall s)((\exists s_3)Ss_3s \to (\exists s_1)(Ss_1s \wedge \sim(\exists s_2)(Ss_1s_2 \wedge Ss_2s)))$.

(A21)　　$(\forall s)(\forall s_1)(Sss_1 \to (S1s \vee (1 = s)))$.

(A22)　　$(\forall s)(\forall s_1)(\forall s_2)((Sss_1 \wedge Sss_2) \to (Ss_1s_2 \vee (Ss_2s_1 \vee (s_1 = s_2))))$.

(A23)　　$(\forall s)(\exists s_1)Css_11$.

(A24)　　$Cq^m a_1 \ldots a_n q^m q^m a_i q^m i$, where all a_i are atomic and of lower type than m, $1 \leqslant i \leqslant n$.

(A25)　　$(\forall s)(\forall s_1) \sim Csqa_1 \ldots a_n q s_1$, where $n > 1$.

(A26)　　$(\forall s_1)(\forall s_2)(\forall s_3)(Cs_1s_2s_3 \to (\text{finite } s_3))$.

(A27)　　$(\forall s)(\exists s_1)(\forall s_2)(\sim Css_2s_1 \wedge (\exists s_3)Ss_1s_3)$.

(A28)　　$(\forall s)(\forall s_1)(\forall s_2)(Css_1s_2 \to (\forall s_3)(Ss_3s_2 \to (\exists s_4)Css_4s_3))$.

(A29)　　$(\forall s)(\forall s_1)(\forall s_2)(\forall s_3)((Css_2s_1 \wedge Css_3s_1) \to (s_2 = s_3))$.

(A30)　　$(\forall s)(\forall s_1)((\forall s_2)(\forall s_3)(Css_2s_3 \leftrightarrow Cs_1s_2s_3) \leftrightarrow (s = s_1))$.

(A31)　　$(e \neq_i e')$, where e is not e', e and e' are in E_s, and the type of e and e' is less than i.

(R1)　　If $\vdash A$ and $\vdash A \to C$, then $\vdash C$.

(R2)　　If $\vdash A$, then $\vdash (\forall v)A$, where v is a variable.

(R3)　　If $\vdash A \leftrightarrow C$, then $\vdash fA \leftrightarrow fC$, where f is any variable in kind $\langle p \rangle$.

We have as theorems the following: change of bound variables, deduction theorem, universal instantiation of the forms $\vdash (\forall v)A \to \check{S}[v/C] A$ | [where v is any qkind, provided that if v is in E, then C is not of a higher type than v] and $\vdash (\forall f)A \to \check{S}[fv_1 \ldots v_n/C] A$ | [where f is in kind $\langle a_1, \ldots, a_n \rangle$, $v_1, \ldots, v_n$ are distinct variables in kinds $a_1, \ldots, a_n$ respectively, and C is in kind p], and that indiscernibility implies co-extensionality.

Section 3
Semantics

We now give an interpretation to the language LS.

Let $E = \{a : a$ is a the first member of the conclusion of an application of formation rule (R4) or (R6)$\}$. W and S are sets such that S is denumerably infinite and $\mathscr{P}(W)$, S and E are pairwise disjoint. D_0 is a non-empty subset of $\mathscr{P}(W)$. Q is a set disjoint from $\mathscr{P}(W)$, S and E.

We define $\underline{D}$ as a set X such that

(a) $S, D_0 \in X$,

(b) if $a_1, \ldots, a_n \in X$, so is a non-empty subset of $D_0[a_1 x \ldots x a_n]$, where $D_0[a_x \ldots x a_n]$ is the set of unary functions that map n-tuples in $a_1 x \ldots x a_n$ and perhaps other things into D_0 (see Appendix 2),

(c) nothing else is in X.

Let E^m be E restricted to type m or less. $D = Q \cup E \cup D$, where Q is a set of partial functions from E into S such that for all $m \geqslant 2$, there is at least one function $f^m : E^m \to S$, where f^m on E^m is one–one and $\mathrm{dom}(f^m) = E^m$. We name one such f^m, $\underline{q}^m$.

A model structure (MS) is a sextuple M of the form $\langle S, Q, E, W, D, O \rangle$, where S, Q, E, W and D are as above, and the following conditions (a) through (u) are satisfied:

(a) $\{O\} \in D_0$.

(b) D_0 is a group under the obvious set theoretic operations and relation.

(c) There exist $\underline{S}$ and $\underline{C}$ such that $\underline{S} \in D \uparrow D_0[SxS]$ and $\underline{C} \in D \uparrow D_0[SxSxS]$.

Where e_i^2 is the ith variable of type 2 in E_s, for $i \in N$, we write i for $\underline{q}^3(e_i^2)$.

(d) $(\forall f \in D \uparrow D_0[S])(f(\underline{q}^m(b_1 \ldots b_n)) = f(\underline{q}^r(b_1 \ldots b_n)))$ for all $b_1 \ldots b_n$ in E, all $m, r \in N$ such that the type of $b_1 \ldots b_n$ is $< m, r$.

(e) $O \in \underline{S}(i, i+1)$, for all $i \in N$.

(f) $O \notin \underline{S}(s, 1)$, for all $s \in S$.

(g) $(\forall x)(\forall y)(\forall z)(\underline{S}(x,y) \cap \underline{S}(y,z) \subseteq \underline{S}(x,z))$.

(h) $(\forall x)(\forall y)(\underline{S}(x,y) \cap \underline{S}(y,x) = \varnothing)$.

(i) $(\forall x)(\underline{S}(i,x) \cap \underline{S}(x,i+1) = \varnothing)$, for all $i \in N$.

(j) $(\forall x)((\cup z \in S)\underline{S}(x,z) \subseteq (\cup y \in S)(\underline{S}(x,y) \cap \overline{(\cup z \in S)(\underline{S}(x,z) \cap \underline{S}(z,y))}))$.

(k) $(\forall x)((\cup z \in S)\underline{S}(z,x) \subseteq (\cup y \in S)(\underline{S}(y,x) \cap \overline{(\cup z \in S)(\underline{S}(y,z) \cap \underline{S}(z,x))}))$.

(l) $(\forall x)(\forall y)(O \in \underline{S}(x,y) \cap \overline{\underline{S}(1,x)}$ only if x is 1).

(m) $(\forall x)(\forall y)(\forall z)(O \in \underline{S}(x,y) \cap \underline{S}(x,z) \cap \overline{\underline{S}(y,z)} \cap \overline{\underline{S}(z,y)}$ only if y is z).

(n) $(\forall x)(\exists y)(O \in \underline{C}(x,y,1))$.

(o) $O \in \underline{C}(\underline{q}^m(a_1 \ldots a_n), \underline{q}^m(a_k), k)$, for all $1 \leqslant k \leqslant n$ and all $m \geqslant 2$, provided that all $a_1, \ldots, a_n$ are atomic in $\underline{E}$ of type $< m$.

(p) $(\forall x)(\forall y)(O \notin \underline{C}(x, \underline{q}^m(a_1 \ldots a_n), y))$, if $n > 1$.

Note that $\underline{S}$ linearly orders a subset of S, call it NS. Then it makes sense to ask whether elements of NS are finite or infinite, relative to $\underline{S}$. We may say that x is a *successor* of y if $O \in \underline{S}(y,x)$. An element c of NS is *infinite* if and only if the set of its predecessors is equinumerous with the set of predecessors of its immediate successor. Two such subsets of NS are *equinumerous* exactly when there is a function f in $D \uparrow D_0[SxS]$ such that for all $\langle x,y \rangle$ and $\langle x',y' \rangle$ in the domain of f, if $\underline{O} \in f\langle x,y \rangle$ and $\underline{O} \in f\langle x',y' \rangle$, then (1) $x = x'$ iff $y = y'$ and (2) x is a predecessor of or identical to c and y is a predecessor of or identical to the immediate successor of c. Otherwise c in NS is *finite*.

(q) $(\forall x)(\forall y)(\forall z)(O \in \underline{C}(x,y,z)$ only if z is finite relative to $\underline{S})$.

(r) $(\forall x)(\exists z)(\forall y)(O \in \underline{C}(x,y,z) \cap (\cup s \in S)\underline{S}(z,s))$.

(s) $(\forall x)(\forall y)(\forall z)(\underline{C}(x,y,z) \subseteq (\cap v \in S)(\underline{S}(v,z) \cup (\cup u \in S)\underline{C}(x,u,v)))$.

(t) $(\forall x)(\forall y)(\forall z)(\forall z_1)(O \in \underline{C}(z,x,z_1) \cap \underline{C}(z,y,z_1)$ only if x is y).

(u) $(\forall x)(\forall y)((\forall x)(\forall z_1)(O \in \underline{C}(x,z,z_1)$ iff $O \in \underline{C}(y,z,z_1))$ iff x is y).

An MS is *atomic* iff $(\forall w \in W)(\{w\} \in D_0)$. M is *SQEW-based* iff D is defined on S, Q, E, W as above. M is *normal* iff

(a) $(\forall w \in W)(\forall X \in X)(\forall Y \in X)(if (\forall d \in D \uparrow D_0[X])(w \in d(X)$ iff $w \in d(Y))$, then $X = Y$ for all $X \in D)$,

(b) $(\forall x,y \in D)(if (\forall d \in Q)(d(x) = d(y))$, then $x = y)$, where Q is as defined.

(c) $(\forall x,y \in Q)(if (\forall z \in E)(xz = yz)$, then $x = y)$.

Where M is a *SQEW*-based MS, a *valuation on M* is a function V from a (possibly null) term extension of LS, its kinds, Q, and E into M such that:

(a) For kinds p and s, $V(p) = D_0$ and $V(s) = S$; $V(Q) = \underline{Q}$; $V(E) = E$.

(b) $V(\langle a_1, \ldots, a_n \rangle) = D \uparrow D_0[V(a_1)x \ldots xV(a_n)]$.

(c) $V(v) \in V(a)$, when v is atomic in qkind a.

(d) $V(q^m) = q^m$, for $m = 2,3,4, \ldots$

(e) $V(q^m e^r q^m) = V(q^m)(e^r)$, for all $e^r \in E$, $m > r$ and all $q^m \in Q$.

(f) $V(q^m e^m q^m) = \underline{V(q^m)(V(e^m))}$, for all $e^m \in E$ and $q^m \in Q$.

(g) $V(A \rightarrow B) = \overline{V(A)} \cup V(B)$.

(h) $V(S) = \underline{S}$; $V(C) = \underline{C}$.

(i) $V(fv_1 \ldots v_n) = V(\underline{f})(\langle V(v_1), \ldots, V(v_n) \rangle)$.

(j) $V((\forall v)A) = \cap V'[v](A) = \{w \in W: w \in V'[v](A)$ for all $V'[v]\}$, where variants are defined as for LPA in Appendix 2.

We say that V *validates* A iff $O \in V(A)$. A *model* $\underline{M}$ is a pair $\langle M,V \rangle$, where M is a normal atomic MS and V is a valuation on M which validates the universal closure of all instances of (A11a), (A11b) and (A12). The definitions of *true* and *valid* are those of LPA.

We claim that LS is sound and complete with respect to the semantics presented.

Notes

CHAPTER ONE

1 We wish to acknowledge here a major debt to Nino B Cocchiarella, whose thoughts on ontological methodology have greatly influenced the approach taken in this monograph. The reader is referred to Cocchiarella's work in ontology [1]–[8].
2 Quine [2], p. 3.
3 Richard Routley [1] has also argued at length and persuasively against Quine's view.
4 Quine [2], p. 4.
5 *See* Cocchiarella [1] and [2].
6 Wittgenstein [1].
7 *See* Frege [1].
8 *See* Daniels and Freeman [4].
9 An independent property is such that it is contingent whether or not any given thing has it and whether any given thing has it is independent of whether any other thing has it.

CHAPTER TWO

1 *See* Borkowski [1] and [2].
2 *See* Bostock [1].
3 The proof that parentheses can be eliminated in this way appears in Appendix 1.
4 *See* Borkowski [2].
5 In Bostock [↑] the language has the added complexity of individual and predicate variables.
6 *See* Daniels and Freeman [2].
7 Daniels and Freeman [2] does contain an error. The language GCMFC2 does not decompose uniquely. This fault is easily remedied, however, by writing '(∀v)A' as '∀Av', as we show in Appendix 1.
8 *See* Borkowski [2] and Bostock [1].
9 We part company with Bostock when he becomes reductionist. The comprehension axioms required for standard second-order logic are, on our view, *ontological*, not logical axioms. Now Bostock might claim to reduce quantification over properties to quantification over propositions. 'With this reading of the quantifiers one might well say that all occurrences of

quantification as ordinarily understood are reduced to quantification over propositions, and one might well add that to come to a proper understanding of this we shall need to know *what propositions there are*' (p. 75). But when he says later '. . . the leading idea in my motion of a quantifier is that a quantifier can always be regarded as stating of a propositional form that certain ways of completing that form yield a true proposition. Thus the universal quantifier and the existential quantifier can certainly be regarded as stating that *all* or that *some* ways of completing the form yield a true proposition, and it is easy enough to see a numerical quantifier as stating *how many* ways of completing the form yield a true proposition' (p. 84), his ontology seems to include not only propositions, but two other basic categories—*propositional forms* and *ways of completing them*. A theory of propositions, propositional forms and ways of completing them will doubtless have comprehension axioms. So the claim that arithmetic is being represented in 'logic', rather than, say, in an ontological theory, is suspect.

10 *See* Freeman and Daniels [2].

11 In relevance, as opposed to classical, logics there may be more than one 'necessary truth', so the ' $\vee p \sim pp$ ' may 'represent' a set containing more than one proposition. An example of a logic providing for more than one such truth is found in Freeman and Daniels [3].

12 Compare the formulation of (p5) with that in Mendelson [1] and Bostock [1].

CHAPTER THREE

1 We here wish to acknowledge what any philosopher familiar with the contemporary literature concerning mental attitudes and indexicals must recognise: the importance and originality of the work of Hector-Neri Castañeda who, almost two decades ago, drew philosophers' attention to the key problems that have to be solved by anyone attempting an ontology of mind. Castañeda's own solutions to these problems are complex and proceed in a direction quite opposite to the ontology we propose here. Suffice it to say that we would not have an ontology to propose in any serious sense had not Castañeda turned his attention to mental attitudes. A list of Castañeda's writings in this area will be found in the bibliography.

2 This point is also argued for in Castañeda [4], [5] and [7], in Daniels [1], and in Perry [1].

3 The 'you yourself' here is what Castañeda terms a *quasi-indexical*. For discussion of quasi-indexicals and their importance in mental attitudes, see his [1] and [4].

4 This is also argued for in Castañeda [4], [5] and [7], and in Daniels [1].

5 *See* Castañeda [3].

6 This analysis was proposed in 1972 in Daniels [2].

7 Here we have assumed that the proposition that the archaeologist believes is the same whether he believes it via the meaning of 'I'm going to Crete' or via the meaning of 'I'm going to Atlantis', given that Crete is identical to Atlantis. Some argument is due.

Suppose that x is indiscernible from y, i.e., that $(\forall F)(Fx \leftrightarrow Fy)$, where 'F' ranges over the properties of individuals. Suppose further that the *proposition* Gx is discernible from the proposition Gy, i.e., there is some property of propositions (some 1–0 unsaturated entity), q', such that $q'Gx \wedge \sim q'Gy$. Then, by an instance of the comprehension axiom for properties of individuals, $(\exists F)(\forall X)(FX \leftrightarrow q'GX)$, there is a property that discerns x from y contrary to hypothesis. So the proposition Gx is indiscernible from the proposition Gy, i.e., $(\exists q)(qGx \leftrightarrow qGy)$, where 'q' ranges over 1–0 unsaturated entities.

Suppose that x is identical to y. Then for the reasons given earlier in section 2, x is indiscernible from y. Suppose now that the proposition Gx is not identical to the proposition Gy. We have $(\forall q)(qGx \leftrightarrow qGy)$. By instantiation we have $(Gx =_0 Gx) \leftrightarrow (Gx =_0 Gy)$, where '$=_0$' represents identity for propositions. But $Gx =_0 Gx$. So $Gx =_0 Gy$. The proposition the archaeologist believes is the same in both cases.

Two key components in this argument are (1) the notion of equivalence symbolised by '$\leftrightarrow$' and (2) the instantiation of 'q'. '$\leftrightarrow$' can be taken to symbolise any equivalence relation between propositions which obeys *modus ponens*, e.g., material equivalence in classical logic, implicational equivalence in the Anderson Belnap system R, etc. As regards instantiation, we will have it in any appropriate system that has the comprehension axiom $(\exists q)(\forall p)(qp \leftrightarrow A)$ where A is any wff in which 'q' does not occur free.

8 This term is used in Belnap and Steel [1], which contains a very extensive and useful bibliography on the theory of questions and answers.

9 The introduction of the distinction between propositions and meanings (appearances, guises) may bring to mind Kaplan's [1] distinction between *content* and *character*. Indeed, at first blush there do seem to be similarities. But there are important differences as well. On his side Kaplan is attempting to provide a *semantics* for sentences containing demonstratives. Our concern, however, is to provide a place for mental attitudes within an ontologically ideal language. Kaplan's contents are *somewhat* like our propositions, although his emphasis is almost entirely semantical and his propositions have a temporal dimension ours lack. For us, on the other hand, propositions are no more and no less values of sentential variables. Furthermore, as we argue in the next section, there is reason to take meanings (appearances, guises) to be properties of individuals at times, and this we do. Characters on Kaplan's account are not, at least in any obvious way, properties of individuals at times. But the difference between Kaplan and ourselves in objectives and approach does not seem to allow much of an enlightening comparison to be made between his two categories and ours.

10 It might be expected, perhaps, that a brain state would turn out to be the physical correlate of such a property.

11 We draw attention to a connection between the presuppositional aspect of wondering concerning individuals and existence. Most of the time when we wonder, say, which face cards in the deck are missing, we have not only the presuppositional belief that there are face cards in the deck, but the belief that there exist face cards in the deck. The presupposition of existence occurs frequently. But not always. I may wonder which Olympic gods are more powerful than which without believing that there exist Olympic gods. And I do believe there are Olympic gods. Indeed, I can name some—Zeus, Mercury, Apollo etc.

12 Daniels [3], pp. 45–6.

13 This definition of a world proposition is almost that suggested in Prior [1], p. 80. We refer the reader to Prior [1], especially pp. 77–82 for a further discussion of maximal propositions.

CHAPTER FOUR

1 The relationship between token-making properties and the properties that are symbol-types can be seen to clarify much of what E H Gombrich [1] says concerning representation and realism in art. Consider two toilet doors in a restaurant, side by side, one with a stick figure of a man on it, the other with a stick figure of a woman on it. We point to the figures and say 'That's a man there, and that's a woman', despite the fact that the one isn't literally a man and the other isn't literally a woman. Yet in this example we cannot point to an area which contains the figures and say in the same sense 'That's a space in which the man is standing to the right of the woman'.

In art, sometimes a figure that is metaphorically a dove will *represent* the Holy Ghost, a figure that is metaphorically an old bearded man will represent God and a figure that is metaphorically a young man will represent Adam. The Holy Ghost is not literally thought to be a dove and God not literally thought to be a man. Yet Adam is literally thought to be a man. In this kind of representation a quality that is a symbol-type need not represent a thing that has that quality literally. Gombrich can be interpreted as saying late Egyptian wall-relief is like this.

In Greek art, however, an art work is, metaphorically, a space, and the metaphorical men, women, flora, fauna and other things in that metaphorical space have metaphorical spatial relations to each other. This metaphorical space, in Greek art, represents a literal space, and each metaphorical spatial quality which functions as symbol-type, e.g., *being a man standing to the left of the woman wearing the shawl*, represents its literal correlate in the literal space or spaces represented.

So Michelangelo's *Creation* can be taken two ways. The painting is, first, metaphorically a space containing a bearded old man reaching down to touch a young man; as such it may (perhaps wrongly) be taken in the Greek way as representing a scene in which a bearded old man is reaching down to touch a young man. Indeed, I have seen a parody of the painting in which the young man has a cigarette in his hand and the old man a Zippo lighter. This slight change forces a Greek interpretation of the picture.

But in the Michelangelo painting, the metaphorical bearded old man represents God, the metaphorical young man represents Adam and the metaphorical touching from a superior position represents creation. Taken in this second Egyptian way, the painting says nothing about the spatial relationships between God and Adam.

2 We take it that one way or another the words of utterances *must* connect to mental attitudes and to their relata—minds, times, propositions and guises. Mental attitudes at bottom provide the impetus for the use of signs. In our characterisation of communicative acts we try to stay true to this insight and to add no more detail than it seems to require. In particular we do not even mention *the meaning of words*, which, we take it, may have meanings in many, many ways. It is our intention to try to keep our ontological characterisation of the lines of connection between signs and mental attitudes as abstract and as far from the controversies as to whether and how words have meaning as possible. For those with a desire to take the plunge into the messy thick of things Putnam [1] serves as a fine introduction.

APPENDIX 1

1 A few words are appropriate concerning this axiom schema and the following. Not only do we commit ourselves to the values of sentential variables, propositions, we commit ourselves to world propositions—not only to truth*s*, in the modal sense mentioned in section 8, but to the *whole* truth. That is, we posit that there is a true proposition from which all true propositions follow. Of course, this posit is also a great help in proving completeness.

2 If for some $X \in D[1,0]$, $w \in X$, $F(X) = x \in \chi[1,1] - \omega$, $\Sigma\{F(X): X \in D[1,0]$ and $x \in X\}$ is undefined and so clearly not equal to any $N \in \omega$.

Bibliography

Belnap, Nuel D, Jr and **Steel, Thomas B, Jr** [1] *The Logic of Questions and Answers* (New Haven and London: Yale University Press, 1976)

Borkowski, L [1] On Proper Quantifiers, *Studia Logica* **8** (1958)
[2] Reduction of Arithmetic to Logic Based on Types Theory Without Axiom of Infinity and Typical of Arithmetical Constants, *Studia Logica* **8** (1958)

Bostock, David [1] *Logic and Arithmetic: Natural Numbers* (Oxford: The Clarendon Press, 1974)

Castañeda, Hector-Neri [1] 'He': a Study in the Logic of Self-Consciousness, *Ratio* **8** (1966)
[2] On the Logic of Self-Knowledge, *Nous* **1** (1967)
[3] Omniscience and Indexical Reference, *Journal of Philosophy* **64** (1967)
[4] Indicators and Quasi-Indicators, *American Philosophical Quarterly* **4** (1967)
[5] On the Phenomeno-Logic of the I, *Internationalen Kongresses für Philosophie* **14** (1968)
[6] On Knowing (or Believing) That One Knows (or Believes), *Synthese* **19** (1970)
[7] On the Logic of Attributions of Self-Knowledge, *The Journal of Philosophy* **64** (1968)
[8] *Thinking and Doing* (Dordrecht and Boston: D Reidel Publishing Company, 1975)

Church, Alonzo [1] *Introduction to Mathematical Logic* (Princeton, NJ: Princeton University Press, 1956)

Cocchiarella, Nino B [1] Some Remarks on Second Order Logic with Existence Attributes, *Nous* **2** (1968)
[2] A Second Order Logic of Existence, *The Journal of Symbolic Logic* **34** (1969)
[3] Properties as Individuals in Formal Ontology, *Nous* **6** (1972)
[4] Whither Russell's Paradox of Predication? in *Logic and Ontology* (Ed M K Munitz; New York: NYU Press, 1973)
[5] Fregean Semantics for a Realist Ontology, *Notre Dame Journal of Formal Logic* **15** (1974)
[6] Formal Ontology and the Foundations of Mathematics, in *The Philosophy of Bertrand Russell: a Centenary Tribute* (Ed G Nakhnikian; London: Duckworth Press, 1974)
[7] A Second Order Logic of Variable-Binding Operators, *Reports on Mathematical Logic* **5** (1975)

[8] Second-Order Theories of Predication: Old and New Foundations, *Nous* **9** (1975)

Cresswell, M J [1] Second-Order Intensional Logic, *Zeitschrift für mathematische Logik und Grundlagen der Mathematik* **18** (1972)
and **Hughes, G E** [1] *An Introduction to Modal Logic* (London: Methuen and Co, Ltd, 1968)

Daniels, Charles B [1] 'I' as a Definite Description, *Australasian Journal of Philosophy* **46** (1968)
[2] Reference and Singular Referring Terms, *Journal of Philosophical Logic* **1** (1972)
[3] *The Evaluation of Ethical Theories* (Halifax, N S: Dalhousie University Press for the Canadian Association for Publishing in Philosophy, 1975)
and **Davison, John** [1] Ontology and Method in Wittgenstein's *Tractatus*, *Nous* **7** (1973)
and **Freeman, James B** [1] Classical Second-Order Intensional Logic with Maximal Propositions, *Journal of Philosophical Logic* **6** (1977)
and [2] A Logic of Generalized Quantification, *Reports on Mathematical Logic* **10** (1978)
and [3] A Second-Order Relevance Logic with Modality, *Studia Logica* **38** (1979)
and [4] Two Notions of Truth, *Pacific Philosophical Quarterly* **61** (1980) See also the Corrections in **62**, N 2

Davison, John and **Daniels, Charles B** [1] Ontology and Method in Wittgenstein's *Tractatus*, *Nous* **7** (1973)

Freeman, James B and **Daniels, Charles B** [1] Classical Second-Order Intensional Logic with Maximal Propositions, *Journal of Philosophical Logic* **6** (1977)
and [2] A Logic of Generalized Quantification, *Reports on Mathematical Logic* **10** (1978)
and [3] A Second-Order Relevance Logic with Modality, *Studia Logica* **38** (1979)
and [4] Two Notions of Truth, *Pacific Philosophical Quarterly* **61** (1980) See also the Corrections in **62**, N 2

Frege, Gottlob [1] On Sense and Nominatum, *Readings in Philosophical Analysis* (Ed Herbert Feigl and Wilfred Sellars; New York: Appleton-Century-Crofts, 1949)

Gettier, Edmund L [1] Is Justified True Belief Knowledge?, *Analysis* **23** (1963)

Gombrich, E H [1] *Art and Illusion* (Princeton, NJ: Princeton University Press, 1969)

Henkin, Leon [1] Banishing the Rule of Substitution for Functional Variables, *The Journal of Symbolic Logic* **18** (1953)

Hughes, G E and **Cresswell, M J** [1] *An Introduction to Modal Logic* (London: Methuen and Co, Ltd, 1968)

Kaplan, David [1] On the Logic of Demonstratives, *Journal of Philosophical Logic* **8** (1979)

Klein, Peter [1] A Proposed Definition of Propositional Knowledge, *Journal of Philosophy* **68** (1971)

Mendelson, Elliott [1] *Introduction to Mathematical Logic* (Princeton, NJ: D van Nostrand Company, Inc, 1964)

Perry, John [1] The Problem of the Essential Indexical, *Nous* **13** (1979)

Prior, Arthur [1] *Past, Present, and Future* (Oxford: The Clarendon Press, 1967)

Putnam, Hilary [1] The Meaning of 'Meaning', in *Mind, Language and Reality*, Philosophical Papers V 2 (Cambridge, London, New York, Melbourne: Cambridge University Press, 1975)

Quine, W V O [1] *Word and Object* (Cambridge, Mass: The MIT Press, 1960) [2] *From a Logical Point of View* (Cambridge, Mass: Harvard University Press, 1961)

Routley, Richard [1] On What There Is Not, *Philosophy and Phenomenological Research* **63** (1982)

Russell, Bertrand [1] *The Problems of Philosophy* (London, Oxford, and New York: Oxford University Press, 1969)

Steel, Thomas B, Jr and **Belnap, Nuel D, Jr** [1] *The Logic of Questions and Answers* (New Haven and London: Yale University Press, 1976)

Wittgenstein, Ludwig [1] *Tractatus Logico-Philosophicus* (Translation by D F Pears and B F McGuinness, London and New York: Routledge and Kegan Paul, 1961)